THE PSYCHOLOGY OF RELIGIOUS FUNDAMENTALISM

The Psychology
of Religious Fundamentalism

RALPH W. HOOD, JR.
PETER C. HILL
W. PAUL WILLIAMSON

THE GUILFORD PRESS
New York   London

© 2005 The Guilford Press
A Division of Guilford Publications, Inc.
72 Spring Street, New York, NY 10012
www.guilford.com

Printed in the United States of America

This book is printed on acid-free paper.

Last digit is print number: 9 8 7 6 5 4 3 2 1

Library of Congress Cataloging-in-Publication Data

Hood, Ralph W.
  The psychology of religious fundamentalism / Ralph W. Hood, Jr., Peter
C. Hill, W. Paul Williamson.—1st ed.
      p.   cm.
  Includes bibliographical references and index.
  ISBN 1-59385-150-2 (hardcover)
  1. Religious fundamentalism—Psychology. I. Hill, Peter C., 1953– II.
Williamson, W. Paul (William Paul) III. Title.
  BL238.H66 2005
  200′.1′9—dc22

                                                              2004030394

About the Authors

Ralph W. Hood, Jr., was raised in the Unity faith for the first 12 years of his life. Since then, he has not identified with any religious tradition. After earning his PhD in a combined sociology and psychology program at the University of Nevada–Reno, Dr. Hood began to explore religious experience, heavily influenced by reading William James. He has always taught at a secular state university. While not identified with any church, he is committed to the belief that religious claims have ontological implications. They purport to be about what is real and, as such, allow one to experience the world in ways that psychology can explore but not necessarily explain. Although not a fundamentalist, Dr. Hood believes that fundamentalist religion has been poorly portrayed in the psychology of religion by researchers and scholars who are so distant from the assumptions and worldview of fundamentalists that they offer explanations for a phenomenon they have not adequately or fairly described.

Peter C. Hill was raised an evangelical in a family strongly committed to the church. He considered ministry as a career option until he took a general psychology course, where his interest in social psychology was kindled. He earned his PhD in social psychology at the University of Houston and has spent much of his professional career applying social psychology to the study of religious experience. Dr. Hill is also the editor of the *Journal of Psychology and Christianity,* which welcomes "theoretical and research articles [that] have a bearing on the relationship between psychology and Christian faith, including the interface of psychology with theology and the psychology of religion." He is currently a professor of psychology at Biola University's Rosemead School of Psychology. Biola University played a significant role in the early days of the Protestant fundamentalist movement and today identifies itself as an "interdenominational and yet theologically conservative" institution. The Rosemead School of Psychology seeks to advance a psychologically and Christian theologically integrated understanding of human nature. As one who works at an institution where an intratextual model is held by some, Dr. Hill has acquired an insider's understanding of both the insights and limits of a fundamentalist perspective.

W. Paul Williamson was born the son of a Church of God (of Prophecy) (COG[OP]) minister in Sewanee, Tennessee. At age 23, he followed in his father's footsteps and became an ordained minister in the denomination, serving 17 years of full-time ministry in various capacities, including Tennessee State Youth Director, pastor, senior pastor, and district bishop. Becoming increasingly interested in psychology as a profession, he earned an MEd in community counseling from the University of Tennessee–Chattanooga and a PhD in experimental/social psychology from the University of Tennessee–Knoxville. During his doctoral studies, he felt the need to resign from the clergy and from his affiliation with the church. After completing his education, Dr. Williamson taught psychology for 3 years at Sterling College, a conservative Presbyterian-affiliated school in central Kansas. Desiring to continue his academic career in a secular institution, he left Sterling College to accept a faculty appointment at Henderson State University in Arkadelphia, Arkansas, where he is presently an assistant professor of psychology. Dr. Williamson draws upon a wealth of experience in a Pentecostal tradition, both as a former member and as clergy, allowing him unique insights into its fundamentalist worldview.

Contents

Introduction   1

1 Fundamentalist Religion as an Intratextual Search for Meaning   11

2 Fundamentalism as a Meaning System   30

3 The History of Protestant Fundamentalism   47

4 Fundamentalism in a Pentecostal Denomination: 84
   The Church of God (of Prophecy)

5 Fundamentalism among Religious Serpent-Handling Sects   115

6 Fundamentalism among the Amish   133

7 Fundamentalist Islam   155

8 Intratextuality, Stereotyping, and Quasi-Fundamentalisms   183

   Epilogue   211

   Notes   215

   References   225

   Index   239

Introduction

Fundamentalism is Luther's Biblicalism in a new phase.
—BARZUN (2000, p. 10)

In the introduction to his excellent book, Joel Carpenter (1997) carefully distinguishes between broad and narrow definitions of "fundamentalism." A narrow definition is necessary for historians of religion, according to Carpenter, so that their field of study will not be obscured by a generic understanding that obscures the distinctive and unique identities of specific religious traditions. He points to the masterful works of historians George Marsden and Ernest Sandeen (and we would now add Carpenter himself), which trace Protestant fundamentalism as a historically distinct religious movement with constitutive beliefs that set it apart from other conservative forms of Protestantism, including evangelicalism. Marsden (1980) identifies several definitive characteristics of fundamentalists that, at first glance, appear common to all evangelical movements. Such characteristics include a particular set of beliefs, especially premillenialism (regarding the second coming of Christ) and Biblical inerrancy (which implies a host of other doctrines). Other distinctive features include revivalism, self-perceived patriotism, antiliberalism, an emphasis on cognitive and ideological factors, and a commonsense realist philosophy rooted in the views of Thomas Reid. But members of other evangelical groups, who do not identify themselves (correctly so) as fundamentalists, also claim each of these beliefs and characteristics. So what sets apart Protestant fundamentalists from these others? According to Marsden, a militant opposition to modernism, both theologically and culturally, is what distinguishes Protestant fundamentalism from its conservative Protestant cousins. Such a view is also associated with the Fundamentalism Project, directed by Martin E. Marty and R. Scott Appleby, who apply this initially Protestant term (though not uniquely a Protestant phenomenon) to a host of other faith

1

traditions across a wide range of cultures. In accordance with Marsden's view of Protestantism, Marty and Appleby (1991) identify fundamentalist faith traditions by their militant opposition to modernity. Much of the militancy addressed in the Fundamentalism Project consists of overt acts of violence; this is particularly evident in its treatment of Islam within many different cultures. Unfortunately, this approach supports a stereotype too common in the West (especially after the attacks of September 11, 2001—hereafter referred to simply as "9/11") that fundamentalist Islam is inherently violent and its believers are likely to be terrorists.

Despite this reservation, we applaud the work of Carpenter, Marsden, and the Fundamentalism Project and selectively utilize their scholarship, particularly in Chapters 1 and 2. Their analyses highlight the frequent misuse of the term "fundamentalism" as, in Carpenter's (1997) words,

> a synonym for bigotry, fanaticism, or anti-intellectualism. . . . The problem is that *fundamentalist*, like *puritan*, has become a word of wide usage and immense symbolic power. It has been spoken with derisive loathing and, no doubt, some fear in intellectual circles, for *fundamentalist* evokes images—such as the Scopes "monkey" trial in Dayton, Tennessee, in 1925 or, more recently, the widespread demonstrations against abortion—that represent deep and long-standing cultural conflicts in modern America. (p. 4; emphasis in original)

Yet the term "fundamentalist," Carpenter (1997) acknowledges, can also be applied in a more generic fashion to describe a religious and cultural phenomenon worldwide, including Jews, Muslims, Hindus, and other religious groupings, only some of which are to be found in the United States. Carpenter finds value in conceptualizing fundamentalism as a universal phenomenon, as do most of the authors associated with the massive Fundamentalism Project (now completed in five large volumes). Of particular value for both Carpenter and the Fundamentalism Project is the search for both commonalities and distinctions among various fundamentalisms, and their different expressions in various cultures. Yet Carpenter opts for a narrow definition, fearing that the broad definition "obscures more than it illuminates" (1997, p. 4). We too have this fear, and thus we have developed a model that accommodates both concerns: a respect for the specifics of each fundamentalist faith, and an appreciation of the commonality of fundamentalisms. Our model (discussed in Chapter 1) focuses upon the idea of a sacred text and what we term the principle of "intratextuality." Although sacred texts are unique within each tradition (e.g., the Bible of the Christians compared to the

Quran of the Muslims), each sacred text reveals structural similarities to others. Thus fundamentalism most clearly exhibits its distinguishing qualities in an understanding of a sacred text and how it is to be read and implemented. Furthermore, to understand how a sacred text is read is to understand a cognitive psychology that results when one conforms to the requirements of the text.

Weber's notion of "ideal types" (see Collins, 1986) is useful in discussions of intratextuality. Fundamentalisms represent the ideal types of our model of intratextuality: When a single text is absolutely authoritative and judged to be the final arbitrator of all other textually based knowledge, the model of intratextuality is ideally expressed. Other texts are judged by their compatibility with this *single* text. The text also specifies normative behaviors and criteria by which norms may be changed through processes outside the text, such as the *Ordnung* among the Amish or the *Shariah* in Islam. However, as one moves away from fundamentalisms as ideal types, the sacred text is less absolute, even though it may remain privileged. It is not simply one book among others, but is a book of privileged status to be consulted and revered. And yet (and this is the key) the sacred text is not granted absolute authority over all other knowledge claims. This is a common position among contemporary evangelicals—one tempered by the long-standing recognition among Protestant fundamentalists (as we note in Chapters 1 and 2) that they do not have their sacred text in original manuscript form. The appeal to an absolute applies to the original manuscript; this was long lost even to the compliers of the King James Version of the Bible, which has become the standard bearer for Protestant fundamentalists. Islam has an advantage, given that fundamentalist Muslims accept the Quran as the actual words of Allah. Here no translation is possible except as a commentary that must be explicitly acknowledged as an interpretation. Allah's words are read and recited in what is believed to be the original God-given language. Yet even among Muslims, as we move from the ideal type, the text becomes privileged but not absolute. Islam too has other than fundamentalist expressions of the faith, as one moves away from the ideal type of pure intratextuality. Again, our focus is on ideal types, most empirically supported in those faiths that are self-identified as fundamentalisms or can be readily identified as such by their approach to their sacred texts.

However, the approach of identifying ideal types does not focus upon the personalities of fundamentalists. Empirical psychology has failed to find distinctive personality traits that differentiate fundamentalists from other believers. Even conversion to fundamentalistic faiths, like most conversions, fails to produce basic personality changes (Paloutzian, Richardson, & Rambo, 1999). Earlier claims to have identified fundamentalism with an authoritarian personality have been resoundingly dismissed on methodological grounds (Christie & Jahoda, 1954). Stark (1971) has noted that the persistent tendency of social scientists to assert a link between authoritarianism and fundamentalism is simply false. The persistence of this claim, in Stark's view, is an example of the social sciences' prejudice against fundamentalists. Perhaps the most persistent empirical finding among American fundamentalists is a correlation between fundamentalism and dogmatism. If one accepts dogmatism as a measure of personality, then, as Paloutzian (1996) concludes, "these findings hint at a link between personality and religiosity. But the link is weak" (p. 243). Furthermore, as Kirkpatrick, Hood, and Hartz (1991) have noted, even the modest correlation between dogmatism and fundamentalism is contaminated by the fact that over half of the items used to measure dogmatism refer to specific beliefs that fundamentalists differentially accept (e.g., items viewing the self in purely humanist terms, items assessing an opposition and threat from the larger culture).

A renewed interest in authoritarianism and fundamentalism is associated with Altemeyer's (1988) development of what is claimed to be a relatively content-free measure of "right-wing authoritarianism" (RWA). It includes authoritarian submission, sanctioned aggression, and commitment to societal norms. However, Altemeyer's scale is explicitly a measure of RWA conceived not as a personality trait, but rather as learned social behavior. Reviews of studies using Altemeyer's measure are consistent in finding correlations between prejudice and fundamentalism, but primarily when the target of prejudice is well defined within a tradition, such as religious opposition to homosexuality (see Spilka, Hood, Hunsberger, & Gorsuch, 2003, pp. 457–479). What is most important about Altemeyer's measure is the fact that it is conceived to be content-free and thus identifies fundamentalism across various faith traditions; it does not restrict the term to a particular tradition, such as Protestantism. A final point is that since the RWA scale is not conceived as a measure of personality, it documents the futility of trying to explain fundamentalists by a distinctive personality type. We must look elsewhere for psychological insight.

The most consistent empirical findings in the psychology of religion are not in terms of basic personality functioning, but rather in terms of identity, meaning, and a sense of purpose in life (Paloutzian et al., 1999). Numerous psychologists have suggested that meaningful empirical relationships can be hypothesized when one considers the use of religious schemas involved in what, for the faithful, are distinctive religious worldviews (McIntosh, 1995). Such views not only meet personal needs for meaning (Baumeister, 1991), but also prevent a sense of fragmentation (Antonovosky, 1987) and provide motivation as one strives to fulfill ultimate concerns (Emmons, 1999). More concrete religious traditions, such as fundamentalism, also provide a sense of completeness and moral certainty. Even RWA can be an effective protection in which the individual, as Welford (1971) said of the classic "authoritarian" personality, "is prepared to sacrifice some spontaneity for stability, some permissiveness for the sake of order and peace, some immediate pleasure for the pursuit of long-term aims, and some sentimental toleration for the sake of efficiency" (p. 47).

Thus, from a psychological perspective, we present fundamentalism as a meaning system. We believe that the meaning fundamentalists derive from their religious beliefs is what allows them to persevere in an inhospitable culture: It creates a way for them to interpret the world, as well as themselves in relation to the world. This meaning system encompasses all of life and is strongly felt, for it deals with issues of eternal importance. It also provides a framework for motivation, and in the process helps meet several personal needs for meaning, such as purpose, value, efficacy, and self-worth. Meaning, for fundamentalists, is found wholly within the pages of the sacred text. Thus we propose that the primary criterion for understanding fundamentalism is its insistence that all of life be understood in relation to the text.

All three of us are psychologists of religion, and it is tempting to rush in with our psychological models to explain why people stubbornly hold to their fundamentalist ideals. Though we believe that psychological models have much to offer, particularly with regard to fundamentalism as a meaning system, we have resisted this temptation for several reasons. First, we are not convinced that adequate models of meaning making currently exist, though the efforts of Baumeister (1991), Emmons (1999), Wong (1998), and others hold some promise. Second, even if sophisticated theoretical models of meaning did exist, they might not apply to religious fundamentalism. Third, and most importantly, we believe that applying a psychological model without first understanding the sociocultural and historical context of fundamentalism as a meaning system violates an important principle that psychologists typically ignore: To adequately describe fundamentalism, we must first understand it on its own terms. If we only view it from afar as outsiders and attempt to provide secular models, then the true essence of the phenomenon will have escaped us. By explaining fundamentalism only through a comprehensive psychological model (if one existed) and ignoring fundamentalism's embedded culture, we would not only do injustice to the phenomenon under investigation, but would provide psychologists with the illusion that they can explain away fundamentalist claims of truth.

As a result, the reader will find that our accounts in this book describe much of the historical and sociological context of various fundamentalist belief systems. The theoretical foundation of fundamentalism as a meaning system and its connection to our intratextual model presented in the first chapter is interwoven throughout each of the four chapters (Chapters 3–6) where we discuss specific fundamentalist systems. However, we carefully resist imposing our theoretical system without a careful historical and sociological (and, in some cases, theological) analysis of each belief system itself. It is not until Chapter 8 that we attempt to come full circle by returning to our original position: From a psychological perspective, fundamentalism can best be thought of as a religious meaning system that relies exclusively upon a sacred text.

The psychology most appropriate for understanding our intratextual model of fundamentalism is not personality but social psychology. Furthermore, it is a social psychology consistent with the call for a new *multilevel interdisciplinary paradigm* in the psychology of religion (Emmons & Paloutzian, 2003, p. 395; emphasis in original). As Belzen and Hood (in press) have argued, the psychology of religion requires that psychologists return to the original meaning of "empiricism" and not restrict their research to laboratory and measurement-based studies. As important as such laboratory studies are, they have limited utility for understanding fundamentalism in terms of the social psychology of its history, its permutations, and its expression in various cultures. If the psychology of religion is a field in crisis, as Wulff (2003) claims, then the empirical study of religion in general and of fundamentalism in particular must adjust its methodologies to be appropriate for the complexity level of the phenomenon studied. Consistent with the call for a new paradigm is the recognition of methodological pluralism (Belzen & Hood, in press; Roth, 1987).

The methods employed throughout our text vary. Chapter 1 presents our model within a broad psychological framework that stresses how religious beliefs serve as a source of meaning. The model itself is then presented with some sense of history, and with the view that the structure of a sacred text implicates the processes of thought constituting the cognitive psychology of the fundamentalist believer. Chapter 2 revisits the religion-as-meaning thesis, with a special focus on the specific religious beliefs of fundamentalism. Chapter 3 describes the history of Protestant fundamentalism in America, a knowledge of which is essential to situating the origin of the term. Consistent with the call for a new multilevel interdisciplinary paradigm is what Belzen (2000, 2001) calls the "historiocultural approach"—the recognition not only that psychological processes occur in a historical and cultural context, but also that psychology itself is history.

In Chapters 4 through 7, we apply the model to various traditions, ranging from those that are Protestant (but not always fitting a narrow definition of Protestant fundamentalism) to the Islamic tradition. Chapter 4 explores the Church of God in terms of our intratextual model. It relies heavily upon interlinking the psychology of its early major leader, A. J. Tomlinson, with the emergence of doctrine rooted in an intratextual understanding of the Bible. This church's doctrine emerged largely through Tomlinson's understanding of the Biblical writ. This social psychology is a version of psychohistory—not in the classic sense dominated by psychoanalysts, but in the current sense of "employing psychology in historical research" (Belzen, 2001, p. 13). Chapter 5 continues this psychohistorical approach, but adds insights from participant observation, interviews with serpent handlers, analyses of sermons, and an exploration through phenomenological methods of the meaning serpent handling has for those who believe they are being obedient to Jesus's command. Our choice of these two traditions in Chapters 4 and 5 is intentional, in that these are groups that many people assume to be fundamentalist, but that have often (for various reasons) been excluded from the "fundamentalist" designation.

In Chapter 6, we present the Amish as a group that does not fit many understandings of fundamentalism, but one that does fit within our intratextual model. Although not based upon direct participant observation, our discussion of the Amish explores this tradition from original documents and reports of those who have lived with and studied the Amish. Chapter 7 applies the intratextual model intentionally to a tradition outside Christianity (Islam). It focuses upon the clash between an intratextual orientation in which religion and the state are not separate, and an intertextual orientation in which religion and the state are independent. We argue that the clash between a writer freely expressing his thoughts (Salman Rushdie) and a leader within Islam (Ayatollah Khomeini) was structured less by the personalities involved than by the clash between exclusively intra- and intertextual commitments. Understanding the difference between these two commitments provides the necessary understanding of likely cognitive schemas that order and give meaning to lives, but in radically different ways. We illustrate this at a structural level, but flesh it out through the words of a believer who aptly portrays how our model allows an understanding of what cannot be dismissed simply as Islamic militancy.

In Chapter 8, we explore the extension of our model to other than faith traditions. We suggest a variety of methodological possibilities consistent with the call for a new paradigm in the psychological study of religion, and with the recognition that this paradigm must truly be multilevel and interdisciplinary. We also attempt to correct the most common stereotypes found among social scientists, the mass media, and society at large about fundamentalism.

As we emphasize in the first three chapters and demonstrate throughout the text, intratextuality does not assure uniformity of belief. The history of American Protestant fundamentalism is perhaps most instructive. This is why all but one of our examples come from this tradition. The acceptance of the Bible as the infallible word of God does little to diminish the fact that it must be read and comprehended (even in its plain meaning) by those with fallible minds! We note in the Chapter 3 that few of the authors of the essays constituting *The Fundamentals* would precisely agree on all elements of the fundamentals of their faith. However, their disagreement would be bounded by the final arbiter, the text, as interpreted by the principle of intratextuality.

Therefore it is a mistake, for example, to define Islamic fundamentalism in terms suggesting that its opposition to what it rejects is always violent or militant. The same is true of Protestant fundamentalism. Sometimes it has been militant, but as we note in Chapter 3, it was liberal Protestantism that sided most closely with secular views of Darwinian theory suggesting that science had discovered the principles of violence, which assured the survival of the fittest. Fundamentalist Islam and Protestantism selectively oppose different aspects of modernity and selectively utilize different means, only some of which are violent. As a result, the militancy that both Marsden and the Fundamentalism Project claim is essential to their definition of fundamentalism is not, in our view, necessarily "violent." Thus we include the Amish as an example of a fundamentalist group. It is a misguided approach, from the perspective of our model, to contrast their pacifism and refusal to wage war with the all-too-common focus upon "Islamic militancy" after 9/11. Rather, the Amish should be viewed as adopting another form of resistance—one that has been waged in state courts and the U.S. Supreme Court. Likewise, our study of Islamic fundamentalism in Chapter 7 is not concerned with violent acts, but with a perception of blasphemy and a religious ruling as to the fair fate of the blasphemer. This case study concerns a ruling about a novel, rather than retaliation for acts of terror, to underscore the fact that Islamic fundamentalism is no more directly responsible for acts of terror than Christianity (fundamentalist or not) is directly responsible for the response to terrorism.

Thus we propose a psychological model of fundamentalism that, though it is relevant to all forms of religious fundamentalism (and has parallels with quasi-fundamentalist secular ideologies, as we discuss in Chapter 8), can only be fully applied in a movement-specific sociocultural and historical context. In other words, ours is a generic model that we believe applies to virtually all forms of fundamentalism, but the application itself can only take form within a specific context. This context is both historical and best understood not in terms of causes, but in terms of the sense of meaning, purpose in life, and identity it can provide for those who believe. Furthermore, specific attitudes and beliefs of fundamentalists can be understood only as embedded in the sociohistorical context of a tradition. It would be as un-insightful to identify the Amish as "prejudiced" because of their beliefs about blacks as it would be to identify Church of God believers as "prejudiced" because of their views on homosexuality. To do so is no more than to recognize that culture is prejudiced. As Gadamer (1975/1982) reminds us, "the fundamental prejudice of the enlightenment is the prejudice against prejudice, which deprives tradition of its power" (pp. 239–240).

Our intratextual model does not refute what historians of American religion have convincingly argued. Rather, it complements their work by providing a uniquely social-psychological theoretical framework—one that requires consideration of both the structure of sacred texts and the content of a specific text, as individuals struggle with their faith in various cultural contexts at specific moments in history. In this sense, our approach is broadly social-psychological, including both causal and hermeneutical considerations, or what from the time of Aristotle have been identified as "efficient" and "teleological" modes of causation. Insofar as teleological or "in order to . . . " motives entail meaningful action, fundamentalists are more than likely to locate the justification and motives for their actions within a sacred text. Thus, insofar as there is a fundamentalist search for meaning, it must be found within a sacred text. Finally, our approach suggests that the social psychology of religion is enriched when it is focused upon experiences and understandings of a sacred text that are foundational to a particular form of life. Although such a form is unlikely to be one that readers of this text subscribe to, it is one that they can more fully understand in the light of our model.

CHAPTER ONE

Fundamentalist Religion as an Intratextual Search for Meaning

The distinctive nature of religious meaning is not simply that one thing is seen to represent another conceptually. Meaning is not just denotative, as a red light stands for "stop," or the image of a lily stands for purity. Much more specific to religion than cognitive representation is the participatory character of meanings and symbols. Religious symbols and words do not simply signify, they speak and perform—and in so doing they transform perception, punctuate the routine world with their own power, effect felt presences, and engage the participant. The purpose of religious language is not just to represent the world but to act one out. The sacred is enacted through words, stories, images, and the construction of consecrated space and time.
—PADEN (1992, pp. 97–98)

Religious fundamentalism has increasingly captured the concern of America and the world over recent decades. What began in the 1970s as a budding interest among social scientists in the rising political influence of fundamentalism in America has long since flourished into worldwide concern about its cross-cultural presence and sometimes militant role in international unrest, particularly since 9/11. Although historians, political scientists, and sociologists have carefully watched, and have assembled a massive literature on fundamentalism, social psychologists have had surprisingly little to say about the matter. Although we applaud what others have contributed toward understanding this compelling movement, we nevertheless feel the need to address what seems to be an obvious neglect from a psychological perspective, in an effort to comprehend the movement more fully. What we offer here is a psychology of fundamentalism—but one based on a nonreductive approach that takes the fundamentalist worldview seriously, in hopes of providing more insight and larger understanding.

We begin the task in this chapter by introducing a social-psychological model based primarily on "intratextuality"—a principle that we suggest is directly linked to the centrality of a sacred text within its own tradition. More specifically, our model offers insight into how fundamentalists make use of this principle in coming to terms with a tradition-specific interpretation of what the divine author of the text intended as absolute truths to be lived out and guarded at all costs. To set an appropriate context, however, we first present a psychological framework for understanding how religion itself may provide a viable role in offering personal meaning and purpose in life. Within this framework, we then move toward presenting our own model and show how it makes possible such meaning and purpose for fundamentalists.

RELIGION AS A MEANING SYSTEM

One can reasonably ask why people choose to be fundamentalists. After all, not many people, even among religious conservatives, like being called "fundamentalists." Even though they adhere to similar religious beliefs and doctrines, many religious conservatives, particularly among American Protestants, also differentiate themselves from fundamentalists; they are apparently fearful of being embarrassed by association. Distinctions are made even among those self-identified as fundamentalists. Perhaps America's best-known fundamentalist, Jerry Falwell, distinguishes himself as a "real fundamentalist" to distance himself from the "extremist" snake handlers (Falwell with Dobson & Hindson, 1981, p. 3). The president of Bob Jones University, Bob Jones III, has suggested that, while remaining "unashamedly fundamentalist," the faculty and students of the university may begin to identify themselves as "Biblical preservationists" so as not to be lumped with Islamic fundamentalists ("Bob Jones Wants to Shed," 2002). "Fundamentalism" is thus for many a "theological swear-word" (Packer, 1958, p. 30) if we keep in mind that the significance of a swear word is not so much "what it means, but the feeling it expresses" (p. 30). It is among the latest of a whole litany of a vocabulary of insult directed toward religious groups, frequently from others who themselves are expressly religious. For example, "Puritan" was a name coined by others to identify religious conservatives of the early 17th century who sought greater "purity" within the English church. "Methodist" was a name rudely given to the followers of John Wesley as a comment on Wesley's own methodical piety. The effects of such labels, of course, are that their use results in great over-simplification of understanding, and that they often take on stereotypi-cal overtones. Such stereotypes of fundamentalists include being narrow-minded, poorly educated, low in socioeconomic status, and simplistic—hardly a flattering profile. Though some social scientists believe that this stereotype has been empirically confirmed (and therefore that funda-mentalists *are* indeed narrow-minded, poorly educated, etc.), critics of this literature have identified such claims as overstated, and at least partly as reflecting the prejudice of social scientists toward fundamental-ists (Hood, 1983; Stark, 1971).

Despite an inhospitable culture that maintains these negative stereo-types, fundamentalists choose to take what they refer to as the "road less popular" and insist that it will lead them to know all truth. To outsiders, this insistence appears to be stubbornly misguided and based on an out-moded relic; to fundamentalists, however, it is an inspired revelation that others are unable to grasp. To help us understand this mindset, we oper-ate from the underlying premise that religion provides the structure for an implicit belief system that creates meaning and through which pur-pose is experienced. In this section, we attempt to provide a general framework whereby religion is a worldview; that is, it becomes a pri-mary meaning system through which all of life is viewed and under-stood. In the next chapter, we explore more fully how fundamentalist re-ligion in particular serves as an unusually powerful meaning system.

Before examining the religion-as-meaning premise further, two im-portant qualifiers must be noted. First, we do not identify as fundamen-talists all people who take religion as a primary meaning system. What distinguishes fundamentalism from other religious profiles is its particu-lar approach toward understanding religion, which elevates the role of the sacred text to a position of *supreme* authority and subordinates all other potential sources of knowledge and meaning. Second, we do not wish to imply that our (or any) psychological framework necessarily ex-plains away the truth claims of any religious system. We find such a po-sition philosophically untenable and naïve. Social scientists have failed to explain even fundamentalist religions away, though they often declare they have (Hood, 2003; Preus, 1987). In fact, social scientists continue to express surprise and bewilderment that among the strongest and most successfully growing denominations worldwide are those that are most fundamentalist, including those that support theological and moral absolutes (Kelley, 1972). Rather, we hope that our framework will com-plement the work of sociologists and other social scientists, and even re-ligious teachings themselves, in demonstrating why religious fundamen-talism remains surprisingly strong in many cultures (including those such as the United States, which are otherwise thoroughly secular). First, however, we consider the importance of meaning and a sense of purpose to psychological well-being. Our review highlights some well-founded and empirically supported theoretical positions that serve as a useful framework for understanding how fundamentalists may find meaning through their religious systems.

Meaning Systems

A "meaning system" can be thought of as a group of beliefs or theories about reality that includes both a world theory (beliefs about others and situations) and a self theory (beliefs about the self), with connecting propositions between the two sets of beliefs that are important in terms of overall functioning. This is a basic premise of several psychological theories, which suggest that meaning systems aid individuals in setting goals, regulating behavior and experiences, planning activities, and sensing direction or purpose to life, and allow them to make self-evaluations in relation to all of these experiences. Examples of such psychological theories include Higgins's (1987) theory of self-discrepancy, Bowlby's (1969) attachment theory, Carver and Scheier's (1985; Scheier & Carver, 1985) theory of self-regulation, and Epstein's (1973, 1994) cognitive–experiential self theory (CEST). For example, Higgins's distinction between the "ideal self" and the "ought self" as two different standards to which a person compares the "actual self," and his description of how discrepancies between the actual self and each standard lead to distinctly different negative emotional states, necessarily invoke a meaning system. The aspirations and hopes of the ideal self and the responsibilities, duties, or obligations of the ought self are defined only within the context of a personal meaning system. That is, the person's perception of hope, aspiration, responsibility, or obligation must be contextualized within some sort of implicit but coherent belief system. Similarly, Epstein's CEST postulates four implicit belief systems that are developed to fulfill four basic needs: (1) the degree to which the world is perceived as benevolent or malevolent (associated with the basic need to maintain a favorable balance of pleasure and pain); (2) the degree to which the world is perceived as meaningful or meaningless (associated with the need to develop a coherent conceptual system); (3) the degree to which people are comforting, trustworthy, or dependable (associated with the need for relatedness); and (4) the degree to which the self is worthy or unworthy (related to the need to see the self in a favorable way). These theorists argue that such meaning systems are necessary for an individual to function well in the world, particularly when coping with adversity.

Dittmann-Kohli (1991, as quoted in Wong, 1998) summarizes the importance of a personal meaning system to overall functioning quite well:

> It [a personal meaning system] is a dynamic, centralized structure with various sub-domains. It is conceived as a cognitive map that orients the individual in steering through the life course. The personal meaning system comprises the categories (conceptual schemes) used for self and life interpretation. It is a cognitive–affective network containing person-directed and environment-directed motivational cognitions and understandings, like goal concepts and behavior plans, conceptions of character and competencies, of internal processes and mechanisms, various kinds of standards and self-appraisals. (Wong, 1998, p. 368)

In short, a personal meaning system is "an individually constructed cognitive system that endows life with personal significance" (Wong, 1998, p. 368) and consists of cognitive, motivational, and affective components. Of course, the question left unanswered is this: What is capable of endowing life with personal significance? For the self-identified religious person (fundamentalist or not), the search for meaning and significance involves the sacred (Pargament, 1997). For such people, religion is considered worthy of veneration, devotion, and ultimate commitment, and therefore is uniquely capable of providing a meaningful purpose to life. For psychologists and other social scientists of religion, identifying what is sacred is often difficult; a sense of personal growth, an ethic of altruism, and one's communion with nature could all be conceptualized as sacred. Hill et al. (2000) concluded that the sacred "is a socially influenced perception of either some sense of ultimate reality or truth or some divine object/being" (p. 67). Although such a definition may be useful to the social scientist who studies religious behavior, it is unnecessarily pedantic to the fundamentalist. The fundamentalist will identify the sacred as quite simply what has been ordained by the Divine Being through the sacred text. Protestant fundamentalists, for example, are quick to claim that the Bible alone is the direct and literal revelation of God, and that it is therefore the totally sufficient source of meaning and purpose to life. Islam makes similar assertions about the centrality of the Quran as the direct revelation of Allah.

The Search for Significance

A major contention of this book is that religious fundamentalism provides a unifying philosophy of life within which personal meaning and purpose are embedded. In short, for fundamentalists, religion is a total way of life. This is not unique to fundamentalism, for others can be just as committed to a faith that is vitally and centrally important to their existence (e.g., intrinsically motivated believers). For fundamentalists, however, religion is a systematized and complex system that requires an authoritative base capable of subordinating to itself all other elements of human experience. As we shall see, subordinating all else to a supreme authoritative text is an important defining characteristic of fundamentalism. Its psychological staying power is its ability to create a unifying philosophical framework that meets personal needs for meaning and provides coherence to an existence that may otherwise seem fragmented. It is therefore not surprising that the most successful religions, in terms of both growth and maintenance of membership, are those with absolute, unwavering, strict, and enforced normative standards for behavior (Iannaccone, 1994). Such standards are characteristic of fundamentalist religions worldwide.

Personal Needs for Meaning

Baumeister (1991) points to four overlapping needs for meaning: "purpose" (seeing one's life as oriented toward some imagined goal or state), "value" (seeing one's actions as right or justifiable), "efficacy" (having a sense of control over events), and "self-worth" (seeing one's life as having positive value). It is clear that a well-developed religious meaning system, imbued with power and rooted in an authoritative base, is capable of meeting all four of the meaning needs identified by Baumeister. For the fundamentalists (as well as many nonfundamentalists) in most religious traditions, there is the promise of a blissful afterlife whereby people can live in God's presence and glorify God (need for purpose) as a result of living righteous and God-fearing lives here on earth (need for value). A recognition of and surrender to a sovereign God may enhance a sense of control (need for efficacy) and may provide a personal sense of value and importance (need for self-worth).

There is evidence (Sethi & Seligman, 1993) that religion may promote optimistic explanations of events. Smith and Gorsuch (1989) found, for example, that the attributional logic of religious conservatives may encourage optimism. Specifically, they (1) attribute greater responsibility to God for everyday life events, especially those that are positive in nature; (2) view God as active through multiple channels, rather than through a single modality (e.g., God may "speak" to a person through various means); and (3) see God as working conjunctively with or through natural causes, including their own personal behavior (i.e., they see themselves as "agents" of God). Such reasoning helps meet the needs for efficacy and self-worth.

A Sense of Coherence

A common conception is that much contemporary life is characterized by a stressful sense of fragmentation, which is not conducive to psychological well-being. Antonovsky (1987) has proposed that people who are best capable of coping with such fragmentation are those with a well-developed "sense of coherence," formally defined as

> a global orientation that expresses the extent to which one has a pervasive, enduring though dynamic feeling of confidence that (1) the stimuli deriving from one's internal and external environments in the course of living are structured, predictable, and explicable; (2) the resources are available to one to meet the demands posed by these stimuli; and (3) these demands are challenges, worthy of investment and engagement. (p. 19)

Antonovsky has further identified "generalized resistance resources," such as money, social support, preventive health orientation, and cultural stability, which have the potential to provide individuals with three key components of a sense of coherence: comprehensibility, manageability, and meaningfulness. We suggest that religion could be added as another such resource. Indeed, the sense of coherence provided by religion may serve as an important mediating variable in what has now become a well-established linkage between religion and both mental and physical health (George, Ellison, & Larson, 2002; Powell, Shahabi, & Thoresen, 2003; Seeman, Dubin, & Seeman, 2003; Seybold & Hill, 2001). We also suggest that fundamentalism enhances generalized resistance resources through its clarity of belief rooted in absolutes.

Emmons (1999, in press)—drawing upon the work of existentialist theologian Paul Tillich (1957), who posited "ultimate concern" (singular) as the essence of religion—proposes that people are constituted to strive for goals and purposes to help satisfy "ultimate concerns" (plural). Fundamentalists return to *an* "ultimate concern" (singular), supporting Antonovsky's (1987) view that their strivings toward this concern not only may be influenced by their own sense of coherence, but in turn may help further solidify that sense. That is, given that religion provides "an ultimate vision of what people should be striving for in their lives" (Pargament & Park, 1995, p. 15), religion provides a coherent global orientation that establishes the framework through which goals and purposes are identified and defined. In addition, the establishment of goals and purposes may help crystallize the sense of coherence derived from religion.

From a psychological perspective, religion's lure for many is that it provides moral certainty and stability, thereby contributing to a sense of coherence in an otherwise chaotic world. For some people, this is a primary function of religion. To understand this further, we find Wuthnow's (1998) distinction between a spirituality of "dwelling" and one of "seeking" helpful:

> A spirituality of dwelling emphasizes *habitation*: God occupies a definite place in the universe and creates a sacred space in which humans too can dwell; to inhabit sacred space is to know its territory and to feel secure. A spirituality of seeking emphasizes *negotiation*: individuals search for sacred moments that reinforce their conviction that the divine exists, but these moments are fleeting; rather than knowing their territory, people explore new spiritual vistas, and they may have to negotiate among complex and confusing meanings of spirituality. (pp. 4–5; emphasis in original)

Wuthnow (1998) explains that a dwelling spirituality stresses security, provides clear distinctions between the sacred and the profane, promotes a sense of community and interrelatedness, and emphasizes a spiritual home. A seeking spirituality, by contrast, stresses faith as a quest, makes fewer distinctions between the sacred and the ordinary, and offers individuals greater freedom from the restraints of community expectations.

In terms of the dwelling–seeking distinction, fundamentalists are spiritual dwellers: Their religion produces a sense of certainty and stability. Dwellers are also often surrounded by others with similar beliefs, who constitute a community where conformity of belief and behavior to the values and "rules of the house" is stressed. People with a dwelling orientation may best achieve their sense of meaning or purpose through "measuring up" to certain moral standards as outlined by the religious belief system. Such standards can be conceptualized as striving toward the positive (e.g., obedience to religious laws or performing the "right" behaviors) or as avoiding what is unhealthy (e.g., striving to overcome sin). Meaning-related virtues or character strengths may also be developed. For the dweller, the development of temperance or self-control over sinful tendencies (e.g., the Biblical notion of "lusts of the flesh") is an important marker of spiritual maturity; it thereby meets what was designated by Baumeister (1991) as the need for a sense of efficacy.

Social support may be another factor that draws people to a spirituality of dwelling. Legitimation by other dwellers is offered to assure believers that they are engaged in the right search for the sacred; this provides a certain level of security. In addition, research has shown that people connected to others in religious settings (which often tend to be settings of concern and care) display less loneliness, depression, and anxiety (see Ch. 15 in Koenig, McCullough, & Larson, 2001). A spirituality of dwelling or habitation means that the dweller, as part of a family or community, both derives privilege from and bears a responsibility to the collective body. Meaning may thus also be gauged in terms of the dweller's generativity or contribution to the collective welfare of the community. This is a particularly strong theme in Amish society (Chapter 6).

Religion's Ability to Provide Meaning

While it is true that many meaning systems meet personal needs for meaning and provide a sense of coherence, it can be argued that religion, especially of the dwelling type, is a unique source of meaning on the basis of at least four criteria: as a comprehensive system, as an accessible philosophical orientation to the world, as a means of transcendence, and as a direct claim to have meaning and purpose. Though our primary purpose is to describe the fundamentalist criteria and methodology for determining how religion becomes a meaning system, here we want simply to stress how religion and spirituality are unique sources of meaning, whether applied to fundamentalism or not. We briefly consider religion's uniqueness as a provider of meaning in terms of each criterion.

Comprehensiveness

Religion is perhaps the most comprehensive of all meaning systems and can subsume many other sources of meaning, such as creativity, personal relationships, achievement, work, enduring values and ideals, and so forth. It is in this sense that Baumeister (1991) identifies religion as a "higher-order" meaning system. That is, it has a longer time perspective and contains a large number of associative links with other objects or events in life.

An Accessible Philosophical Orientation

Since religious meaning systems are comprehensive, they often function as philosophical orientations to the world. Thus religion can be thought of as a "core schema" (McIntosh, 1995) that may be born out of the need to comprehend many of life's deepest existential issues (Geertz, 1973). At the very least, it helps people cope with many of life's questions and dilemmas (Pargament, 1997), and it has been empirically established as a sufficient meaning system to deal with such issues as chronic pain (Kotarba, 1983), breast cancer (Baider & Sarell, 1983), serious spinal cord injuries (Bulman & Wortman, 1977), and bereavement (Park & Cohen, 1993).

Furthermore, within many traditions, religion is a philosophical orientation that is readily available and often promoted. For example, it is not unusual within the Christian literature to see emphasized the importance of a Christian worldview—"a complex of knowledge, opinions, assumptions, and so forth that determine the way we view the world around us" (Curtis, 2000, p. 186). Curtis claims:

> We [Christians] need an awareness of the process by which our worldview is established and refined in order for us to filter out extraneous elements that do not belong in the value system of a Christian. We also need such an awareness in order to focus our attention on principles and methods that will establish biblical truth more solidly in our hearts. (p. 6)

Thus religion not only meets personal needs for meaning and alleviates a sense of fragmentation, but it also provides a worldview (or what psychologists might call a "schema"—see McIntosh, 1995) through which experience is interpreted.

Issues of Transcendence

Religion, more than any other system of meaning, focuses on that which is "beyond me." "At the end of the road," claims Clark (1958), "lies God, the Beyond, the final essence of the Cosmos, yet so secretly hidden within the soul that no man is able to persuade another that he has fulfilled the quest" (p. 419). For many, religion may be the most satisfying meaning system, if for no other reason than its belief in a transcendent and perhaps sovereign God, and in many cases the affirmation of an afterlife (Wong, 1998).

Direct Claims of Meaning and Purpose

By its very nature, religion claims to have meaning and purpose. Within other systems, meaning or purpose is often imposed on the event or object, but for religion, meaning is contained within its sacred character. For example, when Jesus claimed in John 14:6 that "I am the way, the truth, and the life: no man cometh unto the Father, but by me" (King James Version[1]), he was making a bold statement about what is ultimately meaningful and in which the religiously penchant may find sufficiency.

On the basis of these four criteria, it is not surprising that religion functions as a primary meaning system for many individuals, and thus we find claims such as Clark's (1958):

> Religion more than any other human function satisfies the need for
> meaning in life. . . . The journey is unending, and the quest is capable of
> subordinating to itself all other human activities. . . . He [a person] is
> baffled when he broods over that which may best explain his sojourn
> among the living, whence he has come, and whither he is so swiftly has-
> tening. But more often that any other explanation it is religion that
> seems to satisfy his restless spirit. (p. 419)

We concur with Clark that religion is perhaps the most satisfying system
of meaning for a good many individuals, even in an age of secularization. Fundamentalists are no different, in that they too find religion as a
most capable provider of meaning. Indeed, it is our contention that fundamentalists differ from other religious persons not so much in *whether*
they derive meaning from religion, but in *how* they derive that meaning.

We have maintained up to this point that a religious belief system
serves as a convincing and unifying philosophy of life for many individuals. Religion provides a framework that both meets personal needs for
meaning (Baumeister, 1991) and helps people cope with an otherwise
personal sense of fragmentation (Antonovsky, 1987; Emmons, 1999) by
establishing a cognitive "schema" (McIntosh, 1995) or "worldview"
centered on issues of moral certainty and stability. Religion, as revealed
in the sacred text, is *uniquely* capable as a primary meaning system, in
that only it can comprehensively meet these needs. In Chapter 2, we suggest that religion's capability to provide meaning is perhaps most powerful when expressed in fundamentalist forms that to outsiders seem
closed-minded at best. We propose, however, that fundamentalism can
be viewed in another light, and we hope to provide that light with our
model of intratextuality. It is to the presentation of this model that we
now turn.

A NEW APPROACH TO
UNDERSTANDING FUNDAMENTALISM

If the focus is on a sacred text, then it is obvious that a proper understanding of fundamentalism has no need to find explanations for deviant
or strange beliefs. Rather, we must look at the texts that fundamentalists
hold dear and describe how the text molds the belief, the commitments,
and even the character of those who adhere to its words. In this sense,
the centrality of the text is what permits us to understand fundamentalism from within. Many of the recent studies of fundamentalism that offer most insight are textually based. These include Boone's (1989) sensitive effort to read the text *with* fundamentalists, Crapanzano's (2000)

comparison of the more "literal" readings of the Bible with those of the U.S. Constitution, and Harding's (2000) perceptive study of the use of scripture by Jerry Falwell. Each of these works in its own way has advanced the study of fundamentalism by taking seriously what fundamentalists take as axiomatic: that there exists an objective truth—revealed, recorded, and adequately preserved—illuminating an original intent that can be grasped and valued as the foundation for understanding all of life. In short, we must go to the text to understand why so many fundamentalists refuse to leave what, according to modern and postmodern thought, is at best a quaint and outmoded way of understanding what words are about.

An Intratextual Model

We contend that a model based on the principle of intratextuality is essential to understanding the psychology of fundamentalism. Figure 1.1 presents this intratextual model of fundamentalist thought. Observe that the model makes no reference to belief content. Our concern is to understand both the structure and the process of fundamentalist thought. We assume that fundamentalists are correct when they argue that a reader must go into the text and allow the text to speak for itself. In terms of the dialogic nature of sacred texts, an openness to what the text actually says and intends is crucial. It can, within fundamentalist thought, come only from within the text. Thus our model is intratextual.

The bold circle in Figure 1.1 encapsulates three necessarily interrelated phenomena. The first is the principle of intratextuality, which focuses on the process of reading a sacred text. The logic of this principle refers not to content, but to process: The text itself determines how it ought to be read. Thus no discussion of fundamentalism can proceed meaningfully if it refuses to enter into the text and be obedient to the imperatives of the text (Boone, 1989; Bruce, 2000).

Associated with the principle of intratextuality are two related content claims: a sacred text and absolute truths. Note that we do not specify what the sacred text is (the Quran, the Bible, etc.) or what absolute claims are made. The reason is that only the principle of intratextuality can specify what text is sacred, and only a sacred text can specify what truths are absolute. Thus the tautology is apparent but not vicious. In other words, reading the Bible in terms of the principle of intratextuality will both determine that the Bible is the Word of God (a sacred text) and indicate what truths are to be held as absolute (e.g., there is no other God than the Christian God). Similar claims can be made for the Quran.

The process within the bold circle involves a dialogic encounter that emerges between the reader and the text—based on the principle of

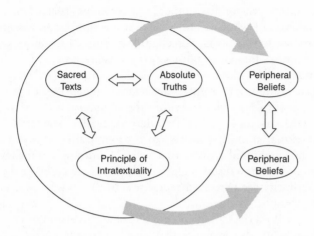

FIGURE 1.1. The structure of fundamentalist thought.

intratextuality—in which the revelation of the Divine Being becomes illuminated in the form of absolute truths. What emerges as absolute truth
is whatever is of immediate necessity for maintaining the fundamentalist
worldview. No sources outside the tradition (e.g., other texts based on
other authorities) are consulted or are even necessary for this to occur;
the authoritative text is sufficient in and of itself toward this end, according to the principle of intratextuality. As absolute truths are revealed
in the interpretive process, they harmonize and are generalized into an
objective reality for the reader (Marsden, 1980, p. 55). This constructed
reality is considered to exist beyond the reader as an *objective* fact, and
it provides a basis for the individual to attribute meaning to all other aspects of the world.

    For example, the person in this stance has gained access not only to
self-knowledge in relation to the Divine Being (say, as a redeemed child
of God), but also to a means of perceiving elements in the world as being
either good or evil, sacred or sinful, spiritual or worldly, and so forth.
Since the only objective reality for the person is that which is based on
belief in the authoritative text, all who do not share this same belief cannot participate in the same reality and are thus viewed as outsiders and
as sources of opposition. Even the Divine Being of the text is mysterious:
Without the fixed and enduring text itself, this being would be an ambiguous, inarticulate revelation, and thus knowledge would be uncer-
tain—hence the importance of the written text.[2] Oral traditions are authoritative, but most so when fixed in a sacred text. For instance, as we

note in Chapter 7, the orality of the Quran remains crucial to a tradition whose recitation of what was once only oral is now both oral and written. It is the written text that is recited. Likewise, Christianity was once an oral tradition. Fundamentalist Christians may preach, but the criterion is always to be "in the word." Thus the acceptance of the text as sacred gives it status as an "overarching symbol" that serves to protect and sanction the worldview shared within the fundamentalism (Barr, 1977, pp. 314–315). As suggested earlier, the principal characteristic of this symbol is textual authority, which leaves room in the constructed world only for those who subscribe to its belief. Critics and unbelievers are eliminated or kept at a distance, for all who refuse to embrace the text as the sole authority are perceived as a threat to the security and purity of the fundamentalist worldview.

Not only does the closed circle indicate an exclusion of other interpretive factors; it also suggests that absolute truths derived from the dialogic process are themselves protected from outside influences and are not subject to outside criticism. An example of an absolute truth among fundamentalist Muslims (Shia) is that there is no God but Allah. For them, this truth is above criticism and not subject to debate. As absolute truths emerge from the interpretive process, they extend (as represented by the one-way arrows in Figure 1.1) into the objective world, which includes less certain truths known as "peripheral beliefs." Since peripheral beliefs exist outside the circle, they are subject to modification based on their relation to absolute truths, personal experience in the world, and even interactions with other peripheral beliefs, as indicated by the two-way arrows. Furthermore, these beliefs include all beliefs (both religious and nonreligious) outside absolute truths. An example of a peripheral belief among fundamentalist Pentecostals is that believers are to trust God for divine healing of illnesses. Although some might hold this as an absolute truth (and be willing to die from an illness while trusting *only* God for healing), those for whom it is a peripheral belief might allow personal experience of illness to modify the belief in some way and thus justify the use of medicine in conjunction with faith healing. As we shall see in Chapters 4 and 5, the early Church of God and the contemporary serpent handlers of Appalachia eventually parted ways on their understanding of what for some is still an imperative to handle serpents. The point here, however, is that neither peripheral beliefs nor external factors are allowed to penetrate the bounded psychological process that produces and maintains absolute beliefs among fundamentalists.

The encircled dynamic, involving the principle of intratextuality and the general content claims (a sacred text and absolute truths), allows us to resolve an issue that has perplexed researchers at the conceptual level—how to interrelate belief content, structure, and process. For instance, although fundamentalists need not have authoritarian or dogmatic *personality traits*, their belief systems are "authoritarian" in that sacred texts often demand absolutes, as we have seen, that are derived from the dialogic relationship. This ideological authoritarianism is inherent in a belief system that emerges from the principle of intratextuality, which allows a sacred text to speak authoritatively.

Fundamentalists are not "closed-minded," but rather seek to search their sacred text for all knowledge. Ammerman (1987, p. 51) cites the amusing case of a fundamentalist who was pondering whether to purchase a tent. At Sunday school, he recounted how upon reading Deuteronomy 14 (which lists animals permissible to eat), he found the word "roebuck"— and hence went to Sears, Roebuck & Co. to purchase a tent. We cite this example because it is illustrative of several things. First, neither our readers nor many fundamentalists would perceive this as other than the idiosyncratic interpretation of a scriptural directive. However, its humorous nature should not distract us from the more interesting fundamentalist view that scripture is a guide for everything in life and ought to be the overarching guide. The use of scriptural verses as "decision guides" in specific instances has powerful as well as trivial exemplars.[3] We note more powerful exemplars in subsequent chapters of this book.

In any case, our model sensitizes us to expect that fundamentalists will use their sacred text as the framework and justification for all thought and action, however trivial some such uses may appear from the outside. Our earlier discussion of the psychological structure and process of peripheral beliefs is helpful here and allows a common misunderstanding of fundamentalist thought to be clarified. Fundamentalists do, in fact, support other forms of knowledge, including science and historic criticism. Indeed, fundamentalism in the United States is almost synonymous with education—from the days of the dominance of fundamentalists at Princeton Theological Seminary, to their struggles within such schools as Fuller Theological Seminary and Wheaton College, to their marginalization in readily identified "fundamentalist" schools such as Bob Jones University and Liberty University. What makes fundamentalists unique is their insistence that whatever peripheral beliefs emerge (in our model's terms), they must be ultimately judged and seen as harmonious with what is contained within the bold circle—the interrelation between absolute truths and the sacred text as maintained by the principle of intratextuality. Our model allows us to explore the conditions under which particular fundamentalists may or may not find various peripheral beliefs' claims problematic. Interesting differences among fundamentalists on such issues as evolution and abortion are seldom appreciated a priori, and unless the beliefs of a specific fundamentalist group are considered, little meaningful can be said. The result is the continuing use of stereotypes about these people. Such stereotypes then serve to provide "explanations" that ultimately say more about those who describe fundamentalists in this manner than about what actually determines fundamentalists' thought and behavior.

The Intertextual Alternative

It will be helpful to understand the *intra*textual model of the structure of fundamentalist thought by contrasting it with what we refer to as "*inter*textual models," as presented in Figure 1.2. Observe that we do not offer a specific structure to contrast with fundamentalism. Rather, we suggest that intertextual models virtually define modernity and are what fundamentalisms oppose. Instead of a firm, bounded circle, there is a broken circle, indicating that very permeable boundaries exist in the thought processes of nonfundamentalists.[4] Thus the principle of intertextuality maintains that no single text speaks for itself. All texts are authoritative and interrelated, and may be consulted in the process of deriving truth, which is more properly understood as relative truth.

In further contrast to fundamentalist thought, the broken circle in Figure 1.2 suggests that factors external to the dynamic also influence the interpretive process. The larger two-way arrows are meant to illustrate not only that relative truths extend outwardly to peripheral beliefs, but also that peripheral beliefs may filter back into the interpretive process and exert continual influence on the understanding of texts and relative truths. Hence, no single sacred text is esteemed in the dynamic process. Instead, a multiplicity of authoritative texts suggest various relative truths, each tentatively held as long as the "evidence" is supportive. Thus the structure of intertextuality permits and fosters change and openness; it is much less bounded than fundamentalist thought. The bidirectional arrows also reflect the basic assumption of the principle of intertextuality: that a plurality of authoritative texts and relative truth claims is inevitable when a single text no longer defines truth. In this sense, even an authoritative text claiming to be absolute falters when placed alongside other texts making similar claims. A sacred text is uniquely authoritative only when it is viewed intratextually. Otherwise, it becomes, at best, only another authoritative text. This is to some the basic insight of fundamentalism, and to others its fatal flaw.

A comparison of the intratextual and intertextual models indicates that both rely on authority and authoritarian (in an ideological, not personality-related, sense) systems of belief. However, authorities in intertextual systems are tentative, contingent, and continually susceptible to change. This is a characterization virtually synonymous with mo-

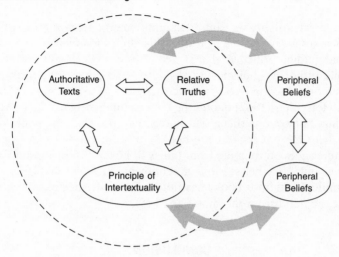

FIGURE 1.2. The structure of nonfundamentalist thought.

dernity and with "knowledge," as many have come to know it within
modernity. It is only when *all* authoritative texts and claims to knowledge are challenged by postmodern claims that supporters of modernity
and its approach to knowledge become as defensive as fundamentalists
became in the face of the challenge posed by modernity. It is as if the
chickens have come home to roost in a manner that may help those of us
who are distant from fundamentalism to be more sympathetic to their
quest.

On the other hand, intratextual structures of thought are open in a
very powerful sense. It is another stereotype to think that fundamentalism has a closed system of thought, consensually held and forever fixed.
As many who study fundamentalism have observed, nothing is more
variable than the perception of absolute truth! Sociologists have focused
on various "megachurches" and have identified fundamentalism with its
various national advocates, appropriately appreciating the successful
institutionalization of this movement. However, they tend to ignore the
smaller congregations and the numerous isolated fundamentalists within
organizations, for whom their sacred text provides the very structure of
their thought and lives. Part of the latent potential of religious thought is
that fundamentalism can coexist in congregations that would neither
identify themselves nor be identified by others as "fundamentalists."
Fundamentalists easily separate when they disagree on what their sacred
text says, indicating that, like all who seek to understand, they are open
to change and interpretation. Note that in both our models, the princi-

ples of intratextuality and intertextuality emerge from the use of texts and their respective claims to truth. This allows for their basic assumption and guiding principle: that sacred texts can proclaim themselves as religious authority—holistic and absolute—and can thereby resist either criticism or reduction to other basic categories of explanation (Machen, 1923). Hofstadter (1962) quotes the famous fundamentalist D. L. Moody as saying, "I have one rule about books. I do not read any book, unless it will help me understand *the* book" (p. 108; emphasis in original). Hofstadter goes on to quote from James B. Finley's autobiography a less extreme, but nonetheless similar, sentiment: "I have wondered if the great multiplication of books has not had a deleterious tendency, in diverting the mind from the Bible" (p. 125).

CONCLUSION

It seems that much of the difficulty for scholars in reaching a consensus on a definition of fundamentalism stems from the rich diversity of thought and belief claims made by fundamentalists, even within a given faith tradition. The principle of intratextuality is no easy assurance of agreement among fundamentalists, for at least two reasons: First, it applies across various sacred texts; second, it can be applied with much variation within a single sacred text. Differences among fundamentalists themselves may reflect deeper or more meaningful appropriations of truths that remain as much assured and absolute as they are evasive and problematic. This aspect of fundamentalism has yet to have its proper hearing in the more scholarly and academic community. We hope to remedy this problem with this book.

The employment of our model ought to reveal aspects of fundamentalism ignored in the existing empirical literature. In each one of the last three decades of the 20th century, scholars committed to an empirical and measurement-based social psychology have found the literature on fundamentalism to be so consistent with cultural stereotypes of fundamentalism that they have become suspicious of this literature (Hood, 1983; Kirkpatrick, Hood, & Hartz, 1991; Stark, 1971). In the first decade of the new century, scholars are repeating the same suspicion (Bruce, 2000). The *Encyclopedia of Fundamentalism* (Brasher, 2001) accepts the arguable claim that "fundamentalism" (originally a term applied to Protestantism in America, as we discuss in Chapter 3) can legitimately be applied to other faith traditions as well. This encyclopedia seeks to encourage comparative work among fundamentalist movements within a variety of faith traditions, such as Hinduism, Islam, and Judaism.

To this end, we briefly examine the historical and cultural contexts of each of the fundamentalisms discussed in this book, with a more complete description of the history of Protestant fundamentalism in Chapter 3. Before looking at that context, however, we revisit the primary psychological tenet of this book—that fundamentalism provides a source of meaning for its adherents.

CHAPTER TWO

Fundamentalism as a Meaning System

> As long as there is a modern world characterized by
> seeming chaos, there will be believers who react to that
> world by refusing to grant it legitimacy. Although some
> may do so in solitary reflection, most will seek out social
> structures in which certainty can take the place of doubt,
> in which clear rules and authority can take the place of
> subjectivity, and in which truth is truth, without
> compromise.
> —AMMERMAN (1987, p. 212)

The underlying premise of our intratextual model as presented in Chapter 1 is that fundamentalist religion remains alive and well because it provides a convincing system of meaning to its adherents. To understand how this is the case, we must look more specifically at how fundamentalist beliefs serve as a viable meaning system.

THE SACRED TEXT AS THE SOLE SOURCE OF MEANING

For fundamentalists, there is but one true avenue for finding meaning. How others find meaning in life—creative work, personal relationships, raising children, personal growth, personal or career achievement, and so on (see Reker & Wong, 1988)—can only be meaningful if interpreted and legitimated through a sacred text. Thus even what creativity means, why one maintains personal relationships, why having children is important, how one conceptualizes personal growth, and how one defines career achievement are subject to the authority of the sacred text. As already pointed out, fundamentalists may not be alone in such views of meaning and purpose. Others who are expressly religious may also interpret ultimate meaning and purpose, and the associated ultimate strivings (Emmons, 1999, in press), within a religious or spiritual framework. It is important to clarify, however, that fundamentalists' striving for meaning differs from that of other religious and spiritual individuals, in that it is totally defined by, and interpreted through, the sacred text itself.

We have pointed out in Chapter 1 that religion, including fundamentalist religion, is a unifying philosophy of life (a "worldview") that meets personal needs for meaning (Baumeister, 1991) and provides a sense of coherence (Antonovsky, 1987; Emmons, 1999). What may be surprising to some is that fundamentalists would heartily agree with such assessments, though with an important caveat. Whereas psychologists might entertain the notion that these factors explain (and perhaps "explain away") the religious impulse, fundamentalists see such needs only within the context of the truth claims of the religious system itself. Thus Protestant fundamentalists maintain that we humans were created by God to have personal needs for meaning and purpose, and that such needs can only be interpreted through God's intention and design. We are, in the minds of these fundamentalists, worshipful creatures whose primary purpose is therefore to know God—and the only way to know God and God's intention is for God to reveal himself and his purposes through direct communication.[1] Furthermore, God reveals himself in the most direct manner possible, and this usually means that the Bible should be taken literally (though, as pointed out in Chapter 3, most Protestant fundamentalists do not insist on a literal reading of every Biblical passage). These same principles apply equally well to the Islamic tradition, where Allah communicates directly through the Quran.

For a fundamentalist, this system is comprehensive, highly complex (yet simple enough for the common person to understand), experientially based to varying degrees, and often highly regulated. For example, Protestant fundamentalism exhibits great complexity and sophistication in the theology of "dispensationalism" (discussed in further detail in Chapter 3)—a position regarding the history of God's revelation with direct implications for the "end times" that originated during the 19th century, but remains popular in many fundamentalist circles today. A fundamentalist as a spiritual dweller (Wuthnow, 1998) also believes that the sacred text speaks with clarity in regard to behavioral regulations. Some behaviors (e.g., some forms of sexual immorality) are so clearly prohibited by the text (and perhaps the culture) that they become issues on which virtually all members of a religious tradition, even liberals, are likely to agree. But fundamentalists tend to apply the regulation to a broader range of behaviors that largely depends on their specific interpretations of scripture. Thus some Protestant fundamentalists emphasize regulations that prohibit dancing, smoking, card playing, or social drinking, on the basis of scriptural injunctions such as 1 John 2:15: "Love not the world, neither the things that are in the world. If any man love the world, the love of the Father is not in him." In this case, the "world" is identified as sinful culture with associated behavioral pleasures. Even though within some fundamentalist traditions the Divine Being can speak directly to an individual through personal experience or visions or through the collective wisdom of others, the veracity of such claims must ultimately be subjected to some reference that is granted authority. In virtually all major world traditions, this authority is the sacred text, and fundamentalist religion is unique in its insistence that all truth claims must be subjected to the sacred text as the single final arbiter.

As we shall see, there is little of greater importance than raising children in the faith. This holds for all fundamentalisms. Most fundamentalists view child rearing as a divinely conferred responsibility, and there is nothing more important than making sure that children are well grounded in the faith. (Again, however, many nonfundamentalists would concur with the importance of child rearing.) For example, among fundamental Protestants who stress a "covenantal" theology (i.e., an agreement or contract that God has initiated with humans through the Abrahamic promises of the Old Testament), there is a strong sense of parental responsibility, as commanded by such scriptures as Deuteronomy 6:1–7. Though some children when they reach the "age of accountability" become apostates and others modify many fundamentalist claims, the teachings and social structures are self-perpetuating. During the important formative years, meaning and purpose are interpreted only within the context of the faith, and all other human functions are subjected to this ultimate meaning. Thus education and vocation are good only to the extent that they facilitate the divine intention and design for each person in relation to the community of believers. Should, for example, higher education or career advancement undermine these higher purposes, they become tools of the devil, which Protestant fundamentalists interpret literally. It is for this reason that many such fundamentalists will send their children only to Christian schools (or provide home schooling). Similarly, many Protestant fundamentalists believe that some vocations, particularly those that represent full-time Christian service (e.g., pastors and missionaries), represent higher and more meaningful callings than others. Fundamentalist religion therefore has staying power. An ultimate authority is established, and a mechanism for reinforcing that authority is provided through responsibility placed on the family, church, and ordained educational institutions. This staying power is even greater when fundamentalism characterizes a majority orientation or where there is no distinction between church and state, as with Shia Islam in Iran.

It should also be noted that fundamentalists are just as subject to many self-justifying tendencies as are other people. Fundamentalists remain firmly committed to their beliefs, despite frequent ridicule from the larger culture; in fact, the primary defining characteristic of fundamentalism identified by many sociologists and historians of religion (Ammerman, 1987; Bruce, 2000; Lawrence, 1989; Lechner, 1985; Marsden, 1980) is its defensive reaction to modernism. Like other people, fundamentalists do not appreciate seeing or hearing things that conflict with their deeply held beliefs, especially if these things are intentionally offered. And yet, by nature, fundamentalists are not masochists. They want to be accepted by others, but not at the price of compromising that in which they believe so strongly. The claims of modernists and their associated ridicule of conservative religion often, in themselves, create cognitive dissonance for fundamentalists; that is, the meaning system fundamentalists have chosen to hold so dearly is the same system clearly held in contempt by the larger culture. As we know from the social-psychological literature, postdecision dissonance is frequently resolved by seeking out exclusively positive information about the chosen alternative, and thereby avoiding negative information associated with it. Thus it is not surprising that the reference group for fundamentalists will be other fundamentalists, just as scientists may use other scientists as their primary identity group. But, once again, the fundamentalists will look only to the text for justification. Therefore, Protestant fundamentalists frequently separate themselves from the world and its philosophy, and justify their position on the basis of selective scriptural passages such as Colossians 2:8: "Beware lest any man spoil you through philosophy and vain deceit, after the tradition of men, after the rudiments of the world, and not after Christ." Indeed, many such fundamentalists even take comfort and pleasure in finding meaning through their status as "a peculiar people" who have been called "out of darkness into [Christ's] marvelous light" (1 Peter 2:9). Fundamentalists within other traditions, whether Hasidic Jews or Shia Muslims, find similar justifications through the texts sacred to their tradition.

HOW FUNDAMENTALISM PROVIDES MEANING

Yea doubtless, and I count all things but loss for the excellency of the knowledge of Christ Jesus my Lord: for whom I have suffered the loss of all things, and do count them but dung, that I may win Christ . . . That I may know him, and the power of his resurrection, and the fellowship of his sufferings, being made conformable unto his death . . . Brethren, I count not myself to have apprehended: but this one thing I do, forgetting those things which are behind, and reaching forth unto those things which are before, I press toward the mark for the prize of the high calling of God in Christ Jesus. (Philippians 3:8–14)

These are familiar New Testament words to Protestant fundamentalists. Like the Apostle Paul, who penned these words, Protestant fundamentalists, like most other fundamentalists, admit they have not "apprehended" everything. But they do know, with zeal and great comfort, their purpose for living: "that I may win Christ" (Philippians 3:8). Many such fundamentalists are quick to offer reasons why others are unable to find such zeal for living—the lure of worldly pleasure, the just rewards of humanity's sinful nature, or simply the lack of God's Spirit-filled direction. Whatever the reason, it is clear that Protestant (and all other) fundamentalists believe that they alone have received and benefited from divine leading that is fully communicated and interpreted through the sacred text. It is this belief that provides confidence in the text as the source of life's meaning and purpose, which others simply "do not understand."

The guiding psychological premise that underlies our intratextual approach to fundamentalism is that fundamentalism is unusually capable of providing meaning through giving a sense of coherence to a fragmented world. To explore this concern for meaning, we discuss fundamentalism's staying power in the form of three questions:

1. How does fundamentalism provide a unifying philosophy of life?
2. How does fundamentalism provide a sense of coherence?
3. How does fundamentalism meet personal needs for meaning?

We attempt to answer each of these questions within the framework of each tradition's own first principles, but also by noting both commonalities and differences among traditions.

A Unifying Philosophy of Life

Fundamentalism provides an organizing framework for understanding how the world is perceived and experienced. It does so by relying upon a single, authoritative, all-encompassing text in which answers to the significant questions of life can be found. The nature and meaning of life are not simply described, but proscribed as well. Moral codes are provided that are absolute and, once internalized, need not be constantly debated. Adherence to such codes provides a "form of life" or "lifestyle" that often is in opposition to the larger world—not simply as rejection, but rather as adherence to values that the larger, often secular society has abandoned. Furthermore, life is embedded in a larger horizon that includes not only a sense of transcendence, but an assurance that death is overcome. Hence what may appear as "foolish" to a secular world is salvation to a fundamentalist believer.

Such meaning is rooted in the centrality of the sacred text within a specific tradition and the absolute authority it commands for adherents. Major text-based absolutes (doctrines of faith) are held beyond dispute among believers against all opposition from without, and even the more peripheral beliefs—those that may be nuanced—are derived from going back to the text for personal dialogue and meaning. Everything points back to the text.

For members of the Church of God (COG), as discussed in Chapter 4 through the life experience of A. J. Tomlinson, a cardinal text-based absolute is the belief in "Spirit baptism" and in the experience of a dichotomous spirit world, where God and Satan are at odds for the eternal claim on humanity. The COG believer is convinced of the necessity of being filled (or "baptized") with the Holy Spirit, which provides empowerment for resisting and overcoming personal attacks from Satan and demonic forces. The primary concern of such demonic forces is to thwart the divine plan that fallen humanity should be reconciled to harmony with God in the present world, as well as in the world to come. Whatever occurs in the daily scheme of personal life, either good or bad, is largely understood and explained within this framework of spiritual forces at war with each other. It is the reading of the text that serves as the basis for such a unified view of life and experience.

The discussion of serpent-handling sects (SHSs) in Chapter 5 shows that they believe not only in Spirit baptism, but also in the requirement that believers be *doers* of the text, as exemplified in the text-based mandate to take up serpents. What appears to outsiders (or the unenlightened) as a questionable ritual that courts potential maiming and death is seen by the SHS faithful as a Bible-based command for true believers that places life in perspective and permits transcendence of death, which is the ultimate concern. A common refrain among serpent handlers is this: "You have to make sure you're living right, 'cause you could get bit and die any time you take up a serpent." As one turns to the text for guidance, it dictates an overarching philosophy of right living in terms of obedience to God and abstention from sin. These take the highest priority in conducting one's life, for such is required in the service of true believers.

For the Amish, discussed in Chapter 6, meaning and purpose are found in the *Ordnung*—a Biblically based behavioral code that is orally transmitted and represents generations of accumulated community wisdom. This purpose is to protect the purity of the community and to develop personal character accordingly. The purity of the church is the highest social value, around which all else is evaluated. The *Ordnung's* moral code, despite its lack of systematization, changes little over time and is not subject to personal conscience or other subjective whims. Rather, it prescribes a style of living through which all of life is understood: behavioral practices as clear markers of separation from the world; the development of meekness and humility as reminders of one's subordination to the greater good of the community; avoidance of modern conveniences as a means of promoting social cohesion; hard work as a sacred obligation of stewardship; and so forth.

Chapter 7 reveals that Islamic fundamentalism is unique in many respects. Unlike Christian fundamentalism, the Islamic form makes no distinction between the religious and the secular. Nothing is to be "rendered unto Caesar." Fundamentalist Islam believes that the Quran was revealed to the Prophet Muhammad through the Angel Gabriel as the direct word of Allah. It contains not simply the meaning and purpose of life, but regulations to guide believers in all aspect of their lives. As such, a sense of meaning and purpose is revealed in the Quran, and life is to be lived in accordance to the Quran. Whereas some fundamentalisms separate purely secular concerns from religious ones, fundamentalist Islam makes no such distinction. Hence all life is lived as a sacred journey, infused with religious importance.

A Sense of Coherence

The text does not contradict itself. The principles and teachings found in the narrative yield a consistent picture of what a life pleasing to the Divine Being should look like. It is the blueprint for living, and no "vain philosophy" of the world shall in any way modify the blueprint. This blueprint, fundamentalists insist, communicates a singular "ultimate concern" (as opposed to Emmons's [1999] conceptualization of spirituality as a plurality of "ultimate concerns") that is in itself dictated by the sacred text; this ensures that a clash of "concerns" cannot occur. Thus the intertextual notion that varied sources can promote different ultimate concerns, or that one can "choose" among multiple ultimate concerns, is refuted—as is the postmodern claim that there are no ultimate concerns. In this sense, as we note in Chapter 3, Protestant fundamentalism was ahead of its time in predicting the crisis that modernity would face if "higher criticism" were carried to the extreme.

Therefore, all fundamentalists, regardless of tradition, have but one ultimate concern: living by the dictates of the sacred text alone, because it alone illuminates the path to fellowship with the Divine Being in this life and in the world to come. All other concerns are subordinate and reconciled to this overriding concern. The fact that the text is authoritative, inerrant, and without contradiction means that the believer is capable of knowing, with total certainty, how fellowship with the Divine Being is to be achieved. No other source of knowledge shall in any way alter the true meaning of the text. This blueprint for living provides the coherent framework for resolving all of life's concerns and provides what Antonovsky (1987) refers to as the "dynamic feeling of confidence" (p. 19) that accompanies a well-developed sense of coherence. A well-known phrase among some Christian fundamentalist groups sums it up nicely: "What's done for this world will pass; only what's done for Christ will last."

As will be seen, members of the COG subscribe to Biblical holiness as the basis for moral conduct. In the 1950s, this group forbade such things as movies, cosmetics, and skating rinks, and it continues to demand total abstinence from alcohol and tobacco. Whatever is deemed in conflict with a holy life is regarded as a temptation designed by Satan to draw one away from a close walk with God. Despite how harmless such activities may seem in the eyes of others, an intratextual understanding of the Bible prohibits them and demands denial for sake of the ultimate concern—for "without holiness, no man shall see the Lord."

An even more illuminating example of coherence as defined through ultimate concern is the issue of death in serpent handling. Serpent handlers do experience bites and sometimes die. However, the ultimate concern for those who remain is neither death itself nor criticism from skeptics, but obedience to the unchanging word of God, which continues to mandate the handling of serpents. In response to the issue of death, handlers often say, "If I get bit and die tonight, that doesn't change one word of Mark 16. It will still read tomorrow: 'They shall take up serpents.' "

Coherence, for the Amish, is understood in terms of the purity of the redemptive community (the church). So, for example, if modern conveniences have even the potential to disrupt the righteousness of the community, they are to be avoided. Anything that draws attention to the self or encourages a person to become individuated is suspect as a divisive element. Close friendships, which otherwise provide social cohesion, must be forfeited with those who live in unrepentant sin—even to the point of avoiding or shunning them. Otherwise, the seeds of a disruptive growth that threatens the social sense of coherence are planted.

In an unusual yet striking parallel to the Amish, the issue facing fundamentalist Islam (Shia) is what effect innovations would have on a way of life dictated by the Quran. This becomes a societal issue in those countries where Shia Islam governs. As a coherent "way of life" linked to the ultimate concern that is contained in the Quran, fundamentalist Islam becomes "closed" to other competing values. One interesting example is that Islamic banks do not charge "interest," because this is forbidden in the Quran. So as globalization emerges, fundamentalism is threatened unless it is allowed to exist as "isolated communities of belief" (similar to Amish communities in the United States). The coherent worldview provided within fundamentalist Islam is problematic to the rest of the world, in that it (1) rejects secularization in principle; (2) opposes democracy, in that laws cannot violate the Quran; (3) seeks to convert the entire world to Islam; and (4) allows no conversion from (out of) Islam. The example provided in Chapter 7 illustrates the problem, in that fundamentalist Islam has refused to allow the blasphemy of the Prophet Muhammad even in lands that are non-Islamic. Although this seems absurd to some, it does show the immense power of a totally coherent belief system, in which nothing is allowed to diminish what truly is of "ultimate concern." Indeed, religious fundamentalism maintains that it can specify an ultimate concern and demand it to be binding on all humanity—though Islamic fundamentalism may be unique in its claim that its principles are perhaps legally (not just morally) binding, even in non-Islamic countries. Regardless of whether the ultimate concern is legally or just morally binding, its concern remains ultimate and hence cannot be judged on purely secular terms. Fundamentalisms in general, and Islamic fundamentalism in particular, take transcendence seriously, and thus the criteria for meeting the ultimate concern transcends the purely secular. This is what makes fundamentalism so "dangerous": All other concerns—even a concern for life itself—are subservient to the ultimate concern. Thus some are called to make the ultimate sacrifice, for in the very act of dying for one's faith, one fulfills the ultimate concern of obedience to the Divine Being and is thereby assured of salvation.

Personal Needs for Meaning

Fundamentalists do not deny that they find meaning in their faith; in fact, they are quick to identify their faith as the central meaning of their existence, around which all other life events are interpreted. They are also likely to describe the personal benefits that they receive from their religious faith experience as remarkably similar (though they often use a distinct lexicon) to the personal needs for meaning identified by Baumeister (1991): purpose, value, efficacy, and self-worth. However, fundamentalists are equally quick to remind us that these are not the *reasons* for their faith; they are merely secondary benefits. The reason for faith is that it is instructed by the text, and the reason for faith in the text is that it is the Divine Being's channel of direct communication for how people are to live their lives. For example, Christian fundamentalists fully affirm what the Psalmist David proclaimed: "Thy word is a lamp unto my feet, and a light unto my path" (Psalms 119:05). It is the text itself that provides meaning, and therefore purpose is understood simply in terms of obedience to what the text says.

Thus fundamentalists are particularly likely to affirm those personal benefits and forms of meaning that are legitimized by the text. For example, all Protestant fundamentalists are familiar with the Apostle Paul's claim in his letter to the church at Philippi that "I can do all things through Christ which strengtheneth me" (Philippians 4:13). Such personal empowerment is an indicator of what Baumeister (1991) identifies as a sense of efficacy in meeting a personal need for meaning. However, the emphasis for such a fundamentalist is less on what he or she is capable of doing personally ("I can do all things . . . ") than it is on the expression of faith (" . . . through Christ which strengtheneth me"). Nonetheless, a sense of personal efficacy is still gained, as the fundamentalist views his or her connection to God as a source of power for victorious living.

Purpose

Fundamentalists need not worry when events do not go well, as evidenced in a common saying: "I know not what the future holds, but I know who holds the future." By remaining faithful to the one who is sovereign over all, the religiously fervent can face almost any situation and, even in the face of extreme tragedy, can rest assured that all has meaning and purpose. Furthermore, the text itself defines this meaning and purpose. Life is lived not simply via efficient causation, but via teleological causation. The teleological causation is not "existential" in the sense that an individual creates a purpose; rather, it is conforming to God's purpose for people in general (and for the individual in particular). Thus the irony is that a "closed-minded" fundamentalist is in fact "open" to all that is contained within the text. Intratextuality assures that the world is absorbed into the text, and the fundamentalist is open to God's view of the world, not the world's view of God.

Most fundamentalist groups, and all Christian fundamentalists, believe in an afterlife of heaven and hell. The present world is only a place of preparation for eternal bliss in the presence of God, or eternal isolation from God in the throes of hell. Thus, when instructed by the text to "Lay not up for yourselves treasures upon earth, where moth and rust doth corrupt, and where thieves break through and steal; But lay up for yourselves treasures in heaven, where neither moth nor rust doth corrupt, and where thieves do not break through nor steal: For where your treasure is, there will your heart be also" (Matthew 6:19–21), many Christian fundamentalists see material and spiritual gain as mutually exclusive and eschew the former in favor of the latter. Similarly, the Quran states that "wealth and sons are the adornment of the present world; but the abiding things, the deeds of righteousness, are better with God in reward, and better in hope" (Surah, 18:46).

As we shall see, for members of the COG, the fundamentalist text-based belief that they are the continuation of the Bible church in contemporary times has provided them with a sense of purpose in their responsibility to share the message of unity with all Christians—as well as with sinners—and to proclaim the necessity of one church for presentation to God in heaven as the bride of Christ.

Similarly, serpent handlers see themselves as enlightened by God with respect to what the Bible says true believers will understand from the scripture and subsequently do. Their responsibility is to preach the "whole" Word—not just what is popular or acceptable—which includes all the signs. Despite the ebb and flow of the movement that occurs over time, contemporary serpent handlers strongly assert that there will always be true followers of Christ who will read, obey, and preach the Biblical command: "They shall take up serpents" (Mark 16:18).

An individual's sense of purpose, for the Amish, cannot be understood apart from the person's place as part of the *Gemeinde*, or redemptive community—the expression of all connotations of "congregation," "church," and "community" (Hostetler, 1993). Individual purpose is to remain righteous, for the church, according to Article 8 of the Dordrecht Confession (a major confessional statement used by the Amish), must be a congregation of righteous people that will fulfill the Biblical mandate to be "a glorious church, not having spot, or wrinkle, or any such thing; but that it should be holy and without blemish" (Ephesians 5:27). To assure that the church will remain pure, the Amish set rules and procedures through the *Ordnung*. If each individual accepts his or her purpose and follows the *Ordnung*, the community will remain pure and within the will of God.

As already noted, Islamic fundamentalism is unique in making no distinction between the religious and the secular. Hence all of life is lived within a religious frame for which there is guidance both from the text and from religious leaders. Further guidance comes from the *hadith* (i.e., authoritative examples from the life of the Prophet). The laws of Islam also provide purpose in dictating what should *not* be done because it is in opposition to Allah's will. Thus there is an interesting parallel to the Amish *Ordnung*: Though the traditions may vary, the purpose is always the same—to assure the community of believers that they are following God's plan for them as dictated by the sacred text.

Value

Fundamentalists, in one sense, have a distinct advantage over many others: They can lay claim to absolute values with clear-cut answers to what the others may find quite problematic (alcohol and drug use, attending R-rated movies, abortion, sexual behavior, homosexuality, etc.). Quite simply, values are judged by conformity to the text. Sometimes, of course, the text allows interpretational latitude, and even rather extreme fundamentalists may recognize (contrary to much public misconception) that the text need not be taken literally. But on many matters, the text speaks clearly and with authority. So, for example, homosexuality is condemned by Christian fundamentalists, for here the Biblical text speaks with unmistakable clarity. It is perhaps ironic, however, that fundamentalists sometimes disagree among themselves on issues that they believe to be important and that they believe the text addresses clearly. For example, some groups within some fundamentalist churches believe that it is wrong to eat anywhere in the church building, and therefore maintain that churches should not have kitchens. It is not unusual for groups to "split" on such issues and form separate churches, with each still adhering to "absolute truth." Thus adhering to absolute values can lead to tremendous diversity, and this may help account for fundamentalisms' vitality and "staying power."

Both the COG and SHSs subscribe to personal holiness as a fundamental command of the sacred text. Within its pages, the Bible dictates what can be understood as values for right living. Based on intratextual interpretations of a given tradition or sect, such values may include proscriptions with respect to certain sexual behaviors, dress codes, alcohol/drug use, swearing, marital issues, divorce, and so on. Again, specifics may vary among denominations and sects, although each will surely make reference to the text—as well as to the common saying that "The Bible means what it says and says what it means." Compliance with these dictates ensures a type of morality that places one in proper standing with the author of the text.

The Amish prescribe a value-laden style of life that is entirely directed toward one purpose: maintaining a church that is uncorrupted by secular culture. Romans 12:2 is a Biblical passage well known among the Amish: "And be not conformed to this world: but be ye transformed by the renewing of your mind, that ye may prove what is that good, and acceptable, and perfect, will of God." To "be not conformed" to this world, an Amish person must disregard many of the cherished values held by secular culture. To be "transformed by the renewing" of his or her mind, the Amish person must become wholly committed to the wisdom of the *Ordnung*. Such commitment results in what appears to the outsider as a hodgepodge of behavioral prohibitions and prescriptions, but what to the Amish person blends together into a coherent lifestyle.

The sense of value in the Islamic context is addressed in Chapter 7 in a unique way. Among fundamentalists, whether Islamic or not, one cannot mock the Divine Being, the sacred text, and in some cases prophets and church leaders (e.g., the Pope or the Ayatollah). Fundamentalist Islam makes claims that one cannot blaspheme the Prophet Muhammad. These are absolute values that override all other values, including values of literary or academic freedom. In contrast, intertextuality allows freedom of expression, because one text is not a privileged text relative to another; this freedom can even extend to the point where mockery can be made of a sacred text. Thus, for fundamentalists, there is more than simply a different rank ordering of values à la Rokeach (1969, 1973). Rather, there is a direct clash of value *systems*—a system based wholly on what the text commands versus one based on relative choice between competing texts. Values in fundamentalist Islam, as in other forms of fundamentalism, are not simply "values"; they are "absolute values" commanded by the Divine Being, and as such require complete commitment and devotion.

Efficacy

An important but often overlooked benefit of fundamentalism is that by finding specific meanings in a sacred text, one has a complete assurance that everything has its purpose (even when one cannot understand what that purpose is) and is therefore good, in that it is ordained by God. Virtually all Protestant fundamentalists believe not only that God has sovereign control, but also that he works through his dedicated believers. Hence they are the "salt of the earth" (Matthew 5:13), the "light of the world" (Matthew 5:14), and a "city that is set on an hill [that] cannot be hid" (Matthew 5:14). This is why that, in the face of threat and modernity, they feel compelled to live out these metaphors: salt cures social decay; light not only illuminates (reveals) sin, but also dispels its darkness; and a radiant city is a point of reference for those in need of direction or safe haven. In the face of battle, a true soldier of God is called into service to stand for truth and righteousness against all the wiles of the enemy—whether this service is protesting against abortion or gathering signatures on a petition for a constitutional amendment to prohibit gay marriage. This is what the text mandates.

On the other hand, when one does all that is possible, there is repose in a resolved faith that God will accomplish his purpose. All is left up to a sovereign God who is in complete control. This is true not only in the case of a call to social action, but also in one of a personal attack from the enemy, Satan. For example, members of the COG, like some other fundamentalists, stress a belief in divine healing—trusting in God for a miraculous cure without recourse to medical intervention. The text explicitly states that God heals all infirmities; yet when the healing has not come, surrender to the will of God, based on intratextual considerations, leads to a resolve that things will work out for the best. Whether he heals or decrees death, "God does all things well." This is true not only for a cancer-ridden COG believer, but also for the serpent handler who has received a fatal bite. In both cases, what might be viewed by others as a loss of control becomes a peaceful surrender in the hands of one who controls all things.

The Amish are likely to stress efficacy less as a personal achievement than as a personal responsibility to live a life worthy of the community's redemptive calling. If individuals obey the *Ordnung*, they will experience personal contentment, for their lives are in harmony with the will of the community. With some exceptions (most notably involving educational requirements), the Amish have been allowed to structure their community in terms of what they see as their redemptive calling. This allows the Amish to define how they can best live efficacious lives in light of community values.

Thus, in the eyes of fundamentalist believers, fundamentalism works best when its style of life is allowed by the larger culture. Fundamentalism is more problematic when it clashes with secular and more interstitial views that dominate the secular world. Hence fundamentalists are greatly concerned about maintaining control over their educational systems. The Amish have been successful in several court cases in maintaining such control; other fundamentalist groups have been less successful. Nonetheless, most Protestant fundamentalists have remained resilient and have maintained control over the education of their children, through either home schooling or Christian schools (including the formation of thriving Bible schools at the college level).

Because Islam makes no distinction between secular and sacred, all of life is lived efficaciously. The Quran provides guidance for everything, from dress to interpersonal relations to times and postures for prayer. Hence, as long as believers are in an Islamic country that allows for what the rest of the world may view as religious peculiarities, all is well. Problems arise, however, when Islamic fundamentalists live in a secular culture, where religious traditions and values may conflict with even well-justified laws. Can they wear headscarves to school? Can women be excused from gym due to dress modesty? Efficacy, whether personal or social, is therefore context-dependent, and a sense of efficacy is best met when the context (culture) is uniformly Islamic. In contrast, needs for efficacious meaning are most frustrated when the culture does not allow for the religious impulse. It is thus not surprising that many Islamic fundamentalists push for the creation of theocentric (Islamic) states—and, indeed, some other fundamentalist groups (including Protestant fundamentalists) believe in a theocratic form of government. When this is not possible, some groups (e.g., some Islamic fundamentalists in Pakistan) will attempt to influence legislation prohibiting the passage of any secular law that is in opposition to the sacred text.

Self-Worth

In one form or another, virtually all religious fundamentalisms emphasize that man (again, fundamentalists make no excuses for using gender-exclusive language, since it is the language of the text; see Note 1) is created in God's image—and hence that a human being has intrinsic value and worth. Specific passages in the sacred text (e.g., Psalms 139:13–14: "For thou hast possessed my reins: thou hast covered me in my mother's womb. I will praise thee; for I am fearfully and wonderfully made . . . ") are interpreted to affirm the sanctity of life, including prenatal life. Such interpretations are the basis for the near-virtual unanimity among American fundamentalists (as well as some other religious groups) in condemning abortion.

By its very nature, the notion of self-worth in fundamentalist Christianity is rooted in the text-based belief that though human beings are created in the image of God (the ultimate basis of self-worth), all humanity is born into sin, which is despised by God. Yet the incarnation of God in Christ, who suffered the ultimate punishment to redeem humanity from this corrupt state, is a testament of the true value of humanity in the mind of God. Once they have repented of their sins, those who have felt worthless, hopeless, rejected, and without purpose gain a new sense of value and acceptance not only from a community of believers, but, more importantly, from God himself. Christian fundamentalists draw much encouragement from the belief that they are personally connected to God; hence their claim for lack of need for acceptance from the world.

This is particularly true for the COG and SHSs (both groups are Pentecostal), whose members believe in Spirit baptism. What greater assurance of worth can one have than knowledge that God himself literally dwells within one's being? As one song proclaims, "I may be a nobody to everybody, but I'm somebody to God." Many fundamentalist groups, including the COG, find additional personal self-worth through the belief that they have been "chosen by God" in their Bible-based claim to being the exclusive body of Christ—the real "Church of God of the Bible," as the COG puts it. For serpent handlers, the ritual of handling venomous serpents is a manifest sign, evidenced in the Bible, that they are true believers of Jesus. Both groups thus experience a "specialness" that reminds them of their intrinsic value.

The Amish find their sense of self-worth through their relation to the community. However, self-worth is not a goal and may not be explicitly acknowledged in Amish society, for it may appear to run contrary to the valued traits of meekness and humility. It is in this sense that education is not highly valued, for the purpose of education is not to exalt oneself through the attainment of knowledge, but rather to provide for one's family and to serve the community. For these purposes, an eighth-grade education will suffice; higher education, because it tends to encourage an inflated view of oneself, is seen as fraught with danger. Nevertheless, there is inherent worth to the individual—to be a productive member of the redemptive community by living in obedience, with meekness and humility, to the sacred order of the *Ordnung*. It is only through this prescription that the purity of the church, in accordance with Biblical teachings, can be maintained. In this sense, the Amish are no different from other fundamentalist groups, for ultimately the purpose of life is to please God by being obedient to his commands. In this way a person shows that he or she loves God and is worthy of eternal salvation, but only by God's grace. Hence the *Ordnung* and the text upon which it is based assure self-worth.

The teachings found in the Quran are like those of the two other great Abrahamic faiths—Judaism and Christianity—in that the human being, though a creature like any other created being, is a special creation. The text says that "I [Allah] have breathed into man of My spirit" (Quran, Surah 15:29). Humans are distinct from nature, and the worth of each individual is found in the fact that he or she is given the responsibility of free choice and is capable of responding in obedience to the commands of Allah (Rahman, 1980).

CONCLUSION

We argue throughout this text that religious fundamentalism—because it demands complete allegiance to a totally authoritative text that provides a unifying philosophy of life and a personal sense of coherence, as well as capably meeting specific needs for meaning—is a powerful meaning system to its adherents. It is therefore perhaps foolish to expect, as some did in the 1920s, that fundamentalism will fade away. Evidence indicates that it continues to hold powerful sway over large numbers of people.

However, as we have already noted in Chapter 1, it is not just religious fundamentalism that can meet needs for meaning. Much of what we have said about fundamentalism as a meaning system can apply to other forms of religious expression (and, for that matter, many strongly held ideological positions, whether religious or not). Religion, regardless of its specific form, can supply great meaning and purpose to life's existence—though it may be true that fundamentalism is even more capable of providing meaning than other forms of religious experience. In fact, many nonfundamentalists, especially evangelicals (but even some mainline Protestants), can identify with much that we have said about how the Biblical text is uniquely capable of providing meaning. Perhaps a parallel phenomenon can be found in other religious traditions as well.

To understand more fully how meaning is found through specific fundamental beliefs, it is important to place such beliefs within their historical and cultural contexts. Although we attempt to contextualize each form of fundamentalism discussed in Chapters 4 through 7, we first devote special attention to the historical roots of Protestant fundamentalism—the belief system to which the term was first applied—in Chapter 3. We maintain that when the fundamentalisms are contextualized, much of the laboratory and measurement-derived research on fundamentalists can be seen as masking more of the truth than it reveals, even when certain findings are true within the confines of a given empirical study. If the application of our model begins to unmask the truth about fundamentalisms, and to permit their full range and scope to be explored, we will have achieved our purpose for this book.

CHAPTER THREE

The History of Protestant Fundamentalism[1]

Liberals blame 'Fundamentalists' for not being Liberals;
sacramentalists [blame them] for not being sacramentalists;
[the] neo-orthodox [blame them] for not being neo-
orthodox; and so on. The limitation of this kind of
criticism is clear. It tells us, in terms of some other system,
what 'Fundamentalism' is not, without telling us—often,
indeed, without even asking—what 'Fundamentalism' is in
terms of itself. Consequently, these accounts do not touch
the heart of the matter; for 'Fundamentalism' is something
quite different from these other systems, and can be
understood only in terms of its own first principles.
—PACKER (1958, p. 11)

The intratextual model of fundamentalism stresses that common psychological and sociological dynamics are at work, regardless of
context. The idea that there are parallels among movements across religious traditions is a logical extension of the intratextual model, and
applying the model to various traditions both within American Protestantism (Pentecostals, serpent handlers, the Amish) and outside Protestantism (Islam) is our aim in Chapters 4–7. However, it is also true that
we must consider the unique historical and social context for a complete
understanding of fundamentalism, and we devote this chapter to these
considerations.

The term "fundamentalism" is used here to describe a particular
movement within American Protestantism that was formed in the early
20th century, though Protestant fundamentalists themselves claim that
their movement is simply an extension of historic Christianity and a continuation of the 19th-century American religious consensus. Protestant
fundamentalism still carries marks of its unique historical development

to such a degree that to say "fundamentalist" conjures up immediate images and feelings in many Americans today. Protestant fundamentalism is not merely an abstract category used to define a particular group of people; rather, it is a self-conscious American religious movement arising out of definite historical circumstances. This chapter traces the historical development of American Protestant fundamentalism as a distinct movement within American history.

We contend that the dynamics of this distinctively American Protestant movement are extended to other faith traditions and cultures, insofar as they share what we identify as the fundamentalist commitment, as a reaction to modernism, to the principle of intratextuality—that is, the necessity to accept solely the authoritative and regulatory claims of the sacred text. It is therefore incorrect to assume that intratextual fundamentalism is uniquely Protestant, or even that it originated in Protestantism and was somehow exported to other traditions. Indeed, the principle of intratextuality far preceded contemporary fundamentalist movements, whether Protestant or otherwise. It is correct, however, to think that fundamentalism *as an intratextual reaction to modernism* occurred earlier in Great Britain and the United States than elsewhere, since modernism (not intratextualism) emerged first as a Western European and North American phenomenon. Any primacy attributed to Protestant fundamentalism is thus only a function of this historical consequence; it was not a dominant system that exerted cross-cultural influence. On the contrary, intratextualism is unlikely to have much influence across traditions, since by its very nature it promotes exclusivity and thereby has an isolated impact. It is precisely this isolation-promoting dynamic that is both fundamentalism's strength (in that it lends itself well to group commitment) and weakness (in that it tends to have little influence beyond those who are already committed). In fact, it may help explain why the authors who are perhaps the two most recognized scholars on the topic (Marsden, 1980, 1991; Sandeen, 1970) suggest that Protestant fundamentalism in the Reformed tradition (e.g., Presbyterians, some Baptists, Congregationalists) should be viewed as independent of such traditions as the Wesleyan Holiness and Pentecostal groups—though other scholars (e.g., Brereton, 1990; Ammerman, 1987, 1991) disagree and adopt a more inclusive view of Protestant fundamentalism.

Technically, the most correct description of the term "fundamentalism" is the fundamentalist movement within American Protestantism, since the term was coined and initially referenced only within the American Protestant framework—specifically, in 1920 in reference to militant conservatives in the Northern Baptist Convention. The term has subsequently been borrowed (especially by the secular mass media, their believing public, and academicians) to describe movements within other religious traditions. In recent decades, the term has been used especially to describe the postcolonial Muslim world—most notably in Iran following the 1979 revolution, and in connection with terrorism in the name of religion (most poignantly made conscious to Americans on September 11, 2001). However, historians of religious fundamentalism are reluctant to speak of it outside of American Protestantism (Pelikan, 1990), and many experts of other religious traditions (e.g., Hassan, 1990; Wieseltier, 1990) maintain that the use of the term as defined in the American context is not applicable to those other traditions. Still others (e.g., Lawrence, 1989) argue that many religious protest movements have common characteristics that justify the use of the term "fundamentalism" in a broad, cross-cultural manner; proponents of this view point out that because modernism is global, fundamentalism too will be global.

Still, however, American Protestant fundamentalism is used as a historical case study in this chapter for three reasons: (1) The term itself originates with American Protestantism, and there is considerable disagreement whether the common Western conception of the term is applicable outside of American Protestantism; (2) it is assumed that this form of fundamentalism is what is most familiar and interesting to the readership (as it is to us ourselves); and (3) only one tradition could be handled with sufficient detail in one chapter. Authors who emphasize cross-creedal and multicultural parallels include Armstrong (2000), Kepel (1991/1994), and Riesebrodt (1990/1993). Other authors, such as Dekmejian (1985), focus exclusively on other religious traditions.

Regardless of how broadly or narrowly one conceives fundamentalism, the quotation from J. I. Packer at the beginning of this chapter indicates that many people, including those within the Christian faith, have a good deal to say about what fundamentalism is *not*, especially in relation to their own ideals about what constitutes true religion. It is far more difficult to identify what fundamentalism truly is, particularly on its own terms. Our intratextual model as presented in Chapter 1 provides a structural model that allows fundamentalism to speak for itself in light of its own particular sacred text. We have reviewed massive amounts of literature on fundamentalism, written mostly by sociologists and historians. This literature is impressive, and we are greatly indebted to the fine work that we have been privileged to read and study. We have also studied many of the original fundamentalist documents that these historians and sociologists have analyzed. From our perspective, they have done an admirable job, by and large. But the points we wish to make are that we have assessed their work from *our* perspective, and that both their "take" and our "take" on fundamentalism are largely the views of *outsiders looking in.* Very few fundamentalists themselves have conducted a historical or sociological analysis of the phenomenon.[2] Again, as we have noted in Chapter 1, fundamentalists are much more concerned with intratextual than with intertextual consideration of their tradition.

Fundamentalism, as a social movement in America, grew out of a rich history of religious conservatism. Among the earliest settlers in the early 17th century were English Puritans, a religious group seeking freedom from the Church of England. The Puritans claimed the Bible as the only infallible guide for matters of faith and practice in matters of religion, and sought to shape their entire lives in light of it. They defined Christianity as a revealed religion, communicated by God to humans through the Bible. They stressed such doctrines as the divinity of Jesus Christ, the sinfulness of humanity, the necessity of religious conversion, and the need for religious truths to affect one's feelings and emotions— all of which are views adhered to by contemporary fundamentalists. In addition, and contrary to some fundamentalist thought, the Puritans were strict Calvinists. They emphasized such beliefs as God's sovereign control over all human affairs, as well as "predestination," which stresses that humans are unable to choose God for salvation until God draws the sinner to himself by changing the sinner's heart. The Puritans also had radical ideas concerning the Christian potential for American civilization. They viewed America as the "new Israel," a land governed by the timeless laws of God as they are found in the Bible.

The 19th century witnessed the Puritan vision for American civilization. Nineteenth-century America could rightly be called "Christian America." There was a general consensus among the populace concerning the truth of historic, Bible-centered Christianity as it had been passed down from their Puritan forebears. In addition, the 19th century witnessed the rise of revivalism, in which masses of people were converted and religious excitement grew suddenly in certain areas of the country. Religion became the center of American life, and aside from relatively small pockets of theological liberalism and Roman Catholicism, historic Protestant Christianity was the overriding consensus. Revivals, missions, evangelism, and social work were not uncommon in public life. Both legislation and unwritten laws supported a Christian ethical system. Christianity was a religion that appealed to the common person through a simple belief in the Bible and a virtuous life, but it also received, at least through most of the 19th century, a generally unchallenged defense among the intellectuals of the day. American civilization and Protestantism were mutually supportive, if not synonymous. Highly individualistic and popular Bible-based Protestantism dominated American life throughout the 19th century. As Marsden (1980) says, "The old order of American Protestantism was based on the interrelationship of faith, science, the Bible, morality, and civilization" (p. 17).

This "Christian America" was the ground from which the American fundamentalist movement emerged. The reason for fundamentalism's rise, however, was the sudden breakdown of a conservative Protestant consensus. In the pages ahead, we describe how that breakdown occurred and how, in reaction, fundamentalism emerged as a religious movement.

"IN THE WORLD BUT NOT OF THE WORLD"[3]: CONTEXT AND COUNTERTEXT

Lawrence (1989) contends that an understanding of fundamentalism must consider both the *context* and *countertext* of the social movement. He maintains that though the specific issues facing American Protestant fundamentalism are different from those facing fundamentalist movements in Islam and Judaism (the other two monistic faith traditions), the general *context* is the same: modernity. Their differences are emphasized by how specifically they respond to the modern context (the *countertext*).

"In the World"

Fundamentalists, regardless of tradition, present a countertext (Lawrence, 1989) to modernity—the constituent elements of a modern, secular world.[4] This does not mean, however, that fundamentalists are necessarily antimodern; indeed, one would be hard pressed to pick out most Protestant fundamentalists in a crowd. In many ways, Protestant fundamentalists (except for some special groups) are thoroughly modern in their lifestyles at home, choice of occupation, educational level, and so forth. Ammerman (1987) discovered from her year-long participant observation of a fundamentalist church in a growing industrial Northeastern city that the church was typical of the community in which it was located on the three primary measures of socioeconomic status: income, occupation, and education level. Ammerman's observation applies to most fundamentalist churches; they reflect the communities of which they are a part.[5] This makes good sense, given that most fundamentalists have an interest in evangelizing their communities and wish not to construct artificial barriers that might keep them from proselytizing effectively. In this sense, fundamentalists are very much "in the world."

"But Not of the World"

The American fundamentalist movement is correctly understood, at its core, as a reaction not against *modernity* (with the exception of some isolated pockets), but against *modernism*—"the contingent ideological reshaping of human experience in response to the modern world" (Lawrence, 1989, p. 17). It is important to remember that at its heart, Protestant fundamentalism was (and still is) a self-conscious religious movement in the face of a threatening culture defending the essentials of the orthodox faith—in particular, the complete authority of the Bible and the salvation of sinners through the death and resurrection of Jesus Christ. The target of this defense was modernism. As a result, fundamentalism and modernism were pitted against one another during the latter half of the 19th century, and this resulted in what Marty (1969) has called the "modern schism." The old Protestant dogmas were being challenged and supplanted by new assumptions of industrialism and secularism. For many, the personal solution to this unsettling of religion was what Marty has called a "controlled secularity," whereby religion was relegated to the private sphere of personal belief, family, and leisure, while the public sphere of science, politics, and economics was yielded to secular thinking. In this tumultuous soil, the seeds of fundamentalism were planted.

Though cultural elements were included in their opposition, fundamentalists viewed themselves primarily as warriors for "old-time religion," preserving elements of the faith that were coming under attack from the threats of modernism—threats both internal and external to the faith. Thus fundamentalism provided a countertext to the modernist vision of the world (Lawrence, 1989). This internal–external bifurcation, however, is too simplistic for analytic purposes; internal dynamics occur within the context of a larger social setting, and indeed many of what appeared to be innocuous developments of a strictly internal matter were largely precipitated by a subsuming cultural context. Clearly, modernism was the cultural underpinning for many issues facing the conservative Christian church, and nowhere was that underpinning more pointed than in the theory of evolution. Consequently, fundamentalism's entire internal discussion and subsequent ideological development were framed within what could be described as a fortress mentality characterized by high degrees of distress, tension, and perhaps fear. Therefore, the internal dynamics sometimes reflected issues that were clearly linked, especially in the minds of conservative church leaders, to a deliberate insurgence of modernistic thought that had to be handled directly and immediately. At other times, however, the linkage between concerns with modernism and many of these developments were so complex and indirect that many fundamentalists themselves would have found it difficult to articulate the connection.

PREVAILING RELIGION IN THE LATE 19TH CENTURY

To understand why the religious ground was fertile for a reactionary movement, we must first understand the prevailing views of late-19th-century American religion. We briefly discuss four characteristics[6] of 19th-century Christianity that directly influenced fundamentalism's emergence: (1) a high view of scripture; (2) a high, but limited, view of science; (3) dispensationalism; and (4) the Holiness movement.

A High View of Scripture

Inherent in the mindset of 19th-century conservative Christians was the belief not only that there is an objective truth, but also that God desires and indeed expects every individual to seek knowledge of that truth, that such knowledge is obtainable, and that such knowledge points the individual directly to God. This view of objective truth had important implications for the 19th-century view of the Bible. Scripture was considered a storehouse of facts in propositional form, and the information it contained was believed to be precise and without error not only in religious matters, but also in historical and scientific matters. Scripture was viewed as factual, and since it was thought to come directly from God, it was seem as authoritatively true everywhere that it spoke. Any scientific dogma or belief that contradicted the clear teaching of scripture belonged to the godlessness of liberalism, and needed to be immediately confronted. For the 19th-century conservative Christian, the clear, propositional teaching of scripture directly communicated by God was the ultimate truth and therefore clearer than any other source of truth. The Bible was elevated to the position of being the chief textbook of all life and knowledge.

Carpenter (1997; see also Marty, 1982) points out that for early 20th-century fundamentalists (and likely for fundamentalists today) the words of scripture often became religious "icons," a claim that they themselves would have found disturbing. Though careful to avoid artifacts and images in worship or religious architecture, which carried with them shades of Roman Catholicism or Eastern Orthodoxy, churches frequently had (and still have), Bible verses blazoned across their walls. Even today one might also find in a fundamentalist home needlepoint work with a scripture verse, not only as a visual reminder of spiritual truth, but increasingly also, in Carpenter's words, as "a badge of separation, and an act of witness to a culture whose aphorisms and images [were] increasingly secular" (1997, p. 75).

A High, but Limited, View of Science

A common misconception about American fundamentalism is that it was and is antiscientific, largely because fundamentalism is forever linked in many minds to anti-Darwinism by the famous Scopes trial of 1925. What is conjured up in these minds is a stereotype of fundamentalists as Southern, rural, uneducated, and poorly informed about the sciences. As with all stereotypes, there is a kernel of truth to this claim, but it fails to appreciate the fact that there are also highly educated, middle- and upper-class fundamentalists. As Coreno (2002) has shown, fundamentalism is both a class and a cultural phenomenon. To ignore this fact is to risk believing that "if a person believes what is usually called 'old time religion,' he must, so to speak, have a greasy nose, dirty fingernails, [and] baggy pants, and he musn't shine his shoes or comb his hair" (Gasper, 1963, p. 13). Historically, however, science was greatly *affirmed* by most 19th-century Christian theologians and church leaders. Even today, fundamentalists are well represented among scientists and technicians in contemporary society. For 19th-century conservative Christians, truth was the same for all times and across all cultures, and if proper methods were used, all rational individuals would come to the same correct conclusion. Just as one could study the supernatural world through scripture, one could study the facts of the natural world through inductive, experimental science. Never would these two methods of gaining knowledge conflict with one another, because both gave objective truth concerning the nature of reality. Indeed, the natural scientists of earlier centuries did not find science and religion incompatible. For instance, the Biblical Christian faith of such major scientific pioneers as Newton, Galileo, and Descartes was far more than a generalized religious sentiment. Rather, as Tarnas (1991) notes, "their Christian presuppositions were intellectually pervasive, embedded in the very fabric of their scientific and philosophic theories" (p. 301). Out of this earlier emphasis on the scientific validity of scripture emerged in the 19th century the view of the inerrancy of scripture.

A major influence among conservative religionists during the late 19th century was the emphasis on two different aspects of a similar philosophical position: Scottish common-sense realist philosophy and Baconian science. The unquestioned American philosophical dogma of the 19th century insisted upon an objective understanding of external reality that was available to immediate perception. This approach to general knowledge also dominated American religious thought of that era;

therefore, when philosophical and scientific epistemologies were undergoing radical revision at the beginning of the 20th century, conservative religionists seriously questioned the validity of the subsequent views. In fact, conservative American Christianity often defended its Baconian and common-sense philosophical base as strongly as it did its religious doctrines.

Common-sense realism is a philosophical position made popular by the Scotsman Thomas Reid (among others). It maintains, in opposition to Locke and Hume, that the mind perceives the world as it really is. People are directly aware of external reality; what they perceive is reality itself, not merely an image of reality. The dominance of the modern social-constructionist perspective is tempered by philosophical criticism, such as Bowker's (1973) view that it remains possible that part of our sense of God actually comes from God. This realist position was indispensable to the conservative Christian notion that God had created an ordered universe that was capable of being known by all people. Hence, Newton could appeal to both "books"—of nature and of God—with the same basic philosophical assumptions. Tarnas (1991) points out that "Newton was as zealously absorbed in Christian theology and studies of biblical prophecy as he was in physics" (p. 301). Thus applied, nonelitist, common-sense philosophy was well suited to the prevailing 19th-century ideals of American culture. But this philosophy also provided a firm foundation for yet another exceedingly important tenet of conservative Christian thinking: Just as God's truth could be known directly by the common person through scripture ("special revelation"), it could also be known through empirical science ("general revelation"). The special role of the Bible is obviously a central theme in Christian fundamentalist thought today; with common-sense realism as an underlying philosophical base, general revelation too was vitally central to the belief system of 19th-century evangelicals.

The method (made famous three centuries earlier by philosopher Francis Bacon) of scientific induction—that is, gaining knowledge by moving from observed and measurable particular facts to more general laws about reality based on such facts—was indispensable to a 19th-century religious outlook. To deny it went against all "common sense," and meant entering the realm of the "speculative" and "unscientific." Many 19th-century Americans felt that this objective and fact-based science was as crucial to the maintenance of the Christian faith as any of its cardinal doctrines. However, science during this era was beginning to be influenced by the Kantian notion that the mind plays a vital role in its perception of external reality. According to Kant, the mind imposes categories of understanding upon the world, making the "noumenal world" (external reality independent of human perception of it) unknowable.

These types of "metaphysical speculations," as many religious conservatives were wont to call them, were seen as dangerous to maintaining an objective and fact-based religion. Perhaps, as Noll (1996) points out, one of the difficulties for conservative Protestants even today is that newer scientific explanations and philosophies have been introduced through a Darwinian materialism. As a result, they have rejected not only Darwinism, but also the more organic, developmental understanding of science associated with Darwin. Therefore, the late-19th-century Christians who eventually became fundamentalists were not against science, as they were (and still are) commonly portrayed as being. Rather, they were opposed to a particular version of science that began to prevail during this era—namely, a Kantian view of science that denied their capability of knowing with confidence an objective reality. In fact, these Christians often made it one of their chief claims that they were being scientific; in their minds, if they did this well, it would provide (1) conclusive evidence confirming the order of God's universe and (2) the intellectual basis for Biblical claims about God's active role in that order.

Thus, philosophically, fundamentalists were (and to some extent still are) modernists, insofar that they adopted the position that truth is objective, that it corresponds to an external reality, that it cannot contradict itself, and that it requires a systematic methodology (i.e., a standard scientific methodology as well as a systematic theological hermeneutic) to be discovered. Today, fundamentalists (like scientists) are far more bothered by postmodern thought—with its suspicions of an absolute truth, of an external reality that directly corresponds with human perception, or of a "match" between surface language and deeper levels of meaning.

Dispensationalism[7]

Another development among 19th-century American Protestants that had an important influence on subsequent fundamentalist thinking involved views on eschatology (i.e., the "end times" or the second coming of Christ). Two different doctrinal positions regarding the second coming of Christ have predominated in most of Christian history. Each position involves a particular view not only of the end times, but also of the success of the gospel's spread in this age and the relationship between Christianity and culture. The position that was dominant in America until the late 19th century was "postmillennialism." Postmillennialism was optimistic regarding the spread of the gospel; its adherents believed that more and more people would be converted to Christ, and the world would eventually be Christianized. This would culminate in a "golden age" of Christianity before the coming of Christ—hence Christ's return was seen as "postmillenial," or "after the golden age." However, 19th-century postmillennialism was very supernatural; it was believed that the gospel would spread with success through the preaching of the Word because of the work of the Holy Spirit in bringing people to believe in Christ. This postmillennial view helped to substantiate a very positive view of American civilization as a "city on a hill," the civilization used by God to usher in the millennium.[8] The postmillenial view of culture was also very positive: The mission of the church was not simply to save souls from a wicked culture, but also to transform all of culture to the glory of God.

About 1875, however, the dominant eschatological view among conservative Protestants began to change (Marsden, 1980). A major reason for this was the secularization of postmillennialism. With the increase of modernism, many began to naturalize the optimism of postmillennialism. This modification called for the natural progression of Christian society to be found in evolutionary models of history instead of the supernatural intervention of God. In addition, this progression was seen as advanced through political and social means, rather than the working of the Holy Spirit through gospel preaching. This secularization of the dominant millennial view by modernists alarmed many evangelical Christians near the end of the 19th century. In order to preserve the supernaturalism of their view of end times, many conservative Protestants began to switch to "premillennialism" (also called "millenarianism"). In contrast to postmillennialism, premillennialism was pessimistic about the spread of the gospel and the development of Christian culture. Its adherents stated that the world was slipping into greater decline, which would finally come to a dramatic end at the supernatural return of Christ. At that time, Christ would establish a 1,000-year earthly reign over his church; fundamentalists tended to understand this literally, based on their reading of certain Old Testament prophecies (especially the interpretation of the "seventy weeks" in Daniel 9:24) and key passages from the book of Revelation (e.g., Revelation 20:4–6) Unlike the postmillennial view, this millennial reign of Christ would only be instituted after his return.

The major impact of this millenarian movement, however, was the resulting change in an understanding of culture as a Christian civilization to a view of the world as rapidly declining from which souls needed salvation. Less effort was made at trying to redeem all of culture for the glory of God, and more effort was made at trying to escape from all that was worldly. Perhaps this new view of culture was best expressed by the Chicago evangelist D. L. Moody, whom Marsden (1980) has described as possibly the "principal progenitor of fundamentalism" (p. 33): "I look upon this world as a wrecked vessel. God has given me a lifeboat and said to me, 'Moody, save all you can' " (quoted in Marsden, 1980, p. 38). The need for soul-saving evangelism fit in well with the individualistic and revivalistic heritage of American Christianity. However, the opposition to the building of a Christian civilization and the urgent necessity placed upon separating from a wicked culture were both novel to American Protestantism—but nonetheless were features that later became essential to fundamentalism.

Corresponding to the development of the scientific view of scripture, there appeared near the beginning of the 20th century yet another new millenarian interpretation of scripture, called "dispensationalism." Over the course of the previous 350 years of Protestant Christianity, the most common method of interpreting the Bible was the covenantal view, which emphasized the unity of all scripture, with the Old Testament serving primarily as a foreshadowing of the New Testament. Most Old Testament prophecy was interpreted figuratively, and was seen in some measure as pointing to the person and work of Jesus Christ. Dispensationalism, however, instead of stressing the continuity between the Old and New Testaments, emphasized the discontinuity between the two by setting forth a series of separate "dispensations," each governed distinctly by God. What began to appear in dispensationalist circles was an elaborate, cohesive, and self-contained system of charts and graphs, which detailed each historical epoch in terms of the particular way that God dealt with creation during that time. The methodology involved a familiar inductive approach: Each epoch was isolated, analyzed, and then systematized according to historical and scientific principles.

For example, dispensational teaching stressed seven (an important number in the fundamentalist interpretation of biblical prophecy[9]) distinct epochs, of which the current epoch was the sixth and was identified as the "age of grace." In contrast, the fifth epoch was the period of post-Exodus Israel, identified as the "age of law." The seventh and final epoch was expected to be a 7-year tribulation period of God's judgment that would usher in the new millennial kingdom of Christ. The majority of the era's conservative believers held the position that Christians would escape the great tribulation by being "raptured" (taken up) prior to the great tribulation (a "pretribulation" position), while a smaller number believed that Christians too would have to suffer through the great tribulation for the sins of the current epoch before being taken up with Christ (a "posttribulation" position).

In the eschatological doctrine of dispensationalism, in the absence of any confidence in social or political progress, we find evidence of a variety of theological tendencies—a literal understanding of scripture (when viewed as appropriate, such as the literal fulfillment of many Old

Testament prophecies during the millennium[10]); the interpretation of the Bible according to Baconian scientific methods; and a thoroughgoing supernaturalism (each dispensation ends with a catastrophic supernatural intervention and judgment of God)—all of which are still held by fundamentalists today.

The Holiness Movement

Conservative Christians of the early 20th century did not see salvation as the final transforming step in the Christian life—another view still held by evangelicals and fundamentalists today. Indeed, further transformation was expected, and by the 1930s fundamentalists had developed a common language to code such experiences: "complete surrender," "a consecrated life," "the filling of the Holy Spirit," "the baptism of the Holy Spirit," "proving God," and the "life of faith," among others (Carpenter, 1997). Underlying this development was a general view that Bible-believing Christians should live a victorious life, capable of overcoming sin by exercising the indwelling power of the Holy Spirit. Once again, however, this view can be traced to important historical developments during the last quarter of the 19th century.

Actually, the origins of what later became known as the Holiness movement go back to the 18th-century writings on Christian perfectionism by John Wesley, the founder of Methodism. Further teachings on the "victorious Christian life" were rooted in a Holiness conference held in 1875 in Keswick, England. What became known as the "Keswick movement" resulted in a particular branch of Holiness teaching that appealed to many Presbyterians, Baptists, and Congregationalists. The key to discovering the secrets of a truly transformed life that was holy and wholly committed was a postconversion experience of sanctification. After this, a person could consciously declare that he or she was now fully yielded to God.

Implicit in Holiness teachings was a redefinition of sin. Sin was no longer faithlessness in God—the prevailing view in much colonial and 19th-century American Protestantism. This traditional view assumed that although progress in the battle against personal sin would be hoped for in the Christian life, barriers and obstacles as manifestations of sin should be expected along the way. This imperfection was simply viewed as part of the human condition, and as a stark contrast to the perfection of God. However, the Holiness movement viewed sin as a voluntary transgression of one of God's known laws within a life of warfare between one's new nature (after salvation) and an old sinful nature that still existed. The ability to live a life without sin, which was expected of a Christian, was possible but could only be achieved through entire sanctification. In Wesley's Methodist perfectionism model, the old sinful self was totally eradicated, whereas the Keswick teaching stressed that the righteousness of Christ transplanted one's sinful nature (Marsden, 1980).

Whether the old self was eradicated or transplanted, the resulting "victory" of a subsequent experience to salvation separated, in the minds of many, those Christians who were truly committed from those who were characterized as more "carnal." The emphasis on holiness also stressed the individual's standing before God—one separated unto a holy life. In stark contrast was the liberal social gospel movement, which was seen by conservative Protestants as little more than a gospel of social justice and action, robbing the true Biblical message of its distinctive power. Quite simply, in the minds of these conservatives, the social gospel placed the cart of social action before the horse of the gospel's essential elements (doctrines of individual sin and redemption through Christ). Hence the earlier emphasis on social concern among evangelicals in the 19th century—rooted in traditional Calvinistic doctrine which saw politics as a way of advancing the kingdom of God—began to decline and had almost disappeared by the 1920s.

THE EARLY 20TH CENTURY: CHALLENGES TO THE PREVAILING VIEWS, AND THE FUNDAMENTALIST REACTION

In retrospect, it is easy to see that the late 19th-century dwelling of conservative Protestantism was on shaky ground in a culture that was growing increasingly inhospitable (Marsden, 1980). Still, the cultural challenges were much greater than suspected by even the most concerned. The two major challenges were the theory of evolution from outside the faith and Biblical "higher criticism" (to be discussed below) from within.

By the turn of the century, the damage done to the Protestant establishment by various modernist claims was clearly detectable. Some conservative Protestants were persuaded by these claims and gave up the old orthodoxy. Many conservative Protestants were either not convinced of the severity of the threat or simply decided to do their best in riding out a period of turbulent change by privately remaining true to their beliefs. However, a vocal and sizable minority was determined to fight back. The first quarter of the 20th century witnessed the mobilization of this vocal group of conservative Protestants on two battlefronts: one localized primarily in the North, to regain control in some churches that had been lost to liberal theology; and the other in the South, to fight the teaching of Darwinian evolution in the public schools.

Rallying the Troops

As we shall see, the decades of the 1920s and 1930s, punctuated by the debacle of the Scopes trial in 1925, were critical in the history of American fundamentalism. However, there were important developments both inside and outside American Protestantism in the first two decades of the 20th century that influenced fundamentalism's particular shape. We consider two such developments: (1) the publication of an important set of essays that would help define the emerging coalition, and (2) the onset of World War I.

The Fundamentals

The term "fundamentalist" as a noun came into use just prior to the 1920s. The term itself is credited to Curtis Lee Laws, editor of the *Watchman-Examiner*, a conservative Baptist publication, who first coined the term at an organized protest within the Northern Baptist Convention in 1920. Laws identified "fundamentalists" as those who were ready to defend the fundamentals of the faith. The clearest exposition of such central beliefs was found in a series of essays published as 12 booklets by two wealthy businessmen and brothers, Lyman and Milton Stewart, between 1910 and 1915, entitled *The Fundamentals: A Testimony to the Truth*. These booklets were first edited by A. C. Dixon, a respected evangelist, author, and pastor of the large and influential church established by D. L. Moody in Chicago. By the 1920s, the term "fundamentalists" had become reified to describe a certain group who adhered to the fundamental tenets of conservative Christianity as outlined by these twelve booklets. Dixon and two subsequent editors, Louis Meyer and Reuben Torrey, amassed an impressive array of conservative scholars and popular writers. Sandeen (1970) notes that the authors (including a sizable minority who were part of the Keswick movement in Britain) were seasoned and highly regarded scholars. He further notes that by 1925, some of these authors, though adhering to the fundamental beliefs outlined, bristled at being called "fundamentalists"—a term they perceived as connoting something other than their scholarly excellence.

Though the wealthy Stewarts financed free distribution of over 3 million copies to conservative religious leaders of various sorts throughout the English-speaking world, the response to *The Fundamentals* among conservative Protestants was less than enthusiastic. It did not create negative reaction, nor was it divisive among various conservatives; instead, it created little reaction—a possible sign of more moderate times than those to come in the decades ahead. It also appeared to remain a little-studied set of volumes. But in time, *The Fundamentals* became a major "symbolic point of reference . . . that called to mind the broad unified front of the kind of opposition to modernism" (Marsden, 1980, p. 119) that helped shape an emerging movement. Today, someone reading *The Fundamentals* would be struck by the sophisticated and restrained language in many (but not all) of these essays. The essays are roughly equally distributed around issues involving the authority of scripture; specific theological doctrines (but surprisingly little is said about dispensationalism and premillenialism); and a hodgepodge of other topics, such as evangelism and missions, the menace of various "isms" (e.g., Mormonism, and Roman Catholicism, in addition to the usual liberalism), and practical issues of personal piety. Noticeably missing are essays on social and political issues—topics far more detectable in the fundamentalist literature after World War I.

Of particular interest here is the essayists' view of the relationship between the authority of scripture and the authority of science. Marsden (1980) points out that despite their defense of the supernatural, the authors were also consistent supporters of true science and historical criticism. The key to their argument lay in their definition of true scientific and historical criticism as that which employed open inquiry—an ironic twist to the frequent accusation that fundamentalism itself was (and still is) a closed system. These conservatives accused academicians of some of the very same characteristics that they themselves were being charged with. Their argument hinged on what they saw as two unacknowledged biases in the scientific and historical method of the day: (1) that such methodology was controlled by speculative hypotheses (no doubt in reference to the theory of evolution and higher criticism in interpreting scripture), and (2) that modern science (including higher criticism of scripture) was prejudice against the supernatural. If science could be freed of these biases, it was repeatedly argued in various essays, then "Scripture would always prove compatible with the highest standards of science and rationality" (Marsden, 1980, p. 121). The key point here was that for many of the essays' authors, the tenets of the Christian faith could and must be rationally defended, and such a defense would only be strengthened by the objective evidence of true science. Thus many of the essays offered mediating positions on various topics, including evolution: They stated that though Darwinian claims could not explain the origins of life, it was not beyond the realm of possibility that God could have used limited forms of evolution in the creation process.

Though hardly rallying conservative Protestants on a grassroots level, *The Fundamentals* provided a defense for the supernatural, miraculous elements of the Christian faith, and did so in an intellectually respectable manner. In this sense, *The Fundamentals* became the "gold-standard" defense of the faith that provided shape to an emerging movement. With the publication of these essays, conservative Protestantism could point to a single set of publications that, though tinged with moderation, clearly identified the movement's basic tenets.

World War I

For many religious conservatives in America, Germany's political threat was at heart a moral disintegration resulting from a rational modernism that included such corrupt teachings as an evolutionary Nietzschean "God is dead" philosophy, which equated power with moral superiority. This cultural crisis not only helped energize the emerging fundamentalist movement, but also transformed it into a more politically active and intense effort to arrest morally degenerative social and cultural trends. Conservative Christians began to think that what was being threatened was Christian culture itself. Furthermore, this first worldwide war substantiated many pessimistic claims of premillennialism, thereby further justifying a theological sense of importance and urgency.

In the eyes of these conservatives, the church was not immune to the degenerative trends of culture. In creative ways, leaders associated world events such as World War I and the formation of the League of Nations with personal "sinful" behaviors (such as smoking, dancing, card playing, and going to theaters), all of which represented "the sign of the times"—in their assessment, the nation's dismal moral condition. Marsden illustrates this creative blend of complex association through a quotation from a sermon by the Reverend Oliver W. Van Osdel, a Northern Baptist separatist leader in Michigan:

> Sometimes people ask what are the objections to dancing and theatres and card playing and such things; they say these are not to be severely condemned; but you will notice that the people who indulge in these worldly things are always loose in doctrine . . . the two go together, and when you find people indulging in worldliness they become loose in doctrine, then apostasy easily creeps in, the union of Christendom becomes possible and probably will be united through corrupt doctrine under one head, the Pope of Rome. (Quoted in Marsden, 1980, p. 157)

The Battle Lines

To an outsider, it may appear that fundamentalism was emerging primarily as a reaction to an inhospitable social and political climate, and indeed cultural trends were perceived with great alarm and with calls for action. Of course, one such development was science's increasing allegiance to evolutionary thought and its teaching in the public schools (discussed below). However, as Marsden (1980) points out, "for the fundamentalists the fundamental issues were theological" (p. 160)—particularly, in this case, a premillennial dispensational eschatology. At the heart of the issue was what constituted good theology. In the mind of the fundamentalist, anything short of a literal interpretation of an inerrant scripture was the sure sign of a suspect theology, leading to the other crucial battle (in addition to the teaching of evolution) facing conservative Protestants. This "battle for the Bible" was, in particular, a reaction to the primary European theological task of the latter half of the 19th century—a "higher critical" analysis of the Bible.

Higher Criticism

European Protestantism in the 19th century was very different from American Protestantism. On the European continent, new religious ideas were constantly emerging; a much greater tolerance existed in Europe for a variety of doctrinal views. This difference between Europe and America developed out of different conceptions of truth. In America, truth was considered an absolute body of facts that remained the same, regardless of time or culture. In Europe, truth was generally understood as progressive and developmental over the course of time within the context of particular historical and social situations. In American Protestantism, the Bible was considered the storehouse of religious truth, and the theological task was understood simply to be the interpretation of the Bible. In European Protestantism, however, truth from other sources was seen as reliable, and therefore extra-Biblical sources were used to critique the Bible. Religious truth was understood as emerging and developing through historical processes, rather than as static and fixed. These European efforts at critiquing the Bible became known as "higher criticism," and it was the primary European theological task in the latter half of the 19th century.

Meanwhile, the end of the 19th century witnessed a softening of what had been firm doctrinal stances by conservative Christians in America. Though interdenominational activities and sentiments dominated throughout the entire 19th century, the distinctive doctrinal stances (e.g., Calvinism among Presbyterians, Wesleyanism among Methodists) between the major denominations had been upheld and were still deemed important. The 19th century witnessed a delicate but workable balance whereby most denominations could adhere closely to their particular theological convictions, but at the same time share a willingness to work together on issues and activities of joint interest. By the end of the century, this balance was disturbed by a growing distaste for doctrinal controversy among most Protestants.[11] To these individuals, debating divisive doctrinal issues was far less important than the application of effort to more pragmatic issues such as evangelism.

European "higher criticism" had existed for nearly half a century before its influence came to the United States. This criticism—along with other aspects of theological liberalism, which denied many of the historic creedal statements of the church and promoted more openness and tolerance of a diversity of views—challenged American Protestantism seriously for the first time at about the beginning of the 20th century, and was immediately perceived as a threat. With the definitive doctrinal tone of the 19th-century evangelical consensus quickly slipping away, the vision of America as the "new Israel" was challenged. Not only did theological liberalism bring many diverse doctrinal views, but it also brought a way of thinking and living foreign to Victorian America. The vision for Christian civilization, based on the truth of God's word, was being attacked by European modernism. To fundamentalists, not just America and its allies, but all of Christian civilization was being attacked. In the face of this threat, fundamentalism, as a reaction to modernism, was more necessary than ever.

The influx of theological liberalism from the European continent was only part of what prompted the formation of the fundamentalist movement as a means of defending the old Protestant establishment in America. A second major battlefront that would forever change American religious history and the common perception of fundamentalism was quickly taking form.

The Teaching of Evolution

No analysis of American Protestant fundamentalism would be complete without serious consideration of the role of evolutionary theory and the teaching of evolution in the public schools. Indeed, the fundamentalist image foremost in the minds of many Americans was set at the so-called "Monkey Trial" of a young biology teacher, John Scopes, in Dayton, Tennessee, in July 1925. Though Scopes was initially found guilty of breaking Tennessee's strict law of banning the teaching of Darwinism in public schools (a decision later reversed on a technicality), it was apparent that the fundamentalist-supported anti-Darwinian prosecution, led by two-time Democratic presidential candidate William Jennings Bryan, had only temporarily won the battle. Bryan's eager willingness to be cross-examined by a man many observers considered the country's foremost trial lawyer, Clarence Darrow, was a colossal mistake. Though the confident Bryan had long shown before many audiences the "self-evident superiority of biblical faith to infidelity" (Marsden, 1980, p. 186), it was readily apparent that he had yet to face an antagonist with Darrow's crafty cross-examination skills. In the end, Bryan was no match for Darrow's incisive questioning of a literal interpretation of the Bible, and the weight of public opinion, aided by the derision of the press, was clearly swayed against the fundamentalists. Bryan died shortly after the conclusion of the trial. From that point on, fundamentalism was indelibly associated with Southern and rural ignorance.

Post-1925 Developments

Marsden (1980) contends that there were two major alterations in fundamentalism's image in the wake of the Scopes trial. First, the meaning of the term "fundamentalism" was greatly expanded and stereotyped, so that virtually all perceived aspects of rural Protestant America were included: poorly educated, stubbornly narrow-minded, simple, homogeneous, not experienced with the growing complexities of the world, and fearful of encroachments from a changing world. Indeed, many fundamentalist leaders of the latter 1920s and 1930s confirmed this perception, so that the fair-minded Marsden has concluded:

> The movement began in reality to conform to its popular image. The more ridiculous it was made to appear, the more genuinely ridiculous it was likely to become. The reason was simple. . . . Before 1925 the movement had commanded much respect, though not outstanding support, but after the summer of 1925 the voices of ridicule were raised so loudly that many modern Protestant conservatives quietly dropped support of the cause rather than be embarrassed by association. (p. 191)

Thus fundamentalism had, in the minds of many (including many conservatives), degenerated from a loose but nevertheless influential coalition of conservatives in the early 1920s to a more rigid and defensive group after 1925.

Second, in large part because of this perceived inflexibility, the movement was doomed in the public mind to a marginal societal position, where its views would supposedly forever remain obscure. The only remaining concern of the now-triumphant secular establishment was the sheer number of fundamentalists lurking in American society. The journalist H. L. Mencken colorfully expressed his concern that fundamentalism was still a threat to modern culture when he said in 1926, "Heave an egg out a Pullman window and you will hit a fundamentalist almost anywhere in the United States today" (quoted in Marsden, 1980, p. 188). Indeed, while the more liberal media applauded Darrow's victory, they also succumbed to Bryan's own misunderstanding of Darwin, confusing the fact of evolution with theories of its mechanism. Both

Bryan and the liberal media elevated to moral values the supposed "struggle for life" and the "survival of the fittest." This martial understanding of evolution so worried Bryan that he told the eminent sociologist E. A. Ross that it would undermine democracy (see Gould, 1999, pp. 125–170). Thus Gould (1999) has emphasized that "the usual reading of the [Scopes] trial as an epic struggle between benighted Yahooism and resplendent virtue simply cannot suffice" (p. 135). Still, the outcome is portrayed in most history books as one of religious ignorance receding in the face of objective scientific fact; indeed, to most people of that day, it was simply a matter of time before fundamentalism would eventually disappear in an enlightened age of science. Such was hardly to be the case.

In the wake of the Scopes trial, fundamentalism's influence had also weakened considerably within such denominations as the Northern Presbyterians and Northern Baptists, where just a few years earlier fundamentalism had nearly gained control. Surely the embarrassment of the Scopes trial and the now well-established reactionary image created a desire among many conservatives to distance themselves from the movement. The movement was also weakened by internal strife, much of it centered around the degree of tolerance they should have for modernists within their denominations. Eventually, this disagreement led to debilitating schisms within the fundamentalist camp and contributed to a modernist victory within the mainline denominations. Those fundamentalists who had no tolerance for modernism within these denominations broke off and started new denominations. Marsden (1980) maintains that within 15 years following 1925, the movement was split in three directions: (1) those who still identified with many of the fundamentalist traditions, but who remained in mainline denominations; (2) those who identified with denominations that were neither fundamentalist nor mainline (such as Pentecostal and Holiness groups, though see Note 10); and (3) those who separated into their independent denominations and churches. By 1960, Marsden contends, only the third group would remain comfortable with the fundamentalist designation.

FUNDAMENTALISM'S RESURRECTION: THE 1930s AND 1940s

By the late 1920s and early 1930s, fundamentalism's epitaph was prematurely written. Religious progressives saw the fundamentalist movement as nothing but "a brief, dysfunctional mutation away from the main line of religious evolution" (Carpenter, 1997, p. 13). But Carpenter and other religious historians (e.g., Brereton, 1987; Marsden, 1987, 1991; Sandeen, 1970) claim that such obituaries were nothing more than wishful thinking; they have identified the next few decades as critical in the development of a "thriving popular movement" (Carpenter, 1997, p. 13) that by 1950 was beginning to occupy a far more central place in American life. Fundamentalism's roots by the 1920s were far deeper than most had suspected. In fact, the mainline Protestant denominations were the groups that suffered dwindling membership during this period (and this is still true today for many such denominations), while the churches associated with the fundamentalist movement, though now disorganized, demonstrated substantial growth. What contributed to fundamentalism's persistent attractiveness? How could a movement that looked so foolish to some command such respect and devotion from others? Who were these people, and what guided their thinking?

(Re)Rallying the Troops

In terms of outward visibility and respect, fundamentalism reached its lowest point during the late 1920s and early 1930s. The once formidable movement was in disarray, and the leaders of the crusades against evolution and many of the other themes related to the end times in the wake of World War I had lost their commanding presence. Yet among the fundamentalists themselves, the sting of 1925 was less potent than outsiders supposed it to be. Though many of the intellectual elite wrote off fundamentalism in favor of a more enlightened secularized society, as classical social theorists of the 19th century (such as Comte, Durkheim, and Weber) had predicted, America's growing social complexity provided an opportunity for dissenting sects to survive (Marsden, 1991). It is also true that fundamentalism's newfound place, on the margins rather than at the center of society, provided unusual developmental opportunities with more homogeneous groupings as the movement drew less attention from the media.

Removed from the national spotlight, fundamentalists could now do what they did best: offer like-minded people a sense of certainty and refuge in the face of a hostile culture. Clearly, fundamentalism's reactionary nature provided its driving motivation and power. Fundamentalists were most effective at the local level, often through independent or nondenominational churches that broke away from mainline denominations. Indeed, the lack of cohesion that now characterized the movement was to become not only its strength—allowing it to grow at the grassroots level—but also, as we soon shall see, a prolonged weakness.

As in the past, the fundamentalist movement continued to be led by a number of dominating figures who, in the words of Carpenter (1997), acted as fiercely independent " 'regional warlords' . . . [who were] jealous guardians of their fiefdoms and scarcely able to get along on a personal level, much less any cooperative venture" (p. 15). After 1925, these leaders did indeed feel defeated—perhaps more than the people they led—but only in relation to their vision of a Christian culture. On a theological level, they were no less confident in the fundamental doctrines of the faith. In an effort to find new bearings, some resorted to their old combative posture, but others began to redirect their energies toward efforts in winning new converts.

Evangelism and the Era of Revivals

Evangelism had always been at the heart of the fundamentalist movement. The vision of a return to 19th-century Christian culture—a major premise of fundamentalist thought—required that people change their hearts and minds to accept Christ. Transforming culture was rooted in the Biblical mandate to go out and "make disciples" (Matthew 28:19) of all people and all nations. Not only did this so-called "great commission" mandate serve as a primary motivation for foreign missions (and, indeed, the energy behind the foreign missions movement was highly concentrated in the late 19th and early 20th centuries), but it also became a primary purpose of the local church. Though the culture wars of the first quarter of the century had diluted some of this evangelistic energy, fundamentalists, perhaps because they now found themselves on the margins of society, discovered a renewed zeal for evangelism. "Altar calls" in local churches became common. Members were exhorted to bring family and friends to church as a form of Christian witness, and it was not unusual to denote specific church gatherings (frequently on Sunday evenings) as evangelistic services. Perhaps even more common in urban settings were the large "gospel tabernacles" where evangelistic and revival services were conducted, often for extended periods of times (several weeks or even months). Frequently, the evangelists with their sensational preaching styles would move on to another setting to repeat the same phenomenon. This tried-and-true format remained popular for decades, and it provided a context for the emergence in the late 1940s of a young and dynamic preacher from North Carolina by the name of Billy Graham. Gospel tabernacles also utilized their own resident evangelists for evangelistic campaigns and revivals. Regardless of specific methodology, a dominant message was that a primary function (and perhaps *the* primary function) of the church was to save souls and to equip its members to be effective lay evangelists. To the mainline denominations, including many conservative denominations, this was a narrow and misguided understanding of the church's mission. But it produced results, and the movement experienced radical growth.

Building the Infrastructure

The common perception of fundamentalism has quite understandably been informed by such highly visible indicators as the Scopes trial and, later, the Billy Graham crusades. Yet during the first half of the 20th century, activities far less perceptible but nevertheless just as important and necessary for fundamentalism to flourish were taking place. At more local and denominational levels, fundamentalists were active in leadership training through the establishment of Bible schools and seminaries, which reported phenomenal growth—far beyond that of their secular and more liberal counterparts. Independent mission societies designed to provide more than just a "social gospel" were formed. Summer Bible conferences with strict behavioral rules (see Figure 3.1) flourished throughout the land as platforms for revival and as retreats from the unwelcoming world. Modern publishing houses were established to provide Christian reading material as well as Sunday School curricula. Radio programs such as Charles E. Fuller's "Old-Fashioned Revival Hour," Jack Wyrtzen's "Word of Life," and Percy Crawford's "Young People's Church of the Air" filled the nation's airwaves. Numerous scholars have noted this irony: The very modernism that the fundamentalists so decried (as ideology) nevertheless contained elements that were judged useful for the sake of the gospel.

THE RISE OF EVANGELICALISM: THE 1950s ONWARD

Many conservative Christians today call themselves "evangelicals," not "fundamentalists." Historians and sociologists of American Protestantism, though they differ substantially in regard to how the terms "fundamentalist" and "evangelical" should be defined, generally concur that the two terms represent two groups that are similar, but not identical. Some (e.g., Marsden, 1991; Sandeen, 1970) see evangelicalism as a continuing, vital form of the earlier fundamentalism movement, geared to the second half of the 20th century; others (e.g., Brereton, 1990; Smith, 1962, 1986) see it as a new coalition of sorts, involving other groups (such as Pentecostals, various types of Wesleyans, and other Holiness groups) less traditionally aligned with fundamentalism. However, it appears that perhaps the most common criterion for distinguishing between fundamentalists and evangelicals is how the two groups relate to the larger culture. One group (fundamentalists) tends to view its relationship to culture through the imagery of warfare, while the other (evangelicals) sees itself as distinctive from, yet conciliatory toward, the broader culture. Hence it is common among those who have studied

PLEASE HELP US KEEP MAHAFFEY SPIRITUAL CAMP BY OBSERVING THE

RULES

OF ORDER OF THIS CAMP GROUND

1st. General decorum, such as is becoming a house of worship, must be observed.

2nd. Talking or standing in groups in the aisles or outside the Tabernacle, during divine services is positively prohibited.

3rd. Smoking on these grounds, in cottages or in tents is positively forbidden at All Times.

4th. The having in possession, drinking or offering to others to drink of any alcoholic liquors on the grounds, is strictly prohibited.

5th. Card playing, dancing and the use of profane language is strictly forbidden At All Times.

6th. No dogs or cats shall be permitted on the grounds during camp meeting period.

7th. No literature shall be sold or distributed or any advertising matter posted on these grounds without permission from the district officials.

8th. No salesman or huckster shall be permitted to offer for sale any article without permission from the district officials.

9th. No firearms or air rifles are permitted on the grounds at any time.

10th. No Sunday newspapers shall be sold or delivered on these grounds.

11th. No parties or picnics permitted cottages or on the grounds without permission from district officials.

12th. Ladies are not permitted to appear on these grounds dressed in men's attire or pajamas, shorts or any immodest apparel. Men must not appear on the grounds immodestly dressed. No one may appear on the camp grounds attired in a bathing suit.

13th. At the ringing of curfew bell quiet will be required on the grounds, also in cottages and tents.

14th. Radios are not to be used during the period of camp meeting.

15th. The one mile limit law will be enforced during the time of camp meeting.

The committee will appreciate the co-operation of all the people on the grounds by observing the above rules and we will do all we can for your convenience and comfort.

By ORDER OF THE DISTRICT EXECUTIVE COMMITTEE

FIGURE 3.1. A list of behavioral rules for a summer Bible camp.

these groups to define fundamentalism's "most conspicuous unifying feature" (Marsden, 1991, p. 178) as militancy. This thesis undoubtedly contains some truth. We caution, however, that it is tempting to differentiate the two groups primarily or even solely on the basis of this single criterion, while not recognizing other distinctive characteristics and (even more importantly) not acknowledging many commonalities. Indeed, both groups are far more heterogeneous than most outsiders recognize. The historian Smith (1986), for example, describes evangeli-calism as a kaleidoscope—a forever-changing constellation of pieces, vulnerable to even the most genteel external nudge, with new overlap-ping positions and colors that form fresh boundaries and mosaics.

If, indeed, there has been a "softening" among at least some funda-mentalists, what is its historical context? Certainly it appears as though some major developments, particularly between the 1940s and 1960s, represented a substantial revision in the fundamentalist movement. Eventually, some people who still affirmed many fundamental tenets could no longer identify with the brand of fundamentalism that had de-veloped.

Reestablishing an Intellectual Base

Although the fundamentalist movement grew tremendously during the 1930s and 1940s, it was also victimized by its growth. That era's version became a movement geared to a popular, common audience, not to scholars or to well-educated people. God, it was reasoned, did not mea-sure souls by educational attainment, and leaders were more likely to be preachers and evangelists than theologians. Certainly, in part, funda-mentalism was hard pressed to attract either theological scholars or laypeople who placed a priority on the intellect, given that its "retrench-ment and disengagement in the 1920s seemed to signal the end of intel-lectual vitality" (Noll, 1996, p. 26). Fundamentalism, so it seemed to many, was straying far from what many conservative though robustly in-tellectual defenders (including many of the writers of *The Fundamentals*) had envisioned.

Perhaps the champion of the intellectual conservatives during the 1930s was J. Gresham Machen, who just a decade earlier had been a vet-eran New Testament scholar at Princeton Theological Seminary. Machen's 1923 book *Christianity and Liberalism* was arguably the most intellec-tually premised and convincing book written by a fundamentalist, at least of his era. Machen's combative nature, however, did not endear him to others; he was viewed by many, especially those in mainline de-nominations, as "a troublemaker and a narrow bigoted crank" (Mar-sden, 1991, p. 184). During the fundamentalist–modernist battles of the 1920s, conservative Presbyterians had tried unsuccessfully to rid their denomination of liberal pastors. In the wake of the devastating defeat of fundamentalism in the mid-1920s, the liberals counterattacked, and Machen was an easy target.

Despite a tumultuous career[12] and an untimely death at the age of 56, Machen (1925) challenged conservatives to think more deeply and vigorously about what he called the superficial mentality of a "religion" of liberalism:

> We [religious conservatives] welcome new discoveries with all of our hearts, and we believe that our cause will come to its rights again only when youth throws off its present intellectual lethargy, refuses to go thoughtlessly with the anti-intellectual current of the age, and recovers some genuine independence of mind . . . we are seeking in particular to arouse youth from its present uncritical repetition of current phrases into some genuine examination of the basis of life; and we believe that Christianity flourishes not in the darkness, but in the light. . . . One of the means which the Spirit will use, we believe, is an awakening of the intellect . . . the last thing in the world we desire to do is to discourage originality or independence of mind. (pp. 17–19)

Machen's challenge went unheeded for almost two decades. During the 1940s, however, a new generation of young conservatives with only secondhand experience of the 1920s emerged in no less an intellectual center of liberal theology than the Harvard Divinity School. More than a dozen young, conservative, ambitious, and intellectually gifted students, many from fundamentalist backgrounds, discovered with dismay just how marginalized the evangelical tradition had become within contemporary theological discourse (Carpenter, 1997). Harold John Ockenga, a student under Machen at Princeton, was pastor at the influential Park Street Church in Boston; he became convinced that fundamentalism was not in the position to "win America." Again, to most fundamentalists of this era, "winning America" meant converting souls to Christ. Ockenga, however, reverted to a more classical, pre-World War I interpretation when he defined the battle as one of cultural influence. For Ockenga and the other members of this new cadre of intellectual fundamentalists (though many by now were beginning to distance themselves from the label), the prescription was a positive social ethic with an intellectual grounding—neither of which Ockenga saw in the popular fundamentalism of his day. At the heart of their vision was a renewal of Western culture that could be accomplished only through an influence of the intellect. But Ockenga and his colleagues recognized that they first had to earn a hearing, and the only way they could muster such merit was to establish first-rate educational centers.

Other key figures shared this vision and recognized the need for a well-planned and concerted effort at making conservative Christianity intellectually reputable. Among them were Charles E. Fuller, a radio evangelist who wanted to establish an intellectual center of training for missions and evangelism, and Wilbur M. Smith, a fundamentalist with intellectual interests on the faculty at Moody Bible Institute in Chicago. Fuller convinced Ockenga and Smith to build a new school, Fuller Theological Seminary, "where an evangelical renaissance could begin" (Carpenter, 1997, p. 194; see also Marsden, 1987). One prominent member of the early faculty at Fuller was George Eldon Ladd, who sought to challenge dispensationalism as the dominant view of the end times with a theology that more thoroughly engaged classical Christian beliefs. Given the central role of dispensationalist thinking to fundamentalism, Ladd's efforts were a clear marker of a new era; indeed, dispensationalism became the favorite whipping boy of this more progressive group. Another Fuller faculty member was Carl Henry, who followed his earlier (1947) work, *The Uneasy Conscience of Modern Fundamentalism*, with a three-part series in the conservative *Christian Life* magazine. There Henry outlined several deficiencies in fundamentalism of that era: inattention to modern philosophy, a prophecy-charged worldview, and spiritual isolationism. Henry remained influential among conservative Protestants and later became editor of the influential evangelical magazine *Christianity Today*.

In this analysis, two points are critical. First, there was a supreme effort to draw conservative Protestantism away from the margins of intellectual and cultural life. Indeed, there was a recommitment to the vision of conservatives from the era prior to World War I: namely, a renewed culture based on foundational Christian principles with a firm intellectual grounding. Second, the primary critique of fundamentalism came from within the conservative camp—from comrades who desired to "affirm the great fundamentals but avoid the 'deficiencies' of fundamentalism" (Carpenter, 1997, p. 201). On the one hand, the criticism probably carried far greater weight (and perhaps sting) than if, as in the past, it had been offered by an apostate culture. On the other hand, rankling from within had the potential for substantial internal strife.

External Theological Developments

Another important development that influenced differences among fundamentalists occurred within theology but outside the conservative camp (Gasper, 1963). The increasing influence on mainline Protestants of the European theologians Karl Barth and Emil Brunner and the American theologian Reinhold Niebuhr from the 1930s onward brought a partial return to many classical orthodox beliefs from the teachings of St. Augustine, John Calvin, and Martin Luther. These "neo-orthodox" theologians developed a "theology of crisis," the main tenet of which was that individuals have encounters with God at critical and defining moments in their lives, and are invited to submit to divine justice. As part of the unnerving reaction to the devastation of World War I, neo-orthodoxy replaced what was increasingly perceived as a less realistic and naively optimistic world-affirming liberalism, which had taught that the application of Christian ethics would solve the world's problems. Declaring a centrist position that affirmed neither humanism nor fundamentalism, neo-orthodoxy became an attractive alternative for some moderate conservatives. By 1940, it was the dominant theology system among American Protestant theologians in general. Though it was cautiously welcomed at first by some fundamentalists because of its opposition to theological liberalism and its evident agreement on selected cardinal doctrines (although the frequent use of similar terminology may only have created the appearance of agreement), neo-orthodoxy was later firmly rejected as too compromising (see Gasper, 1963, for a more thorough discussion of these issues).

Few religious conservative leaders, even those who began to distance themselves from fundamentalism, heartily embraced neo-orthodoxy. But in the minds of some, neo-orthodoxy represented a movement away from classical liberalism and thus that provided an atmosphere of reconciliation. For once, the gulf with the broader theological culture had not only *not* grown, but indeed had apparently shrunk; this left open the possibility of viable mediating positions.

Organizational Developments

It was clear that the fundamentalism of the 1930s and 1940s was a movement without organizational leadership. Despite fundamentalism's growth, there was no effective national organization that could provide coherence or even identity of interest, possibly because there was no nationally prominent leader after the 1925 death of William Jennings Bryan. Though the leaders themselves were men of strong character and vision, their influence tended primarily to be restricted to their local churches, or at least geographically limited. It was also clear that, despite the movement's growing numerical strength, conservatives no longer had influence in such ecumenical and mainline organizations as the Federal Council of Churches. By 1940, a group of fundamentalist leaders had acknowledged their decentralization and fragmentation, and their corresponding weakness in an unfriendly culture. They made an effort to form a council for the stated purpose of both testimony to, but also separation from, the world (and especially from the Federal Council). This new American Council of Churches (ACC) was formed in September 1941. Its leader, Carl McIntire, a Presbyterian pastor from New Jersey, confidently proclaimed that at last, a single unified national organization representing all fundamentalists was formed. Nothing could have been further from the truth.

Later that same year, a group of conservatives met at the Moody Bible Institute in Chicago. Concerned that the ACC's adamant stand on separation from the Federal Council was too reactionary and might therefore do more harm than good, a second new organization, known as the National Association of Evangelicals (NAE), was formed by the spring of 1942. The first president was Harold John Ockenga. The NAE, though doctrinally similar to the ACC, differed from it in several regards: It was more conciliatory toward and less exclusive of other organizations (e.g., members could also hold membership in the mainline Federal Council of Churches), more committed to intellectual development, and more engaged in the cultural and social issues of the day. As Gasper (1963) points out, as much as the two groups were agreed in doctrine, they were divided in method.

The NAE's greater inclusiveness had its limits, however. Its differences from McIntire's more radical ACC should be noted as existing only within the context of an adherence to orthodox Christian teaching, based on the principles of the deity of Christ and the authority of the Bible as the inspired and infallible word of God. Those who accepted a seven-item doctrinal statement based on these principles were admitted to membership in the NAE. The NAE's option for an inclusive policy was thus still within the limits of conservative Christianity. Whether or not an individual remained a member of a mainline denomination that was affiliated with the Federal Council of Churches was not a defining issue. Members of other groups ranging from mainline Presbyterians to Pentecostals could be members of the NAE, but only if they could agree with basic doctrines of orthodox Christianity. On these issues, there was no room for negotiation.

"Ye Must Be Born Again" versus "Contend for the Faith": The Role of Billy Graham

It would be difficult to identify anyone more important to the evangelical movement than Billy Graham. Graham's emergence during the late 1940s with his immensely popular crusades gave fundamentalism more notoriety than it had had at any time since the 1920s. As an evangelist employed by Youth for Christ, a popular conservative parachurch organization catering to adolescents and young adults, Graham had discovered his niche by holding several citywide evangelistic campaigns. The 1949 Los Angeles crusade was particularly noteworthy for several reasons (see Gasper, 1963, pp. 130–134, and Carpenter, 1997, pp. 220–226, for more thorough accounts). First, Graham himself had gone through a period of self-questioning just prior to this crusade, and had resolved with renewed energy to be "fully surrendered" to God's leading. From that point on, Graham preached with a conviction second to none. Second, there was considerable friction among the clergy of Los Angeles as to how much support should be given to Graham. Many theologically conservative clergy doubted the possibility of revival in such an apocalyptic age. In fact, rankling among local clergy became an ongoing concern for Graham wherever he traveled. Third, the Los Angeles crusade in particular had drawn the interest of the local media, largely because Graham's crusade was endorsed by several Hollywood celebrities, some of whom were converted during the crusade itself. Fourth, the crusade far exceeded almost everyone's expectations, with a sizable attendance and many new converts. What began as a 3-week crusade lasted for 8 weeks; by the end, Graham was a feast for the sensation-seeking media. Articles on the crusade were carried by *Time* magazine and through the Associated Press as well as other news services, assuring that the crusade would be covered by newspapers throughout the nation and in Great Britain. The success of the Graham crusades broke through the neglect that the secular media had accorded to conservative Christianity since the Scopes trial. Indeed, the effort to bring revival to the land was no longer the secret of evangelicals and fundamentalists.

Yet Graham's success was also a source of division. After a series of successful crusades in other cities such as Boston—which was thought to be perhaps the most difficult U.S. city for evangelicals' efforts, but where 50,000 people gathered on the Boston Common for the crusade's last service—Graham was in the privileged position of no longer being held captive by the interests of any one group, including fundamentalists. With far more invitations to conduct meetings than he could possibly handle, Graham required that the majority of local churches must support his crusades and be willing to organize a force of volunteer workers and "prayer partners." The fact that such a condition could be met in most major cities was in itself testimony to just how much the conservative churches had grown. Graham's motivation to avoid controversy so that he could freely preach the gospel was best accomplished, he thought, through churches' working together toward a common goal that would promote ecumenical unity. For organizations with a more inclusive mentality, such as the NAE, Graham's policy was not a problem and was even welcomed. But for more exclusive fundamentalists, Graham's insistence created serious problems. By the time of Graham's 1957 New York City crusade, fundamentalists such as Bob Jones, Sr., and Carl McIntire, representing the more restrictive ACC, renounced the crusade even before it started. McIntire called the New York crusade a "distinct defeat for fundamentalists" (quoted in Gasper, 1963, p. 142) and a victory for apostate modernists. Preferring now to be called a "constructionalist" than to be identified with what he called the "aura of bigotry" (quoted in Gasper, 1963, p. 142) associated with the term "fundamentalist," Graham spurned the old-time fundamentalist slogan "Contend for the faith" and replaced it with "Ye must be born again." Furthermore, Graham, though hardly an intellectual himself, became associated with the new evangelical scholars (and, in fact, was appointed to the board of trustees at Fuller Seminary) and concurred that perhaps some aspects of scripture (e.g., hellfire) were not intended to be taken literally. To stricter fundamentalists, however, Graham, in the name of avoiding controversy, was now compromising the very gospel that he preached. To this day, the great divide between Graham and fundamentalists has not been bridged.

WHO ARE THE PROTESTANT FUNDAMENTALISTS TODAY?

In reality, it is often hard to separate evangelicals from fundamentalists—and, to be sure, there are many important commonalities. In fact, if we take Ammerman's (1991) five central features of fundamentalism (all with ties to *The Fundamentals*), we discover that indeed it is difficult to separate those who might define themselves as evangelicals (or fundamentalists) from their counterparts on at least three of those issues.

Inerrancy of Scripture

Inerrancy of scripture, as discussed by Ammerman (1991), includes belief in the divinity of Christ and in the efficacy of Christ's life, death, and physical resurrection for the salvation of the human soul—all beliefs to which evangelicals adhere. A number of scholars (e.g., Ammerman, 1987; Bebbington, 1994; Hunter, 1983; Stott, 1956) identify inerrancy of scripture as part of the doctrinal core of contemporary evangelicalism, even though Fuller Seminary formally dropped inerrancy as part of its doctrinal statement in 1972.

Evangelism

Certainly evangelism is at the heart of both the evangelical and fundamentalist missions, and it has been identified by many as a defining characteristic of both groups (Ammerman, 1987; Carpenter, 1997; Marsden, 1991; Stott, 1956). Accepted methodologies may differ between the groups, though even in these there is often far greater consensus than difference. There may be considerable variation on views of evangelism among evangelicals, but they will have greater compatibility with fundamentalists than with members of many mainline churches on the necessity and methodologies of evangelism.

Premillenialism

Premillenialism continues to be the dominant eschatololgical position among both fundamentalists and evangelicals, though evangelicals are likely to hold more varied views. Dispensationalism as a particular form of premillenial doctrine, though still popular in fundamentalist circles, is less likely to be essential among evangelicals. What should be noted, however, is that some contemporary evangelicals discount the importance of eschatology, to the point of either intellectual agnosticism or chosen ignorance; this is less likely among fundamentalists.

To this point, it is difficult to differentiate a fundamentalist from an evangelical. Yet members of each group are often quick to differentiate themselves from members of the other. It appears that the historical bifurcation between these two groups can be attributed to differences on the last two of Ammerman's (1991) defining criteria.

Separatism

The affirmation of orthodox doctrines in the late 19th and early 20th centuries had to be, for the first time, articulated within a cultural milieu that was ultimately antagonistic. Ammerman (1991) claims:

> Their [the fundamentalists'] affirmation, however, was different in kind from the affirmations of the generations that had preceded them. Their times would demand that the defense they mounted be innovative in its own right. Previous generations had accepted the Bible as true and had assented to orthodox dogma in a world where most, if not all, sources of cultural authority upheld those beliefs. Never again would that be the case. Those who would affirm the historical reliability of the Bible would forever be forced to defend their affirmation. *Fundamentalism, then, differs from traditionalism or orthodoxy or even a mere revivalist movement. It differs in that it is a movement in conscious, organized opposition to the disruption of those traditions and orthodoxies.* (p. 14; emphasis in original)

Ammerman's contention is not entirely new. She recognizes a parallel with Geertz's (1968) description of a similar difference found in Islamic societies—the difference between "holding" beliefs and "being held by" them. Both fundamentalists and evangelicals feel uncomfortable with the dominant culture at times. During these times, the fundamentalists find that their religious beliefs lose their taken-for-granted character (i.e., "being held by" their beliefs, or simply *having faith*) and require conscious and even conscientious vindication (i.e., "holding" their beliefs, or *having reasons to defend the faith*). This vindication becomes their badge of separation from the world.

In contrast, evangelicals faced a far less hostile culture during their important formative years, though these came only a few decades later than fundamentalism's defining years (the latter occurred, as described above, immediately after World War I). The rise of neo-orthodoxy, the success of the Graham crusades, and the emergence of a more centrist group of scholars from within all contributed to this more hospitable cultural environment. This is not meant to suggest that culture willingly embraced all that evangelicalism had to offer, but rather that evangelicals were less likely to feel forced to defend an unpopular position.

Biblical Literalism

Though fundamentalists are more likely to adopt the position that the Bible, especially when interpretation is subject to controversy, should be taken literally, this difference is not without qualification. Fundamentalists do not necessarily insist on a literal reading of all scripture. For example, a common fundamentalist methodology when scripture apparently contradicts a well-established scientific "fact" (e.g., the earth's revolution around the sun rather than vice versa) is to suggest that those portions of scripture are written poetically, and therefore are not meant to be read with scientific precision. Also, it is common for fundamentalists (and most Biblical scholars) to depart from a literal reading of scripture when interpreting prophecy; days, for example, may represent long periods of time (Ammerman, 1991). But even here, symbols often have such a precise meaning that a few fundamentalists may go so far as to predict (or to be convinced of by the predictions of others) the precise timing of the end of the world—or, in terms more specific to their premillenial eschatology, "the rapture." Most, however, warn against such speculation, not so much on the basis of reason as because the Bible states: "But of that day and hour knoweth no man, no, not the angels of heaven, but my Father only" (Matthew 24:36; see also Mark 13:32).

A literal reading of the Bible is more common when fundamentalists are accounting for creation. In an earlier publication, Ammerman (1982) suggested that adherence to "a historical, six-day creation may be the most accurate indicator available for a truly 'literal' belief in scripture and membership in the fundamentalist party of evangelicals" (quoted in Kellstedt & Smidt, 1991, p. 171). Evangelicals, as a group, are far less likely than fundamentalists to take the Genesis account literally (Ammerman, 1982), and in general they see far less necessary connection between scriptural inerrancy (a tenet generally held by evangelicals) and scriptural literalism. In fact, Jacobsen (1987) describes a new breed of evangelicals who no longer envision Biblical interpretation along strict "monistic" lines (i.e., the penchant to unify apparently diverse passages into a single, tightly unified system of Biblical truth). These emerging evangelical pluralists argue that the Bible does not necessarily have only one meaning that must reside within its text. Rather, such pluralists suggest that the Bible can be interpreted in a responsible and valid manner by different people using different methodologies. Jacobsen further contends that such pluralism is not limited to hermeneutics, though that is the focus of his discussion. The broad range of evangelical pluralism suggests that in general,

> They [the pluralists] are less defensive than their forebears about the things they claim to know and more open to the possibility that present evangelical ways of thinking may be in need of revision. While they affirm that from God's perspective all things cohere in a unity, they also remind us and themselves that our view of reality is much more limited than God's. And they suggest that, given our limited human state, some form of pluralism is a more appropriate stance than monism. (p. 325)

Still, many evangelicals are reluctant *not* to take the Bible literally, especially on matters involving core doctrinal issues such as the divinity of Christ, the virgin birth, the resurrection, a literal heaven and hell, and specific sinful practices (e.g., homosexual behavior). Thus fundamentalists and evangelicals alike believe that one can know God only through the redemptive work of Christ. Common among both groups is a saying consistent with the Bible's claims (e.g., John 14:6) that salvation "is through none other [than Christ]." As noted in Chapter 1, both fundamentalists and, to a lesser extent, evangelicals believe that scripture itself reveals clearly when it is to be taken literally. Of course, scripture has to be interpreted, and evangelicals may (and do) differ from fundamentalists (both groups also differ within themselves) about when scripture teaches that it is to be taken literally and when it does not. But such differences, both evangelicals and fundamentalists would agree, are not problems with the text itself, but are problems of human limitation in accurately processing the text. Thus both fundamentalists and evangelicals believe that scripture speaks with sufficient clarity when necessary;

however, they may differ in their understanding of what "when necessary" means.

Our purpose here is not to deny differences between evangelicals and fundamentalists. The distinction is crucially important, and to ignore these differences would be to take a step back from the significant strides that have been made in understanding conservative Protestantism. Indeed, many Christians identify with the term "evangelical" but not the term "fundamentalist," and vice versa. However, important commonalities are often overlooked; not the least of these center around the authoritative centrality of scripture, which is the defining criterion in an intratextual understanding of religion and spiritual experience.

CONCLUSION

This chapter has focused on early 20th-century American Protestantism—the movement that gave a name to the fundamentalist phenomenon. From this analysis, we hope to have shown that both the fundamentalist movement and its offspring, contemporary evangelicalism, are indeed complex and defy simple explanation. Any stereotyped caricature is at best of limited value and is most likely misguided.

Fundamentalists themselves could read this chapter (or the many other fine works that have been devoted to their history), identify with the many characteristics and historical events contained herein, and still maintain that their very essence has yet to be captured. Yes, fundamentalists in many regards are militant—largely as a reaction to a dominant culture that disregards and even treats with disdain what they believe to be of ultimate importance. Yes, fundamentalists maintain an apocalyptic view of the future that is narrowly and tightly defined by scripture, and is perhaps even bizarre to outsiders. Yes, fundamentalists tend to separate themselves from the world. Yes, some fundamentalists are anti-intellectual and, though thoroughly modern with regard to Enlightenment science, believe that contemporary science (particularly Darwinian science) is speculative and unsupportable. But fundamentalists would not use these peculiarities to describe themselves.

For fundamentalists, the root issue is not social or cultural; it is theological. Fundamentalist theology is not necessarily lofty, nor does it necessarily address burning issues of the day, particularly as defined by the host culture. Rather, *in the words of fundamentalists themselves*, their theology is summarized in the first few phrases of a familiar tune that many learned as toddlers: "Jesus loves me, this I know, for the Bible tells me so." Even other cardinal doctrines surrounding the deity of Christ rest upon the view that the Bible speaks with authority and clarity. For fundamentalists, the origin of the text is God, so it should be expected to speak with truth. This confidence in the authoritative sacred text, held as objective truth, is applicable whether the text is the Bible (as described in this chapter), the Quran, the Vedas, the Torah, or any other sacred text.

CHAPTER FOUR

Fundamentalism in a Pentecostal Denomination

The Church of God (of Prophecy)[1]

Live by the Bible or die by the Bible, yea, whether we live
or die, if we obey Him we are true soldiers of Jesus Christ:
and we are His for service because we have enlisted in His
army. . . . Let the enemy raise his war whoop and turn his
gatling [*sic*] guns of false teaching and a hireling ministry
against us, we must and will march right up to the
ramparts and over the breastworks, snatch the sword
(Word of God) out of the giant's hands, and with it cut off
his head.

—TOMLINSON (1984, pp. 26, 27)

This chapter is concerned with fundamentalism in the Church of
God (COG), one of the most significant Pentecostal denominations to
emerge in the Southeastern United States at the beginning of the 20th
century. Some may find it puzzling at first to examine fundamentalism
in such a group, particularly since social scientists among both nonfundamentalists (Ammerman, 1991; Barr, 1977; Marsden, 1980, 1990)
and self-proclaimed fundamentalists (Beale, 1986; Dollar, 1973; Sidwell,
1998) have tended to deny that such groups are part of the tradition.
COG members are typically labeled by fundamentalists as heretics for
their doctrinal stand on charismatic gifts—glossolalia, for example—and
as such are distanced from evangelicals. Ammerman (1991) bases this
distinction on speculation that "Pentecostals trust the revelatory power
of experience more than do the more rationally oriented fundamentalists
who seek to confine revelation to scripture alone" (p. 4), thus adopting
what Carpenter (1997) identifies as a narrow definition of fundamental-

ism. Sidwell (1998) seems to agree and even quotes early fundamentalist G. Campbell Morgan in describing Pentecostals as "the last vomit of Satan" (p. 134). Sidwell also observes, however, that the more traditional (i.e., classical) Pentecostals who denounced the rise of the charismatic movement were acknowledged as fundamentalist kin even by Bob Jones, Jr., a renowned fundamentalist, although Jones himself continued to reject their doctrine of supernatural gifts.

However, reasons do exist to consider fundamentalism among Pentecostals. One study (Hunter, 1982), which considered fundamentalism to be an aspect of Evangelicalism, observed the Holiness–Pentecostal tradition as one among four others thought helpful in contributing toward a useful operational definition of evangelicalism; the present-day Church of God (of Prophecy) [COG(OP)] was even listed as a potential resource for investigating this concern. Even if Pentecostalism is viewed as distinct from the early fundamentalist movement itself, it clearly shares basic tenets of the faith with fundamentalism—that is, the inerrancy of scripture, the deity of Jesus, substitutionary atonement, the resurrection, and millennialism (Barr, 1977; *The Church of God Is: Foundational*, 2003; Marsden, 1990). In Latin America and in other countries, Pentecostalism has even been *applauded* as a fundamentalist movement that uses glossolalia as a powerful form of protest against political oppression (Deiros, 1991; Nielsen, 1993). Furthermore, even some among the Pentecostal ranks have referred to themselves as fundamentalists (Conn, 1996). Although Ammerman (1991) tends to distance Pentecostals from fundamentalists for emphasizing experiential over rational understanding of the text, Parker (1996) has observed in a psychological analysis that spiritual discernment among Pentecostals does in fact have a rational aspect, based on the Bible and a sensitivity to traditional cues and affirmations. It is also a mistake to ignore the fact that some Pentecostals have carefully worked out a systematic theology that includes participation of the Holy Spirit in discovering the revelation of scripture (Pruitt, 1981). Furthermore, historical records of the COG document an early concern for establishing a correct understanding of the text as the basis for all doctrine and teaching.

For example, at an early General Assembly, COG General Overseer A. J. Tomlinson began deliberations on church doctrine with a reminder that "Every subject should be carefully, prayerfully dealt with. Every decision must be strictly made by the Bible or in harmony with it" (cited in *Echoes*, 1913, p. 9). At a later Assembly, Tomlinson felt the need to remind delegates of the very reason for which the yearly convocations were first begun: "The Assembly was first called for the purpose of searching the Bible for information concerning the Church and her teaching. . . . The Holy Ghost has always been present to unfold the truths and make them clear and impressive" (quoted in *Minutes*, 1920, p. 16). The fact that the COG has traditionally subscribed to "classic" fundamentals of the faith and has always emphasized the importance of being Biblically grounded in its theology invites investigation into its fundamentalist character from a psychological perspective.

As to the difference observed by some scholars between fundamentalism and Pentecostalism, what distinguishes them is not really a difference in the fundamental truths they claim, or the basis on which they claim them, but rather a distinction between the types of warfare they have historically chosen to engage in (Conn, 1996). While fundamentalists were waging intradenominational wars for control over doctrinal issues in the early 20th century, the COG and other Pentecostals were at the same time warring against "sin and Satan" in their quest to spread the "third blessing" (Spirit baptism) around the globe. Conn (1996) claims that Pentecostals "were not only militantly fundamentalist—in the pure, spiritual meaning of the word—but they had also the positive message of holiness and the baptism of the Holy Spirit" (p. xxviii). This view suggests that the Pentecostals not only were ready to defend fundamentals of the faith, but also were concerned with offering a convincing alternative to what they saw as vapid and powerless living in an increasingly modernist society.

Conn (1996) is essentially correct in observing a parallel of missions between the rise of fundamentalism and Pentecostalism, but we suggest that the COG mission was more complex than simply spreading Pentecostalism and its message of hope. We submit that both the fundamentalist and COG movements were engaged in their early stages with restoration concerns that were not so different in nature. On the one hand, concerned Baptists and Presbyterians were devoted to restoring the purity of apostolic principles and practices that had come under attack from modernism and higher biblical criticism (Beale, 1986; Dollar, 1973). On the other hand, members of the COG were committed to restoring what they believed was the New Testament church—the "real Church of God"—which they felt had been covered over by the gross darkness of "man-made" creeds (particularly the Nicene Creed) and unscriptural doctrines; in addition, they pledged themselves to staving off attacks from critics of the Bible and the corruptive influence of modernism (Davidson, 1973; Spurling, n.d./1921; Stone, 1977; Tomlinson, 1984). This COG mission took complex form in the preaching of a pronounced "church gospel" that was intended to save both the lost world and the blinded denominational churches. Furthermore, it demanded a separation from the world and its apostates, which was meant for safeguarding both membership and Biblical doctrine. On all fronts, the Pentecostal-empowered mission appeared to be a double-edged sword, with aggressive evangelism on one edge and a defense for the truth on the other. The conflict was not only with the temporal world—which was the primary concern for early fundamentalists—but also with a spiritual world.

In this chapter, we use our model to illuminate at least a portion of this fundamentalist Pentecostal worldview and the psychological meaning it affords to believers. Doing so requires us to take a psychohistorical approach: (1) presenting a brief history of the COG, to provide a context for understanding the cultural conditions from which it emerged and the dynamics involved with its leadership; (2) assessing the degree of A. J. Tomlinson's persuasion as its most influential early leader; and (3) tracing the origin of some of its most cardinal Bible-based beliefs, as interpreted by Tomlinson during his own crisis experiences—beliefs that through his influence came to be widely embraced by followers as a way to understand their manner of being in the world, as well as their purpose for existence. As will be seen, the psychology of this stance is indubitably linked to an intratextual understanding of their sacred text, the Bible.

A BRIEF HISTORY OF THE
CHURCH OF GOD (OF PROPHECY)

As successful Pentecostal denominations, the two descendants of the original COG—the present-day COG and COG(OP) (see Note 1)—both have international offices located in Cleveland, Tennessee. Recent reports indicate that the COG has a worldwide membership of over 6 million with a presence in nearly 150 countries (*A Brief History*, 2003), whereas the COG(OP) has 546,000 international members in 120 countries (Church of God of Prophecy, 2002). Begun as a single Appalachian sect, both denominations have grown considerably in their century-plus histories, and together they account for a significant number of adherents around the world. Although several factors have contributed to their growth, these worldwide Pentecostal denominations owe much of their existence to heartfelt Wesleyan Methodism of the 19th century (Synan, 1997).

During the late 1800s, Appalachian religion's blend of Calvinist grace, Baptist revivalism, and (in particular) Methodist pietism typified much of the fervor so common among American camp meetings of earlier revival periods (McCauley, 1995). Although geographic isolation and the mingling together of different religious traditions were by themselves sufficient sources for disputes and schisms, other issues of concern were soon beginning to surface in reaction to the rise of modernism, in the forms of evolutionary theory and modern Biblical criticism (Ammerman, 1991). It was in such a context that Richard Spurling, a Baptist-ordained minister of Monroe County, Tennessee, became greatly troubled concerning the prevalence of religious creeds and doctrines that had crept in among denominations and even in his own church (Stone, 1977). In Spurling's thinking, Protestant Christianity needed another reformation—one that denounced what he saw as institutional creedalism and man-made laws in view of the New Testament model based on principles of Jesus and the "law of love" (*Book of Minutes*, 1922; Spurling, n.d./1921). Two years of failing to convince his own church of its error led to his pastoral resignation and the subsequent organization of a small group of eight like-minded persons on August 19, 1886, under the name "Christian Union." A covenant of agreement required that each member reject all creeds and traditions for a life governed by principles declared in the New Testament; furthermore, each member was to have freedom to interpret the Bible as led by personal conscience, and to be responsible to sit with others as the "Church of God" for business purposes. The aging Spurling was immediately chosen as pastor, although his son, Richard G. Spurling, was selected as his replacement only 1 month later. The new group struggled to exist, and how long it actually survived remains in dispute (Conn, 1996; McCauley, 1995; Synan, 1997; Tomlinson, 1984). Nevertheless, it was the elder Spurling's vision of restoring the New Testament church, passed on through his son, that gave both birth and mission to what later became the COG.

Through the influence of Richard G. Spurling during his travels, the Holiness Church at Camp Creek, North Carolina, was organized in 1902 as a belated consequence of the 1896 Holiness revival at nearby Schearer Schoolhouse (Conn, 1996; Synan, 1997; Tomlinson, 1984). The revival had met with fierce opposition from the community for its unusual Pentecostal-like manifestations; thus its converts, under the care of the Baptist-ordained W. F. Bryant, encountered severe persecution. Lack of organization among the group allowed discouragement, strife, and sedition to arise, which probably would have destroyed its existence had Spurling not intervened some 6 years later. Spurling persuaded them to reorganize and was immediately installed as pastor of the 20-member group. Once again the mission to restore the New Testament church became a central concern, although the new church experienced little success until the arrival of A. J. Tomlinson, a Bible salesman, the following year.

Tomlinson, reared in a Quaker community near Westfield, Indiana, had become interested in the Holiness movement and had preached in times past for both Bryant and Spurling while passing through the mountain region (Conn, 1996; Davidson, 1973; Stone, 1977). Influenced by Spurling's ideas of restoring the church to what it had been in the first century after Christ, he was convinced to join the Holiness Church at Camp Creek on June 13, 1903, with an understanding that its claim was to be the original Church of God of the New Testament— "not going to be, but IS the Church of God" (Tomlinson, cited in Evans, 1943, p. 12; emphasis in Evans). Being an able leader and preacher, Tomlinson was immediately selected as pastor and led the group in gaining 14 additional members the following year (Conn, 1996; Davidson, 1973; Tomlinson, 1984). Within a second year, his leadership resulted in three additional congregations in Georgia and Tennessee. At the end of 1904, Tomlinson moved his office of ministry from the mountains of North Carolina to Cleveland, Tennessee, a town of some 4,500 residents, from where he continued to serve three of the four churches as pastor and to conduct new evangelistic campaigns.

The continued growth of the new organization led to the eventual need for meeting annually as a corporate body for the purpose of coming to agreement on various important Biblical teachings and practices (Conn, 1996; Davidson, 1973; Stone, 1977). Among the many important issues discussed and decided over the years, perhaps its very first decision in 1906 was the most foundational: "We do not consider ourselves a legislative or executive body, but judicial only" (General Assembly Minutes 1906–1914, 1992, p. 8). In other words, they considered themselves only as interpreters of the authoritative scripture. In efforts to adhere only to scriptural principles and to abstain from the corruption of "man-made creeds," the COG throughout its history often referred to this first act of business as a beacon when reaching later doctrinal decisions (General Assembly Minutes 1906–1914, 1992, pp. 40, 58, 257–258). Tomlinson was chosen as moderator and clerk for each of the General Assemblies until 1909, when the sect had grown sufficiently to warrant his appointment as General Overseer of the church—an office he held without contest until dissension arose in 1922–1923 (Davidson, 1973; Stone, 1977).

By 1922, the evangelistic arm of the COG had reached into some 30 U.S. states, Canada, China, the Bahamas, and the West Indies; the total membership included 666 local congregations and 21,076 individuals (Minutes, 1922, p. 56). With growth, however, came internal struggles over the type of leadership the COG now required for its continued success. From the beginning, Tomlinson's inspirational type of leadership was necessarily direct, and this was probably responsible for much of the sect's early success (Williamson, 2000). With expansion and growth, however, came the need for a more diversified approach to leadership— especially in the company of others who were quite capable and willing to share such responsibilities. This created conflict for Tomlinson, who had been selected by the 1914 Assembly as General Overseer for life.

The situation was greatly intensified by action taken in the 1921 Assembly to adopt a Constitution that greatly restricted the power of the General Overseer's office (*Minutes*, 1921, pp. 60–65).[2] In addition, the financial structure of the general church had not been adequately developed over the years, leading to insufficient resources for operational expenses and confusion over distribution of what meager funds were available. The leadership and financial conflicts escalated until 1923, when Tomlinson was impeached and removed from office by a standing Board of Elders who, at a called interterm meeting, handed over the reins of leadership to F. J. Lee (Conn, 1996).

This event brought about much confusion within the general church. As a result, more than one-fourth of its membership and ministry (5,000 to 6,000) followed Tomlinson, who at nearly 58 years of age continued as their General Overseer (Stone, 1977). Both factions struggled to regroup, however, and eventually continued with their own missions. Tomlinson's COG (which was given the distinction "of Prophecy" by a court decision in 1952) persevered and followed his virtually unchallenged leadership for the next 20 years. By that time, Tomlinson had reclaimed lost ground and added more than 65,415 new individuals to his church, 9,659 of whom were dispersed among 20 other countries and provinces of the world (*Minutes*, 1943, pp. 91–92). Despite the devastation of 1923, Tomlinson was able to recover and continue his vision of restoring what he thought was the "last-days" COG of the Bible. This he did until his death on October 2, 1943.

Since Tomlinson's decease, the COG(OP) has had only three other General Overseers in its history. M. A. Tomlinson, the youngest son of A. J., led the denomination in his father's vision for 47 years, allowing virtually no change in church doctrine or teachings. Before his retirement in 1990, the denomination had exceeded a membership of 300,000 individuals in all 50 states and in more than 90 countries around the world (Williamson, 2001). Billy D. Murray, the younger Tomlinson's successor, was more evangelistically oriented and emphasized the church's need to be more inclusive in its outreach. It was also during his 10-year term that the church's 77-year-old teaching against the wearing of jewelry was replaced with one more in keeping with moderation (*General Assembly Minutes 1906–1914*, 1992, p. 337; *Assembly Minutes*, 1991, pp. 81, 85, 90, 107). Despite the loss of a small faction over this issue, the denomination expanded to a worldwide membership of 424,777 (350,000 outside the United States) during Murray's term (*Minutes*, 1998, pp. 116–124). Overall, Murray's leadership was distinct from his predecessors', in that he moved further away from exclusivity and toward a more ecumenical stance—a trend that has continued with his successor, Fred S. Fisher, Sr., who took office in July 2000 upon

Murray's retirement. The developments of recent years are thus moving the present-day COG(OP) further from the sectarian roots that produced it and toward an increasing mainline denominational position with a more educated membership. However, fundamentalism remains alive and well.

THE INFLUENCE OF A. J. TOMLINSON

A very important reason for briefly surveying COG history is to show in context the influence of a certain man, A. J. Tomlinson, on the development and worldview of a particular type of Pentecostalism. The COG tradition does in fact reflect the significant contributions of numerous persons, both men and women, over the course of its history. However, given the factious nature of Appalachian religion (McCauley, 1995), it might be speculated that without Tomlinson's foresight in relocating church operations to Cleveland, the COG might have remained as one of many small congregations still isolated in Appalachia today, if it had survived at all. We will never know for certain the worth of this speculation, although the influence he wielded in the denomination and its early doctrinal views cannot be overestimated.

Tomlinson's affiliation with the COG not only made him popular, but also allowed him various opportunities to communicate his own perspectives on spirituality and the world. These perspectives were based, as we shall see, on the way in which he took up the sacred text. First, he was not at all a passive administrator who governed church affairs from a remote office. Rather, he was an active one who spent the majority of time "on the field," encouraging the membership and preaching evangelistic campaigns (Duggar, 1964). Second, except for a brief period, Tomlinson was editor of the church's weekly/biweekly publication from its first issue in 1910 until his death in 1943; this allowed him to contribute several hundred articles that influenced the vast readership.[3] Third, Tomlinson was perhaps most persuasive in the celebrated annual addresses he gave to the several thousand clergy and lay leaders who gathered for the COG's General Assembly each year to receive inspiration and direction for their work. These addresses, printed later in the church paper and the Assembly minutes, contained not only sermonic material but also his vision for the church, as well as personal views on certain issues to be taken up by the Assembly for discussion and (almost always) approval as official church beliefs and practices.

Finally, it was apparently common practice in early years for an appointed committee to receive doctrinal questions from Assembly delegates that were later presented to the General Overseer for his response before the entire Assembly body (*General Assembly Minutes 1906–1914*, 1992, p. 190). For example, the following question was presented along with others to Tomlinson for his response at the conclusion of his 1913 annual address:

> Q. Can we afford to adorn our bodies with gold or pearls or costly array? (See Tim. 2:9, I Peter 3:3). (*General Assembly Minutes 1906–1914*, 1992, p. 224)

His response:

> A. Unnecessary jewelry, such as finger rings, bracelets, earbobs, lockets, and other kinds for mere adornment should not be worn. Gold teeth, gold rimmed spectacles, watch cases and things specially useful are left for the individual to decide. (*General Assembly Minutes 1906–1914*, 1992, p. 224)

Tomlinson's own input was often taken by delegates as *the final answer* to such questions and accepted as official church ruling.[4] Such was the persuasion of the first General Overseer of the COG. It was through the affordance of such opportunities that his personal experiences and views came to be regarded as certain absolutes in the COG.

Simply stated, Tomlinson's worldview eventually became that of the early COG through his powerful influence as a charismatic leader for some 40 years. Hence, to understand the psychology of fundamentalism in the COG, we must examine how Tomlinson himself came to take up the text, interpret from it various absolute beliefs, and successfully communicate these certainties to adherents who were persuaded to share his view of and meaning system for the world. We suggest that an understanding of his own experiences with the text, in regard to these absolutes, is helpful in illuminating the COG worldview. We conduct this examination in the context of Sundén's role theory—a psychological approach that focuses on the importance of a sacred text within a tradition and how it is understood (Holm, 1995).

According to Sundén (see Holm, 1995), religious experience, especially the type encountered as supernatural, can be understood in terms of taking up the roles or structured models provided by traditional narratives found in sacred texts. Such narratives contain two roles: that of a human party and that of God. In becoming familiar with the narrative, a person acquires a foundation from which future spiritual experiences can emerge, and also a template that provides such experiences with structure. At such times, says Sundén, motivation for seeking these events is triggered by feeling a sudden loss of security in an environment previously felt to be safe (i.e., one in which Baumeister's [1991] sense of efficacy was experienced). When this occurs, the person (unconsciously) assumes the role of the protagonist in the narrative as a performance, and also takes on the role of God, in the sense that whatever happens in the context of experience can be perceived as an act of God—a discernment of God's immediate will and control. It is in this way that the person senses a "concrete" persuasion that God has been divinely responsible for the occurrences in the experience. In this mental shift, a "Thou with a purpose" has been encountered in pure relation through an experience that becomes all-encompassing—one that takes over complete control. Eventually, the person experiences a mental shift from this religious context of encounter back to the secular realm of existence, but feels altogether transformed by the experience. Hence role theory provides insight into the psychology of religious experience within a tradition that privileges its text as absolutely foundational to meaning and existence.

Sundén's theory is useful in describing the psychological import of intratextual interpretations. As we shall see, it seems especially applicable to Tomlinson and his encounters with the text; furthermore, it suggests how a particular process of role taking from the text could be transmitted from a charismatic leader such as Tomlinson to a devoted group of followers, who not only came to embrace their leader's view of the world, but also reinforced it by going back to the text in the same manner he did. From text-based narratives that he experienced first himself, Tomlinson provided a model for adherents who came to experience and understand religion and life for themselves as he exemplified it, by certain behaviors and beliefs derived from personal encounters with the text. As role theory would predict, his conduct, perceptions, and convictions were modeled by followers who were persuaded by the same text-based certainties about life and the way of the world. These certainties, or absolutes, can be considered as fundamentals of a meaningful worldview. It is to some of these fundamentals, encountered first by Tomlinson and later embraced by the COG that we now turn.

FUNDAMENTALS OF THE CHURCH
OF GOD'S TRADITION

In addition to subscribing to and defending classic fundamentals of the Christian faith (e.g., Biblical inerrancy, the deity of Jesus), the COG holds to other beliefs that give it distinctive character as a unique denomination. An analysis of these other beliefs reflects a few of what might be described as absolutes, based on an intratextual interpretation of the Bible, that weave together an "objective" psychological reality for adherents. This reality is "objective" in the sense that it is perceived as standing beyond an individual's subjective experience, and that it serves as a basis for understanding the person's relation to the world and as a framework for maintaining a sense of purpose in life. Although there are several such beliefs in the COG, perhaps three of the most interesting for consideration are holiness, the church's existence as the "Church of God of the Bible," and Spirit baptism. Each of these contributes in part to a fundamentalist reality—one in which the objective world for COG believers appears as holy, exclusive, and spiritual.

In the remainder of this chapter, we consider each of these absolute truths in more detail and illustrate how they were intratextually abstracted from the Bible. As discussed above, such an enterprise requires a major concern with A. J. Tomlinson, who wielded a significant influence in the denomination and its eventual acceptance of these and other important beliefs. Although he was not the originator of any of these beliefs, Tomlinson first had to struggle with them for himself as living realities, understand them intratextually as objective truths, and then articulate them theologically before passing them on to others. The psychological transformation he underwent as a result of his own experiences thus became a locus for emphasizing these truths to the COG as absolutes and for keeping them foremost in their worldview of meaning (Tomlinson, 1984). We now examine each of these absolutes in terms of the way it was intratextually derived from Tomlinson's own experience with the text, the manner in which he forged it into COG thinking and practice, and the subsequent effect it had on the COG's perception of reality.

The Fundamental of Holiness

Although Richard Spurling and his son were Baptists, the COG emerged in large part from the Holiness tradition that characterized the 1896 Schearer Schoolhouse revival (Conn, 1996; Synan, 1997). It remained for Tomlinson as an early leader, however, to help establish the vitality of this small group and hence the doctrine of holiness as one of its fundamental truths. For this group, holiness was and is understood as a sinless state of being in the world made possible by "sanctification"—a process through which a believer is supernaturally cleansed from innate sinfulness and enabled to live a godly life unencumbered by "desires of the flesh" (e.g., fornication, debauchery, rebellion, selfishness). By no means was Tomlinson the first to experience sanctification among the COG, but he was foremost in articulating on a large scale what its members already believed. It was because he himself had encountered sanctification as a powerful experience rooted in the sacred text that he became convinced of its truth and the holiness-based view of the world it constructed. Once persuaded by the text, he was compelled to declare the fundamental truth of holiness both before and after his initial encounter with the COG.

A key to understanding Tomlinson's view of holiness—and hence that of the COG—requires some knowledge of his own experience, which had its basis in an intratextual understanding of the Bible. Because Tomlinson had no religious training as a child, it was not until adulthood that he first took an interest in religion. Shortly after his marriage, he began experiencing a troubled conscience, which left him with what was described as a terrible sense of dread (Tomlinson, 1984). Some time later, he was nearly struck by a lightning bolt that shot through his house during a severe thunderstorm. Knowing nothing of conversion, and even less of scripture, he read some verses from his wife's Bible and had her pray with him. Although he experienced no immediate change, it was from this moment that he claimed to have committed himself to a sincere seeking after God.

Not long after this conversion, Tomlinson described a spiritual conflict that constantly troubled him (Tomlinson, 1984). Seeking relief, he even thought of constructing a small booth in the midst of a field on his farm for spending time in prayerful searching of the scriptures. He claimed to have read his Bible both day and night, despite having to rise at dawn to plow his fields. It is clear from his writings that he studied the following passages:

> Knowing this, that our old man is crucified with him, that the body of sin might be destroyed, that henceforth we should not serve sin. (Romans 6:6)

> That ye put off concerning the former conversation the old man, which is corrupt according to the deceitful lusts; And be renewed in the spirit of your mind; And that ye put on the new man, which after God is created in righteousness and true holiness. (Ephesians 4:22–24)

In reading the text, he struggled to find meaning for his life in terms of a conflict with the "old man" of sinful nature. Learning the final outcome of the matter, and feeling more spiritually prepared, he finally resolved that this "old man" must die. He wrote:

> At last the final struggle came. It was a hand to hand fight, and the demons of hell seemed to be mustering their forces, and their ghastly forms and furious yells would no doubt have been too much for me had not the

Lord of heaven sent a host of angels to assist me in the terrible hour of peril. But it was the last great conflict, and I managed, by some peculiar dexterity to put the sword into him up to the hilt.

It was about twelve o'clock in the day. I cried out in the bitterness of my soul: "Now! Now! You've got to give it up now! Now! I felt him to begin to weaken and quiver. I kept the "Sword" right in him, and never let go. That sharp two-edged "Sword" was doing its deadly work. I did not pity him. I showed him no quarters. There we were in that attitude when all of a sudden came from above, like a thunderbolt from the skies, a sensational power that ended the conflict, and there lay the "old man" dead at my feet, and I was free from his grasp. (Tomlinson, 1984, p. 226)

This self-description of Tomlinson's own sanctification—a life-changing event that seems to have provided foundation for constructing his view of holiness—can be considered in light of the psychological framework of meaning making discussed in Chapter 1. Tomlinson experienced a crisis of meaning in all four of Baumeister's (1991) categories discussed in Chapter 1: purpose, value, efficacy, and self-worth. Hill (2002), in discussing the role of negative emotions in religious experience, identifies one's sense of "wrongness" in life as an unmet need for meaning. For a religious person such as Tomlinson, this sense of wrongness, according to William James (1902), is quite a powerful transforming agent:

The sense of present wrongness is a far more distinct piece of our consciousness than is the imagination of any positive ideal we can aim at. In a majority of cases, indeed, the 'sin' almost exclusively engrosses the attention, so that conversion is [to quote Starbuck, 1899, p. 64] '*a process of struggling away from sin rather than of striving towards righteousness.*' (p. 205; emphasis in original)

For Tomlinson, the unmet needs resulting from this sense of wrongness motivated him toward overcoming the "old man" of sinful nature.

From Sundén's role theory perspective (see Holm, 1995) as described earlier in this chapter, it seems that a greatly troubled Tomlinson saw himself on some level as the believer in constant conflict with the "old man" of the text—the abiding sinful nature that hinders the freedom brought about by the "new man." He also took on the role of God from the text in discerning God's will for the conflict to be settled by the killing of the "old man" with the "Sword," a metaphor for the word of God. A band of angels was even dispensed to his side for aid, and a thunderbolt of power was divinely hurled to complete the task. The result was experienced as a supernatural transformation that left this seeker resolved and forever changed. But what is crucially important here—particularly for understanding fundamentalism—is the fact of Tomlinson's full acceptance of the Bible as the source of truth, and its critical role in constructing an objective psychological reality that stood beyond his person, giving sense and meaning to his existence.

For Tomlinson, his own experience was now understood within an interpretation of the text, in terms of a conflict with the "old man" who was and forever would remain in his worldview as the sinful nature of fallen humanity. Tomlinson did not arrive at this understanding by an *intertextual* relating of other authoritative texts to the Bible, but rather by taking up the Bible itself in terms of *intratextuality*. That is, he prayerfully entered into dialogue (or process of interpretation) with the text, and struggled to discover a revelation of God concerning the nature of sin and its personal remedy. He made no claim to the discovery of sanctification as a Biblical doctrine, for he had already heard of its teaching elsewhere. However, it was through the process of reading the text for himself and struggling with its intended meaning that sanctification became interpreted as an absolute truth of objective reality for him. His encounter with the text also revealed the word of God as a powerful "Sword," one that was capable of severing the sinful from the spiritual nature within someone. Consequently, he felt freed from sin, and believed that he would never more be the same. Hence we see in Tomlinson's encounter with the text the emergence of a basic absolute that formed a portion of his objective worldview, a truth that never wavered in meaning for him throughout life: All humanity is born with a fallen nature that wars against righteousness, and a crisis experience of sanctification is required to make possible a life of holiness, separated unto God.

Through his own experience of sanctification, the fundamental of holiness became an important aspect of Tomlinson's objective reality that emerged, as we have seen, from dialogue with the Bible, and one that he pointed out from the text with persistence to COG members and others to whom he preached. Furthermore, the sanctification process satisfied the needs for meaning discussed in Chapter 1 as a sense of purpose, value, efficacy, and self-worth (Baumeister, 1991), and it was accompanied by associated positive emotions (see Hill, 2002). Various Biblical passages were brought into this dialogue for intratextual interpretation, which became prominent in the COG through their use in numerous sermons and writings. Examples of the most common verses were quoted in a series of articles that Tomlinson wrote in defense of sanctification and holiness, against attacks from a more recent "finished-work" doctrine that challenged their validity as being distinct from justification and salvation. In one such article, he stated:

When our sins are forgiven [salvation] we stand in the same relation before God as the little child. It is not responsible for the sin principle neither are we responsible for that "old man," "carnal mind," "Adamic nature" until we have the privilege of knowing it is enmity to God and that it can be rooted out or crucified [sanctified], then if we refuse to accept the cleansing after God's order and plan we make ourselves transgressors again [sic].

"Wherefore Jesus also, that he might sanctify (make holy) the people with his own blood, suffered without the gate." Heb. 13:12. "For this is the will of God even your sanctification." 1 Thes. 4:3. "By the which will we are sanctified through the offering of the body of Jesus Christ once for all." Heb. 10:10. "Be ye holy, for I am holy." 1 Pet. 1:19 [sic]. "And the very God of peace sanctify you wholly." 1 Thes. 5:23. (Tomlinson, 1914, pp. 2, 3)

Tomlinson (1914) continued:

These are a few of the many Scriptures that teach sanctification both by showing God's provision for it, and by asserting that it is His will and command. Then if readers do not get sanctified they become transgressors because they ignore His will and disobey His command. The individual must first be reconciled to God and accepted by Him, which is, "Therefore being justified by faith, we have peace with God," then sanctified, or cleansed, the "old man" put off—crucified, that one may be made holy. . . . "Wherefore Jesus also, that he might sanctify the people with his own blood, suffered without the gate. Let us go forth therefore unto him without the camp bearing his reproach." Heb. 13:[12–13]. After being justified by the blood on the inside, go to Him outside and get sanctified. This seems so clear that it looks like any one ought to see it. (pp. 2, 3)

Not only did Tomlinson take such a stand for himself; he also demanded that COG ministers take a strong defense in their pulpits against attacks from advocates for "progressive" sanctification:

Our preachers are instructed to preach sanctification strong and powerful. Show that it is a definite experience and not obtained by gradual growth. These gradual growth sanctificationists never do get sanctified. They are always getting sanctified, but never able to state truthfully that they are sanctified. . . . The "old man" is crucified, and no longer lives in the heart to try to dominate over the new nature put in there at conversion. (Tomlinson, 1931a, p. 1)

The Church of God stands for conversion, sanctification as a second definite work of grace subsequent to being saved from sins. . . . I wish to once more exhort our ministers to emphasize the doctrine of sanctification, and let the people know that we are not compromising or weakening the least bit. We give the "old man" no quarters—he must be crucified. (Tomlinson, 1931b, p. 1)

In other words, as leader of the COG, Tomlinson not only proclaimed and defended his view of sanctification; he also required the ministry to follow suit, lest the denomination should fail in keeping it central as a fundamental belief (Duggar, 1964, pp. 105–106).

Once sanctified, the COG believer was instructed to live in a world of holiness, separated unto God, which was characterized by a life of abstinence from sin and things of the world—or, more specifically, worldliness itself (*Minutes*, 1950, pp. 34–35). A few casual glimpses of church teachings and other guidelines reveal much of how the psychology of the sanctified life was maintained. Under Tomlinson's leadership, several teachings were listed that served not only as boundaries for group identification in a modernist world, but also as protocol for an appropriate lifestyle in preserving holiness (*Minutes*, 1943, pp. 110–111). Aside from a teaching on sanctification itself, another was listed as "Holiness," with reference to supporting scriptures that were interpreted to advocate such requirements of members. For instance, Teaching 22 strictly forbade the use of alcohol and strong drink, as did Teaching 23 for tobacco and drug use. Teaching 26 denounced the wearing of "gold for ornament" and of decorations such as finger rings, bracelets, earrings, lockets, and any jewelry in other forms. COG members were prohibited from membership in lodges by teaching 27, and were taught to refrain from swearing (i.e., the taking of oaths as a pledge of one's truthfulness) by Teaching 28. Family integrity was required by Teaching 29, which warned against the "Divorce and Remarriage Evil." It was held that in abiding by these standards, members not only could be recognized as exemplars of holiness, but also would be protected from the dangers of worldliness (modernism) and its damning influence. Members failing in these teachings were seen as backsliders, who were as lost from God as worldly sinners (*Minutes*, 1950, pp. 34–35).

In addition to church teachings, guidelines in the form of "Advices to Members" appeared in Assembly minutes as early as 1917 (*Minutes*, 1917, pp. 48–49). These guidelines, probably the work of Tomlinson himself, were meant as "kindly instructions" (p. 48) to assist members in their walk toward holiness and to keep them from contamination by the world. Of the several "advices," some were directly related to separation from the world. For example, members were advised to live "straight" both at home and abroad, to avoid charges of hypocrisy. A paragraph was also given to moderation of dress and the abstention from all forms of jewelry. Younger members were forbidden close association with "worldly outsiders," whereas marriage with sinners was never even to be considered. That these advices eventually came to be taken more as prohibitions is evident in revisions made in the late 1950s, after Tomlinson's death (*Minutes*, 1958, pp. 148–150). The paragraph concerning dress became more specific in terms of "paying moderate prices for clothing, [and] wearing dresses of high-enough necklines, low-enough hemlines, [and] sleeves of reasonable length" (p. 149). Other advices included prohibitions against the wearing of sheer fabrics, shorts in public, cosmetics, and expensive perfumes. Members also were admonished to refrain from "worldly attractions," such as "professional ball games, horse races, stock car races, wrestling arenas, skating rinks, motion picture houses or drive-in theaters, bowling alleys and going swimming where men and women both use the same bathing areas" (p. 149).

By compliance with these advices, as well as with church teachings, members came to be assured of both their holiness and their status as faithful COG members. Moreover, such instruments as church teachings and advices—especially those concerned with the truth of holiness—helped to reinforce the psychological reality of a dichotomous worldview in terms of holiness–worldliness, saints–sinners, righteousness–unrighteousness, and the redeemed–lost (Pruitt, 1981). In the contemporary COG, holiness as a truth of reality provides a psychological basis of meaning for proscribing various "sinful" behaviors for the righteous, whose compliance is believed to have both corporeal and eternal implications for right standing with God. Furthermore, this truth serves as a basis for judging the behaviors of others in terms of their righteousness or sinfulness—that is, whether they are fit for the kingdom of God and heaven, or doomed to an eternity in hell. The truth of holiness is not negotiable or subject to criticism; it is the psychological reality of the world for the COG, based on their understanding of the Bible as modeled by Tomlinson. All these beliefs are based on taking up the sacred text, entering into dialogue with its passages, and interpreting the intent of a holy God who requires much from his children, even in an increasingly unholy and sinful world.

The Fundamental of Being the "Bible Church"

A clear understanding of what it means to the COG to be the "Bible church" requires briefly tracing the origin of the belief and how it emerged to provide such a meaningful identity for its followers. From early documents and Assembly minutes, it seems clear that the COG saw itself in terms of a unique institution with a divine mission—the call to restore the New Testament church of the apostles, or the "Church of

God of the Bible." Tomlinson was not the author of this concept, although it seems certain he was the one who sought it out more clearly as a Biblical revelation and gave it impetus as a COG concern (Evans, 1943, pp. 7–9). He duly recognized Richard G. Spurling as one who had introduced him to the "vision of God's Church" (*General Assembly Minutes 1906–1914*, 1992, p. 194).

According to Spurling, the early church was based only on the two great commandments of Jesus—which were, first, to love God supremely, and second, to love one's neighbor as oneself. These, said Spurling, constituted the "law of Christ" (Spurling, n.d./1921, p. 14). Accordingly, this law was said to have dominated the early church until 325 A.D., when the emperor Constantine ordered the writ of the Nicene Creed, the first of many "man-made" creeds and doctrines to follow. The content of the creed itself was not the issue for Spurling, but the fact that a human instrument had been devised that supplanted the law of Christ and the teachings of the apostles (Spurling, n.d./1921, pp. 22–24). Even if the creed was intended for purging heresy from Christianity, said Spurling, apostasy occurred at that moment, and gross darkness covered the true church from visibility. In his view, Christian churches and groups since that time had relied on creeds and doctrines, instead of the law of Christ, as the basis for their faith; hence no Christian institution was deemed by Spurling to be in character as "the Bible church" until the beginning of the 20th century, when the COG—the *true* Bible church—emerged from darkness as a restorative phenomenon. It was this new sect that Tomlinson came to visit on several occasions, receiving exposure to such ideas. However, the invitation to one particular Bible study on June 13, 1903, would prove to be a memorable event both for him and for the COG.

The legendary events of this date have been widely circulated and published in the COG (Davidson, 1973; Duggar, 1964; Evans, 1943). Tomlinson had arrived at the Bryant home for the Bible study a night early. Concerned over Spurling's ideas about the New Testament church, he left the house the next morning for a time of solitude before the meeting was to begin. According to his own words, he climbed to the top of nearby Burger Mountain:

> I looked out a place to pray. I felt heavy responsibilities upon me and that I should pray through. I asked the Lord to give special wisdom and guidance, and to keep me from making any mistakes. I had been a close student of the Bible for many years and I was careful to obey its teachings perfectly. I prayed until I was satisfied and committed myself to God for safekeeping. I then went down to the base of the mountain and entered into the meeting that had been called.

> When I understood fully that those saintly people meant to stand for the whole Bible rightly divided and take the New Testament as their only rule of faith and practice, it appealed to me and I became very much interested at once. I asked many questions and Bible answers were given which perfectly *satisfied all my inquiries* [emphasis added]. I then said, THIS MEANS THAT IT IS THE CHURCH OF GOD [emphasis in original]. To this they assented. . . . Then I ventured to ask if they would be willing to receive me in the Church with the understanding that it IS [emphasis in original] the Church of God of the Bible. They were willing and I took the covenant with sincerity and extreme sacredness never to be forgotten. (*Minutes*, 1941, p. 18)

And with that, Tomlinson became a member of what he believed to be the "last-days" Church of God of the Bible.[5] Such membership signified the affirming sense of coherence (Antonovsky, 1987) that an intratexutal fundamentalism can provide, in that, for Tomlinson, it "satisfied all my inquiries."

In the years following, Tomlinson continued his study of the Bible with regard to the last-days COG—a study of scripture that might account for many of his retrospective details about the celebrated 1903 event. In terms of our model of fundamentalism, he engaged the text (primarily the books of the Old Testament prophets), entered into dialogue with it, and struggled with what he came to believe was a divine revelation intended from God concerning the true last-days Bible church. His early writings are replete with interpretations of various Biblical passages abstracting this truth, although the scriptures most often cited were in Jeremiah and Isaiah.

In terms of his role as a reformer, he saw himself as the key figure in a specific Biblical prophecy: "and I will cause him to draw near, and he shall approach unto me: for who is this that engaged his heart to approach unto me? saith the Lord" (Jeremiah 30:21). By his own admission, Tomlinson came to the COG as a troubled person, unsettled in direction for life or even in commitment to any religious group (Tomlinson, 1984). It was in this psychological state that he came to struggle with the text in his revelatory experiences on Burger Mountain and at the Bible study that followed. Once again, Sundén's role theory (Holm, 1995) offers insight into Tomlinson's approach to the passage in his taking on the role of the providential seeker under the direction of God's will. In the process of dialogue with the text, he was able to interpret its meaning intratextually, in relation to himself as the predestined seeker drawn to God for the purpose of receiving understanding of God's divine intent concerning the last-days church of the Bible—which he saw as a unique honor indeed. In reference to this distinct privilege, Tomlinson (1984) later wrote of Martin Luther's role in receiving the revelation of Protestantism, which he described as a "limb" extending from the "trunk" of larger truth—namely, the COG. To John Wesley was revealed the "limb" of sanctification, to Albert B. Simpson the "limb" of divine healing, and to William J. Seymour the "limb" of speaking in tongues (glossolalia).[6] It was divinely reserved for Tomlinson, however, that he should receive the revelation of the "trunk" of truth itself—the revelation of the last-days COG, from which all other truths extended as "limbs." In reflecting on his role in the event, he later wrote:

> I believe I can say as well as Paul that for this purpose God raised me up. Why not? Who else did it? Who else could do it? Like the Apostle Paul said, "I magnify mine office." And like John the Baptist, I was just a voice of one crying in the wilderness. You never saw my name in there [in the Bible], but without a name I was there. It just turned out to be me and nobody can help it. Where would this [the COG] have been if it hadn't been for me? I am not boasting only as God has done this for me. You are all Church of God because I am. (Quoted in Evans, 1943, p. 13)

Concerning the revelation of the COG itself, Tomlinson often investigated other Biblical passages for dialogue and interpreted their meaning from within the text. He found a scriptural basis for Spurling's ideas about the apostasy of the early church in Isaiah:

> For a small moment have I forsaken thee; but with great mercies will I gather thee. In a little wrath I hid my face from thee for a moment; but with everlasting kindness will I have mercy on thee, saith the Lord thy Redeemer. (Isaiah 54:7–8)

Although most Biblical interpreters would agree that the passage is directly related to the restoration of Israel, Tomlinson, troubled by his seeking for a meaningful church affiliation, interpreted its meaning as a revelation of the momentary lapse of the New Testament church in its adoption of the Nicene Creed. In this substitution of a man-made creed for the divine law of love, God's anger would first isolate the erring church as a means of discipline but then finally relent in view of its restorative efforts, as seen in the following passage:

> Arise, shine; for thy light is come, and the glory of the Lord is risen upon thee. For, behold, the darkness shall cover the earth, and gross darkness the people: but the Lord shall arise upon thee, and his glory shall be seen upon thee. (Isaiah 60:1–2)

Using this scripture in dialogue with the earlier passage, Tomlinson saw the early church emerging from the darkness of apostasy as a glorious institution, loosening itself from the shackles of man-made creeds, and reverting to the scriptures as the only rule of faith, practice, and government. For Tomlinson, this was a direct prophecy concerning the 20th-century reemergence of the COG, whose solitary business was restoring the true Bible church and saving the lost. He believed that the COG's shining character and stand for truth, as opposed to denominational creedalism, would draw all true Christians into its fellowship, which was destined to become the bride of Christ.

As evidence for the correctness of this interpretation, Tomlinson observed an interesting phenomenon that coincided with the "arise–shine" of the COG, as well as with a prophecy of the church in Isaiah. It is clear that he recognized June 13, 1903, as the time the church emerged from darkness into visibility (Davidson, 1973; Evans, 1943; Stone, 1977). However, he also viewed the first successful flight of the Wright brothers' airplane 6 months later (December 17, 1903) as more than mere coincidence, for the same chapter of Isaiah that prophesied the arise–shine of the COG also foretold the flight of the airplane: "Who are these that fly as a cloud, and as the doves to their windows?" (Isaiah 60:8). Tomlinson pointed out not only that these events occurred in the same year and were mentioned in the same chapter of Isaiah, but also that they occurred 6 months apart and were mentioned six verses apart. Furthermore, both events occurred in the same state, North Carolina: the arise–shine in Cherokee County, and the plane flight in Kitty Hawk (Evans, 1943).

Based on the manner in which Tomlinson came to the text, and his means of staying within the text for interpretation, he emerged as a transformed individual who held in his grasp an absolute truth that forever changed his view of the world. For him, the truth of the COG as the last-days Bible church became generalized into an objective psychological reality that directed his mission for the remainder of his life—a mission dedicated to spreading the gospel and the message of God's divine church. Tomlinson proclaimed the message of the church strongly in his preaching and writing, never failing to defend it in the face of any opposition.

In his most comprehensive work, *The Last Great Conflict* (1984), Tomlinson dedicated three chapters to the COG's history, its prophecies, and much of its theology as the last-days Bible church. He began the first of these chapters by observing the unrest among contemporary denominational churches, and concluded that the cause was a sincere searching among true Christians for the authentic church of the early apostles. In his view, the Spirit of God was the mastermind at work in leading unwitting persons to dissolve sects and denominational ties, as a preparatory move toward a coming together of all true believers. He went on to say: "But few, and probably none of these instigators know of the undercurrent or influence that is at work, neither do they understand the purport of such actions, but it is God wielding his mighty scepter preparing the people for the Bible church—the Church of God" (Tomlinson, 1984, p. 145).

His annual addresses to General Assemblies were replete with the church message for the purpose of enlisting recruits and spurring the COG forward in what he believed to be its worldwide mission. Here is an example:

> It was the mission of the early Church to propagate the principles and doctrine taught and advocated by the Lord Jesus Christ, and it is no less the mission of the Church of God to-day. . . . The Church of God is the very same sacred institution, only having made its appearance in these last days after a period of years of having been obscured under a cloud of the dark ages and creeds. It is coming out all the brighter for the storms of the past. It is beginning to claim the attention of the world again. . . . Its members only have to be possessed with a more perfect white heated love for each other and the principles it holds dear to itself to raise it to heights of glory and power that will attract the attention of all peoples of the world. (*Minutes*, 1921, pp. 15–16)

In the face of opposition, Tomlinson would not relent, but demanded the membership to stand as the true church—a stance he believed God would honor with ultimate vindication:

> There must be no retreat! No surrender! But by steadily marching forward we will reach the goal! By the help of the Lord we will hoist the standard to the very top of the mast, and by faith in God smite every opposing force, and cast all the mountains of difficulties into the sea, and still march on and on. The Church of God shall win! (*Minutes*, 1916, p. 18)

In his final annual address, at nearly 78 years of age, Tomlinson's focus was still on planting the COG in every state across America (*Minutes*, 1943, p. 25). To the end, he remained convinced of an absolute truth that only the COG had the true message for lost humanity; for him, it was God's institution on earth, divinely revealed in the Bible for all who would seek it. Not only did Tomlinson hold to this objective reality, but so did the scores of thousands whom he had converted to the COG vision. For them, as well as for Tomlinson, there was no other church; all other religious institutions were steeped in creeds and doctrines without scriptural basis.

For many in the COG, the psychological reality of being *the* Bible church continues as Tomlinson's legacy. To live within such a worldview of meaning takes into account more than a mere distinction between the church and the world; it also makes distinction among such polarities as false churches versus the true church, the many called versus the few chosen, kingdom saints versus church saints, and wedding guests versus the bride of Christ. In believing that they have forsaken creedalism and man-made doctrines, members of the COG see themselves in each of these situations as the favored who are now responsible for declaring the revelation of God's true church to unknowing Christians, as well as to the lost. This belief not only helps structure their view of reality, but also affords them a powerful sense of uniqueness and a compelling inspiration in their efforts to carry out the great commission. This meaningful truth is precisely what motivated Tomlinson, and it continues to motivate those who share in his Bible-based vision today.

The Fundamental of Spirit Baptism

From its inception until 1908, the COG professed largely to be a Wesleyan Holiness institution, along with its claim to being the New Testament church. Both Spurlings of the Christian Union were of the Baptist tradition, as was W. F. Bryant of the Holiness Church at Camp Creek. At the 1896 Schearer Schoolhouse revival, however, these early leaders were introduced to the Holiness movement, which at that time was characterized by highly emotional worship resembling Pentecostalism. It was not until the 1906 Azusa Street revival that speaking in tongues became widely known as the single criterion for Spirit baptism, although the doctrine was first practiced on a small scale by Charles Fox Parham in Topeka, Kansas, in 1901 (Synan, 1997). Despite modern claims that the COG was in fact a Pentecostal movement predating Azusa Street (Conn, 1996; Davidson, 1973; Stone, 1977), even Tomlinson himself gave credit to William J. Seymour, evangelist and pastor of Azusa Street, for discovering the doctrine of speaking in tongues (Tomlinson, 1984, pp. 156–157; see our comment in Note 6). For the early COG, it would be Tomlinson's own 1908 Spirit baptism with glossolalia that would begin its transformation from a small Holiness sect toward a Pentecostal denomination and its adoption of a more spiritualized view of the world. As with the fundamentals of holiness (sanctification) and of being the Bible church, his personal experience was key in coming to an intratextual understanding of the Spirit baptism and establishing it as a fundamental truth among the COG. If we are to understand the psychology of the COG with respect to Spirit baptism, we must again examine the experience of the critical figure who was so influential in establishing this truth as a meaningful part of the church's worldview.

By late 1906, Tomlinson clearly had read a description of the widely publicized Azusa Street revival and its compelling Pentecostal manifestations, for the title of his sermon on Saturday night of the 1907 General Assembly was "The Baptism of the Holy Ghost and Fire" (*General Assembly Minutes 1906–1914*, 1992, pp. 37, 39). Throughout the remainder of 1907, he preached constantly on this new doctrine of tongues, although he had yet to experience the phenomenon for himself (Tomlinson, 1984, p. 232). After giving a sermon on the Holy Ghost, it appears that he was frequently among the first at the altar to seek the experience for himself. Having a great desire for the "blessing," he invited C. B. Cashwell, who had recently received the baptism at Azusa Street, to speak at the Cleveland COG on Saturday evening and Sunday morning, January 11–12, 1908.

As Cashwell was preaching the Sunday sermon, Tomlinson described feeling a physical sensation that moved him from his seat to the floor directly behind the speaker (Tomlinson, 1984, pp. 233–236). So powerful for him was the resulting experience that his detailed description required four pages of print. In sum, he experienced movements in his arms, legs, and head that seemed beyond control, while his entire body felt as though it were being shuffled and tossed about the floor. He claimed a sense that his body was levitating at times, and reported experiencing moments of both "great joy" and "excruciating pain." He described visions in which he visited various countries around the world and spoke in each of their native languages. He also experienced a vision in which he directly encountered "the devil," with whom he struggled and eventually overcame. He concluded his description by saying:

> This was really being baptized with the Holy Ghost as they received Him on the day of Pentecost. . . . With all I have written it is not yet told, but judging from the countries I visited in the vision I spoke ten different languages. It seemed that the Spirit was showing me these countries with a view to sending me there. Each place I saw large numbers of people coming to the light. I saw multitudes coming to Jesus. I don't know whether God wants me to go to these places or not, but I am certainly willing to go as He leads. (Tomlinson, 1984, p. 236)

Although Tomlinson described experiencing various supernatural manifestations of God at this time, the specific evidence he claimed for receiving Spirit baptism was his speaking in unknown languages, as outlined to him by the Bible (Tomlinson, 1984).

The Biblical passages that afforded the Azusa Street participants and Tomlinson such profound experiences were those that eventually found their way as permanent citations into the title heading of the *Church of God Evangel*, from the very first issue published in 1910 (*The Evening Light*, 1910) until a change in publication format in 1923

(*Church of God Evangel*, 1923). As quoted in the *Evangel*, these key verses state:

> And when the day of Pentecost was fully come, they were all with one accord in one place. . . . And they were all filled with the Holy Ghost, and began to speak with other tongues, as the Spirit gave them utterance. (Acts 2:1, 4)

From the perspective of Sundén's role theory, Holm (1991) has provided a psychological analysis of how believers experience Spirit baptism, based on this Pentecostal narrative from the text. According to the narrative, Jesus, just before his ascension into heaven, instructed his followers to wait in Jerusalem until he sent the Holy Spirit as a spiritual empowerment. The Spirit arrived on the day of Pentecost as a "rushing mighty wind," with such force that recipients supernaturally spoke in languages (tongues) they had never learned. The textually modeled ability to speak in such tongues eventually became understood as Biblical evidence for Spirit baptism. Whether those so baptized were Azusa Street participants, were Tomlinson and his COG, or are even contemporary believers, all can be understood as taking on the role of disciples in the text and reproducing the phenomenon of glossolalia, which is perceived as a supernatural event controlled by God. Like the disciples on the day of Pentecost, later recipients claim a profound experience that transforms life, as described by the Biblical text.

Again, the key here is the power of the text not only to provide the basis for an experience, but also to allow for an intratextual interpretation of its truth. Although it is clear that Tomlinson's Spirit baptism was immediate and indeed intense, it must be recalled that he had already spent the previous year struggling with the text, engaging in dialogue with it for meaning, and seeking its intent from God, until finally the passage became a matter of revelation that took form as a compelling reality. He could become passionate about receiving Spirit baptism with tongues only after he had interpreted and believed it to be an objective, or factual, reality that could be pursued. Once obtained, this baptism was a life-changing experience that influenced his psychological worldview and the manner in which he led the COG. Furthermore, it provided him, and others who would receive it, with what was believed to be a supernatural source for effecting evangelism and growth in the COG (Williamson, 2000).

As did other Pentecostals of his time, Tomlinson enlarged the narrative of Acts 2 by taking up other passages in the sacred text and bringing them into dialogue for intratextual interpretation. Not only did this solidify the fundamental of Spirit baptism and glossolalia as objective truth; it widened the Biblical platform from which he strongly encouraged others in seeking the reality of its blessing. In an article written for this concern, he stated:

> When the Apostles received the Holy Ghost they all spoke with other tongues as the Spirit gave them utterance. No one can deny this.
>
> "And they were all filled with the Holy Ghost and began to speak with other tongues as the Spirit gave them utterance." (Acts 2:4) [sic] But there were others there with the Apostles that were afected [sic] in the same way. This was shown in Acts 1:14,15. Men and women all received the Holy Ghost and all spake with other tongues as the Spirit gave them utterance.
>
> Ever since that time all who have received the Holy Ghost have talked in tongues.
>
> It may seem to some like this statement is too strong, but we are not without plenty of proof. . . . These [scripture] references will be perfectly satisfactory to all unprejudiced lovers of truth. (Acts 10:44–46, Acts 19:1–6, Mark 16:17). (Tomlinson, 1915, p. 1)

In continuing, Tomlinson referred to other passages that, when interpreted in relation to Acts 2:4, presented Spirit baptism and speaking in tongues not only as a "promise" for believers (Acts 1:4, 5; Acts 2:38, 39), but also as an experience even *required* by Jesus (Luke 24:49). For example, said Tomlinson, "when He breathed on them and said, 'Receive ye the Holy Ghost;' if this is not a command then I take the ground that water baptism is not a command or [that] repentance is not a command" (Tomlinson, 1915, p. 1). Furthermore, he cited John 15:14, in which Jesus declared to the disciples that friendship with him was contingent upon obeying his commands. On this Tomlinson commented, "This shows that they would have proved themselves to be His enemies if they had not received the Holy Ghost . . . [and] If this command was binding on the disciples in the days of the apostles it is equally as binding on us today" (p. 1). From this and other intratextual interpretations, it seems that the experience of Spirit baptism and glossolalia had become so much a part of the COG worldview as to characterize those who had not received it as the disobedient, and even as the "enemies" of Jesus. Hence dialogue with such scriptures led to an intratextual interpretation of Spirit baptism as an absolute truth that dichotomized the world into two groups: the obedient, who speak with tongues, and the unbelieving, who do not.

Perhaps some the most interesting consequences of Tomlinson's transformation were observed in his evangelistic efforts and in patterns of COG growth, the details of which were captured in his personal journal (see Tomlinson, 1901–1923). After his 1908 Spirit baptism, he conducted a series of revival campaigns that were among the most remarkable for him at that time. For example, a meeting in Chattanooga continued for a period of several weeks and resulted in the organizing of a new church with 49 members. Upon reflection, he stated in a journal entry dated August 4, 1908:

> I preached last Sunday under the power of the Spirit to about 1000 people, and God wonderfully confirmed the word with signs following. Glory! What followed is almost indescribable. Shouts, speaking in tongues, a sister played organ controlled by the Spirit [sic]. I was enveloped in a kind of sheet of power and controlled, and they said my hair stood up on my head. Glory! It was wonderful. Since our meeting commenced there the first of May until the close last night there have been about seventy-five who received the baptism of the Holy Ghost and spoke in tongues, which is the Bible evidence. . . . I preached to about 5,000 people on a lake shore where we were baptizing. (see Tomlinson, 1901–1923)

Only a few weeks later, Tomlinson wrote of a revival he had conducted in Cleveland, Tennessee, in which manifestations of the Spirit were reported to be so convincing that as many as 100 seekers at a time would respond to his invitations. In his journal, dated October 14, 1908, he described the meeting:

> Closed out tonight after a 10 weeks successful battle [sic]. 105 professions and 163 received the baptism of the Holy Ghost. 78 baptized in water [sic]. 106 accessions to the Church [sic]. Quite a number healed [sic]. We had a glorious meeting tonight. About 75 in the altar [sic]. (see Tomlinson, 1901–1923)

These entries serve only as a sample of numerous other accounts recorded in church literature, which reflect a marked increase in the evangelistic success of Tomlinson and the COG. Not only did the results of his revivals change; so did his preaching in terms of encouraging others to be filled with and empowered by the Spirit. Before long, Tomlinson's encounter with Spirit baptism ushered the COG into the reality of being a Pentecostal church.

Supernatural manifestations of the Holy Ghost thus became established as a fundamental aspect of the COG worldview, as evidenced in numerous writings and sermons in which Tomlinson proclaimed and encouraged them among the group. Only one of many examples is necessary here:

> Our people should be encouraged to yield to the Spirit, and even to stir up the gift that is in them. Preaching is necessary, but if all of our services were given to preaching only, the spiritual fire would go out. There must

be testimonies, talking in tongues, interpretations, signs, wonders, dancing, and whatever else the blessed Spirit of God dictates. Our people must be free in the Holy Ghost. . . . The letter alone will kill, but the Spirit gives life. (*Minutes*, 1917, p. 21)

Spiritual manifestations such as these added to the meaningfulness and even to the success of worship services. In the sense that such manifestations were present, God was believed to be in attendance, making possible whatever was deemed necessary among believers for soundness of mind, body, and spirit. The COG thoroughly embraced Tomlinson's teaching on Spirit baptism and tongues-speaking, and fully took on the Pentecostal nature. In years following, the name COG became synonymous with Pentecostalism and glossolalia, and—as we have shown—members were even *expected* to have the experience.

Perhaps more for the fundamental of Spirit baptism than for anything else, members of the COG encountered persecution from the larger society, from mainline denominations, and even from other Holiness sects. In their early years, they were of lower socioeconomic status and often were ridiculed as ignorant and uneducated for their passionate displays of worship. Nevertheless, Pentecostalism was such an undeniable fundamental truth in the COG that Tomlinson was unrelenting in its defense:

> Another source of the enemy's onslaught against us is the "tongues" as evidence of the baptism with the Holy Ghost . . . The religious press is against us. The world's press is against us. The ministers of all denominations, of a hundred millions strong, are in opposition to this truth. . . . [W]ith all these scriptures as proof we are on solid footing. . . . We are not giving our opinion in this matter, we are giving the infallible Word of God for it. We do not shrink from saying that when people teach otherwise they make themselves false teachers. . . . God is now raising up a people to engage in this last great struggle and conflict against formalism, perverted Scriptures and theories of men, who will sacrifice their lives, if need be, rather than surrender any part of the truth that came from the sacred lips of Jesus, and the inspired pens of the Apostles. . . . We admit that this teaching is opposed by many writers and teachers, but no opposition of men and the combined forces of hell can succeed in eradicating this precious truth from the Bible. (Tomlinson, 1984, pp. 27, 110, 111)

There is little need for commentary on this defense for Pentecostalism, whose opponents were perceived as misguided critics and apostates. What seems clear is that such adversaries failed to share in the same objective reality as the Pentecostal COG. With regard to the truth of

Pentecostalism, these critics were either guided by their own texts or else counseled *intertextually* with other authorities besides the Bible—ones that were given equal or greater weight. On the other hand, Tomlinson and his COG had already engaged in dialogue with their text and discovered within it a truth concerning the intent of God that believers enter into a reality of power for living and serving in the world. From this view, all critics and the "combined forces of hell" could never sway them, and the same is true of contemporary COG believers.

For the COG, the intratextual interpretation of Spirit baptism with speaking in tongues affords meaning—not only the perception of the supernatural power necessary for successful evangelism, but also the view of a world characterized by spiritual warfare. Whereas the absolute of holiness casts the world simply in terms of the righteous and unrighteous, the fundamental of Spirit baptism enlarges this view with the belief that the righteous possess supernatural power for the purpose of overcoming the unrighteous of the world. Hence the world is again meaningfully polarized in terms of the Spirit-filled versus the unfilled, the powerful versus the powerless, and the victorious versus the defeated. Ultimately, objective reality involves seeing the world as a prize to be won in a contest between the spiritual forces of good and evil— forces under the direction either of Satan and demons of darkness, or of the Holy Spirit and angels of light. This psychological transformation of the corporeal world into a spiritual one leaves the COG believer in a constant state of spiritual warfare that requires a personal baptism in the Holy Spirit in order to become and to remain an overcomer.[7] Positive life events are seen as the consequence of successful battle gained by the Spirit-baptized believer against Satanic influences, whereas negative life events are often (but not always) interpreted as failure on the believer's part to prevail against such forces, due perhaps to some lapse in personal prayer, devotion, or obedience to the Spirit. Hence the world is constantly viewed, interpreted, and evaluated in terms of spiritual power. So compelling is the truth of Spirit baptism in the COG worldview that it, like the truth of holiness, is neither negotiable nor open for debate (Tomlinson, 1984).

Although Spirit baptism has remained a vital truth among the COG, it is worthwhile to note that the range of spiritual manifestations related to this experience has been restricted in the tradition's move from sectarian toward denominational status (Williamson & Hood, 2004). A once-popular text among the COG in justifying glossolalia as evidence of Holy Spirit empowerment also includes four other "signs" of this experience: casting out demons, laying on hands for healing, becoming invulnerable to toxic drinks, and taking up venomous serpents (Mark 16:17–18). Evidence from the *Evangel* reveals that some members of the

COG demonstrated all five signs in its early history; however, with increasing concern for success in attracting the middle class and pursuing denominational status, serpent handling and the less common sign of ingesting poison were marginalized and ultimately divorced not only from practice, but also from the reconstruction of COG history (Williamson & Hood, 2004; see also Conn, 1955, 1977, 1996). Those among the COG who remained convinced of the intratextual truth of all five signs were eventually forced outside the church to exist as independent sects. In view of its interpretation of scripture, the contemporary COG continues to speak in tongues, lay on hands for healing, and (to a lesser extent) cast out demons, whereas serpent-handing sects persist in practicing all five signs in a modern society that opposes them, even with legal sanctions. As we shall see in Chapter 5, this minority does so on the basis of meaning derived from its own intratextual interpretation of the sacred text.

CONCLUSION

As all fundamentalisms do, the Pentecostal type, as illustrated by the COG, embraces without reservation its sacred text as the authoritative word of God, which it takes as the foundation for all its beliefs. Aside from acceptance of the Bible, we have highlighted what can be understood as a few other absolute truths of this tradition. Based on the principle of intratextuality, these truths emerged from intense dialogue that remained within the sacred text in an effort to discover a revelation of God's intended message. We submit that these resulting truths (and others) have merged to form an objective psychological reality that stands as a backdrop of meaning, or frame of reference, for the COG in perceiving and interacting with the world. Among the most prominent truths that constitute this worldview are holiness, status as a divinely chosen church, and Spirit baptism. These truths can be understood as some of the most fundamental aspects of A. J. Tomlinson's COG that gave it psychological grounding and meaning.

Clearly, the sociohistorical context cannot be isolated from attempts to fully understand the psychology of COG fundamentalism. With a knowledge of its historical roots, one may speculate how the movement came to interpret its sacred text in the manner that it did. It might be suggested that in observing the effects of late-19th-century modernism, especially the perceived consequence of cultural immorality, the movement's key figures (especially Tomlinson) became sensitive to certain parts of the text—those describing a form of holiness that could transcend the immediate situation and serve as an objective standard for moral living. Similarly, the urban isolation experienced by rural migrants might have led to an awareness of particular scriptural passages that afforded belief in an overarching uniqueness, such as might be found in a select community of believers who thought themselves to be divinely chosen by God. The psychosocial distress resulting from modernism and technological development could have highlighted other portions of the text, promising supernatural power that could resist opposition and bring order to a chaotic world. These are only general observations, of course, related to a deeper empirical question concerned with specifically how and in what manner people come to the sacred text (i.e., "What is the psychology that compels them to come to the text as they do?"). Our main purpose here has been to provide, from an intratextual theoretical perspective, a nonreductive psychological description of how the fundamentalist COG, after coming to the text, sees and ascribes meaning and purpose to its world.[8]

CHAPTER FIVE

Fundamentalism among Religious Serpent-Handling Sects

The Bible says, "They shall take up serpents." Honey, it means what it says, and says what it means. . . . It won't change for me. It won't change for you. Amen. Thank God. It won't change. . . . I don't care what you try to do, the Word of God is still the same.

—KINGSTON SERVICE VIDEO (1995)

As we have noted in Chapter 1, understanding fundamentalism from an intratextual perspective requires us to consider the manner in which fundamentalists come to their sacred text and interpret absolute truths—unwavering certainties that together construct a worldview filled with meaning and purpose in life. Based on this concern, the principle of intratextuality allows us to examine fundamentalism not only among the more obvious groups, but also among those that have been marginalized by the host culture and ignored too often by fundamentalist scholars. Yet we would suggest that these atypical groups are precisely the ones that, though not militant in a combative sense, protest most strongly against modernity in seeking to maintain certain text-based absolutes that provide them with uniqueness and identity. Among such groups are those noted for their ritual of handling venomous serpents in religious services (Hood, 1998; Williamson & Pollio, 1999). For these serpent-handling sects (SHSs), the fundamental of serpent handling is an incontrovertible requirement interpreted from scripture that is accepted and practiced by enlightened believers of Jesus. They maintain this revealed truth against all opposition from the larger society, other religious groups, and even the laws of some U.S. states wherein they reside (Hood, Williamson, & Morris, 2000; Kimbrough & Hood, 1995).

Using the principle of intratextuality, we examine this uniquely

American Protestant fundamentalism in terms of the way adherents relate to their sacred text, the King James Version of the Bible. In doing so, we first present a brief history of the tradition, including a psychohistorical analysis of a key figure who strongly influenced the movement; we follow this with a social psychology of the tradition itself. Finally, we review what we describe as text-based fundamentals of the serpent-handling truth, derived from an analysis of personal phenomenological interviews with serpent handlers themselves. Through this approach, we hope to demonstrate a fuller understanding of the believer's psychological reality and worldview of meaning. Now we turn to the much-debated origin of this tradition.

A BRIEF HISTORY OF SERPENT-HANDLING SECTS

In the early 20th century, a small group of believers in a new, emerging Holiness–Pentecostal denomination (the Church of God [COG], Cleveland, Tennessee; see Chapter 4) began handling venomous snakes brought to its worship services by religious skeptics (Williamson & Hood, 2004). The precise time of the birth of this practice has been debated by scholars, although most current sources situate the event sometime around 1910 (Burton, 1993; Kane, 1979; Kimbrough, 1995; Williamson, 2000). At about this time, George Went Hensley, a newly converted Christian, forsook a life of debauchery and bootlegging for the way of Wesleyan Holiness as exhorted by the fledgling COG (Williamson, 2000).

Drawn by its emphasis on right living and its approach to the immediate, heartfelt experience of God, Hensley readily accepted the COG teachings of scripture—particularly a Biblical passage used frequently as a basis for its theology of purpose and supernatural manifestations: Mark 16:15–18. The passage indicates that just before his ascension, Jesus commanded his disciples to go forth preaching his doctrine and manifesting five specific signs as confirmation of their role as obedient believers. Four of these were interpreted as mandatory (emphasis is added here): "they *shall* speak with new tongues," "they *shall* lay hands on the sick," "*shall* they cast out devils," and "they *shall* take up serpents." A fifth sign was thought to be optional: "*if* they drink any deadly thing, it shall not hurt them." For a while, Hensley seemed content with his new conversion experience, but he later became sorely troubled that manifestations among fellow believers were limited only to three signs—speaking in tongues, laying hands on the sick, and casting out devils. If in fact they were to be true believers, he reasoned, they also would take up serpents as Jesus had said obedient disciples would do. Such grave concern eventually led to his first encounter with serpent handling on White Oak Mountain, outside Chattanooga, Tennessee (Collins, 1947; Williamson, 2000).

Hensley described his legendary transformation concerning serpent handling to a local newspaper reporter some 35 years after the event (Collins, 1947). Resolving that manifestations of the signs were indeed commands for believers to obey, he felt that his eternal security rested upon obedience to all five of these mandates. According to Collins (1947),

> His decision was to risk his life in order to have rest from his spiritual burden. Thus it was that he set out on probably the first religious snake hunt in modern civilized history.
>
> In a great rocky gap in the mountainside he found what he sought, a large rattlesnake. He approached the reptile, and, disreguarding [sic] its buzzing, blood-chilling warning, knelt a few feet away from it and prayed loudly into the sky for God to remove his fear and to anoint him with "the power." Then suddenly with a shout he leaped forward and grasped the reptile and held it in trembling hands. (Collins, 1947, pp. 1–2)

It was from this life-changing experience that an inspired Hensley descended the mountain, rattlesnake in hand, to launch his first evangelistic effort with a challenge that believers should practice *all* that Jesus had commanded—including the taking up of serpents.

Hensley and his serpent handling attracted the immediate attention of both leadership and laity in the COG, who for a while welcomed the fascinating sign into the COG's evangelistic arsenal, in hopes of converting skeptics and unbelievers to the faith (Williamson, 2000; Williamson & Hood, 2004). As the sect (which would become a denomination) became increasingly concerned with its middle-class prospects, however, the initial interest in the sign abated over the years, and the serpent-handling believers among its ranks became marginalized. Finally divorcing itself from the practice, and even from its own serpent-handling history, the COG forced adherents outside its membership—where they ultimately came to exist and continue as small, independent, autonomous sects. In the years that followed, Hensley and other believers traveled widely as itinerants throughout the Southeast, spreading the belief in serpent handling to all who would receive it (Burton, 1993). At about 75 years of age, Hensley himself met with a fatal rattlesnake bite while preaching in a service at Altha, Florida, on July 24, 1955. However, the seeds sown then continue to be reaped today wherever those remain who take the text of Mark 16 as the literal command of Jesus.[1]

The Psychology of a Fundamentalist Serpent Handler

Whether Hensley was actually the first to handle serpents is of less importance than his manner of "taking up the text" and his charismatic influence on the tradition, both of which have psychological import. A relevant theoretical approach here is Sundén's role theory, as presented in Chapter 4 (Holm, 1995). In this case, the role taken by Hensley was based on the model of the obedient believer found in the text of Mark 16 in the King James Version of the Bible. From this perspective, Hensley's serpent-handling experience can be seen as the result of his feeling troubled by believers' practicing only selected signs among those explicitly stated in a scripture text already embraced by the newly founded COG. When atop White Oak Mountain, and confronted with a serpent in context of prayerful meditation, he took on the role of a true believer constructed from the text; he also took on the role of God, which led to feelings of being divinely directed in the activity. In the mental shift toward this religious experience, God was felt to be directly encountered as a present divine reality who sanctioned the obedience of Hensley as that of a true believer in response to the perceived Biblical command. Never to be the same again, Hensley descended the mountain to launch by example a religious practice that would hold significant meaning for those who would fully believe and obey. Not only was Hensley himself transformed by the experience, but many who would hear him and see his handling of serpents would be profoundly influenced by this live modeling of the text. A number of such persons would come to take on this role for themselves (Williamson & Hood, 2004).

The ability to take on the role of the believer from the text requires the use of the principle of intratextuality. That is, Hensley approached the text in such a way as to understand and interpret the divine intent of God. In assuming the Bible to be absolutely authoritative and to mean precisely what it says, he entered into dialogue only with the text and struggled to arrive at the revelation of what was perceived as an absolute truth from God concerning his intent for true believers. He concluded that the true believer does not have the option of handling serpents, but emphatically *shall* handle them in response to the perceived imperative from Jesus. Becoming convinced of this absolute truth, Hensley generalized the belief of serpent handling into an objective fact of his existence and worldview of meaning—one that stood beyond his person, dictating his reality of experience and interpretation of the world. In this transformation, the absolute truth of serpent handling was integrated with others in his worldview: Not only did true believers in Jesus speak with new tongues, cast out devils, and lay hands on the sick, but they also handled venomous serpents. On the other hand, indicators of unbelief (despite any personal claims to being Christian) were the rejection or, at best, the selective use of the signs required of true believers in Mark 16. For Hensley, the world appeared in a fundamentalist dichotomy—the believers (the handlers) versus the unbelievers (the nonhandlers)—and the side on which a person stood had eternal implications. Such a dichotomy is unusually capable of solidifying an otherwise fragmented worldview, providing what Antonovsky (1987) refers to as a sense of coherence. His worldview was evidenced by his persistent handling of serpents in the face of occasional conflicts with the law, and by his unrelenting defense of this fundamental of the faith—even unto death.

Contemporary Serpent-Handling Sects and Intratextuality

Since the days of Hensley, contemporary SHSs continue much as they did back then, with some exceptions. They tend to remain small Holiness–Pentecostal groups, typifying Wuthnow's (1998) conception of "dwelling" (vs. "seeking") spirituality (see Chapter 1). They emphasize without apology the major text of Mark 16, although they differ among themselves as to whether they are Trinitarian or Oneness in their doctrine of the godhead (Williamson, 2000). They also remain concentrated largely in Appalachia, with the exception of a few congregations that sprang up as families migrated to new regions of the country for work.[2] The autonomy and independence fostered in early years remain characteristic of present-day SHSs, although each congregation typically participates in some type of network, maintaining links with sister churches for the sake of occasional fellowship at "homecomings" and support in the serpent-handling ritual.

One striking contrast with years past, however, lies in the fact that present-day serpent handlers have more access to resources and education (Williamson, 2000). Most families have adequate incomes to meet their needs, and furnish their homes with what is considered typical for most American families. Many of the churches are well decorated and furnished with modern amenities as well. The younger serpent handlers also are better educated today than in the past; some have attended college or vocational schools, and others hold professional jobs. Several serpent handlers communicate frequently with two of us (Hood and Williamson) via the Internet, in stark contrast to the common stereotype of serpent handlers as ignorant and unsophisticated. As Lawrence (1989) and Ammerman (1987) have rightly observed, fundamentalists—even serpent handlers—can be modern without being modernists. Furthermore, the persistence of these more resourceful serpent handlers into the 21st century can no longer be easily explained by deprivation/compensatory theory, which directed much of early research (Williamson, 2000).

Beliefs held among contemporary SHSs remain rooted primarily in the Wesleyan Holiness tradition (Williamson, 2000). The emphasis continues to be on crisis conversion and a heartfelt personal experience of God, with prominent concern for abstinence from so-called "sins of the flesh." A well-known church in West Virginia posts its basic teachings for members on the wall behind the pulpit:

Jolo Church Doctrine:

Women not allowed to Wear Short Sleeves, Jewelry or Makeup
   (I Pet. 3:3, [1] Tim. 2:9)
No Gossiping (James 1:26)
No Talebearing (Pro. 18:8)
No Lying (Col. 3:9, Rev. 21:8)
No Backbiting (Rom. 1:30)
No Bad Language or By-words (Col. 3:8)
No Tobacco Users (II Cor. 7:1) (I Cor. 3:17)
Men not Allowed to Have Long Hair, Mustach [sic], or Beard
   (I Cor. 11:14)
Men not Allowed to Wear Short Sleeves
Women not Allowed to Cut Hair (II Cor. 11:15)
Wear Dresses Above Knees [sic] ([I] Tim. 1:9)
For Members Only! (*Jolo Homecoming Video*, 1998)

Although most SHSs readily affirm Holiness doctrine, the specifics of that doctrine and the degree to which they are enforced vary among congregations and believers themselves. This idiosyncratic approach to such peripheral beliefs stems largely from the movement's inherent tendency toward independence and autonomy. It is not uncommon for members to change churches frequently or simply to drop out of attendance for a time because of disputes arising over such differences. Hence specific peripheral beliefs are not what bind SHSs together; rather, the binding element is the meaning in the absolute fundamental of serpent handling they find in their sacred text.

Not only does the emergence of serpent handling require the principle of intratextuality, but so does its persistence among contemporary practitioners who live in the postmodern world. As in Hensley's case, essential to this process is the fundamental truth they hold with respect to the Bible (specifically, the King James Version) as being the undisputed word of God. The Bible is believed without reservation to be divinely inspired, authoritative, inerrant, and unchangeable. As the long-time preacher's proclamation quoted at the beginning of this chapter clearly illustrates, a "sugarcoating" of the plainly understood text for the sake of compromise or ease of comfort will never suffice: "it means what it says, and says what it means." No serpent handler (or any other fundamentalist, for that matter) would disagree with this pastor, at least as far as his stand on the unchanging character of the Bible is concerned.

In addition to belief in the immutability of the text is the strong conviction that its intended meaning is derived not simply from a common-sense reading, but even more from prayerful meditation upon its words (i.e., from dialogue with the text), in such a way that the true interpretation comes directly from the divine author and not from other sources. A serpent-handling preacher with 35 years of experience could just as easily have spoken for all SHS members as for himself:

> I believe the Bible said, "Study to show thyself approved, a workman that needeth not be ashamed." I believe it says, "Rightly dividing the word of truth," doesn't it? Rightly dividing. Glory to God, you can't rightly divide it unless you've been called of God to do it. Praise the name of the Lord, you can go to all the colleges you want to, and you can learn the Bible from Genesis to Revelations. You can learn the words that's in there. Anybody with any education at all can read those words, but they can't bring any understanding to those words unless they've got the power of God. I believe the Bible said they were spiritually discerned. . . . I'm not a mama-called, papa-sent. Praise the name of Jesus. I didn't go to college to learn how to preach God's word, but I declare to you that I've got a degree. I've got a BA degree. . . . [He asked of himself:] "Where'd you get it, Brother Bill?" I went to the college of kneeology. Praise the name of Jesus. The BA degree I've got is the Born Again experience. (*Sand Mountain Homecoming Video*, 1998)

The school of "kneeology" is indeed a common place among serpent handlers for understanding what is perceived as the true spiritual meaning of the text. Once revelation of an absolute truth is obtained, particularly of such a truth as serpent handling, a believer cannot be persuaded otherwise by any reason or debate from other recognized authorities on scripture. To enlightened serpent handlers, such so-called authorities and skeptics are simply blinded from spiritual truth by Satan and by their reliance upon worldly knowledge and wisdom. According to the believers' worldview of meaning, critics simply cannot see truth, and hence they resist it.

Clearly, the principle of intratextuality is involved in the manner in which serpent handlers take up their sacred text and seek its truth. Moreover, the fact that serpent handling is understood by believers in terms of a world-transforming truth is underscored by their unrelenting defense and practice of the sign. For instance, in our 10 years of field research, we have known fewer than five handlers (among scores of others) who have been successful in escaping the fang of the serpent. With frequent handling over the years, most have suffered at least one or more painful bites; some of these have led to twisted hands, gnarled and missing fingers, atrophied limbs, near-death experiences, and even the loss of beloved family members to death. Yet, for these enlightened believers, the reality and meaning of their worldview dictate that they continue as obedient followers of their Lord. To do this, they must continue to study the text. And as they do so, their worldview of serpent handling is not only maintained, but also is enlarged with the incorporation of other related truths that serve to enhance meaning. We devote the remainder of this chapter to examining the enlarged understanding of the sacred text that has led to the expanded fundamental beliefs of serpent handling.

FUNDAMENTALS OF SERPENT HANDLING

As all fundamentalists do, serpent handlers seek to understand the meaning of their religious experiences from within the pages of their sacred text. Here again, the principle of intratextuality is involved: They remain within the text and enter into dialogue with passages in attempts to make sense of their own serpent-handling experiences, and those of others, within the context of their tradition. For instance, for nearly a century, believers most often have handled serpents without harm on any single occasion; however, as occasions of handling become more frequent, most do encounter serious bites—and some even die.[3] In coming to terms with what others might call "successful" and "unsuccessful" handling, serpent handlers themselves consult the Biblical text to find meaning in these and other experiences. That is, they bring various other passages into dialogue for consultation with the main text of Mark 16, each one shedding light on the others as believed to be revealed by God. What have emerged as consistent beliefs over decades from such dialogues with the text may be understood as *fundamentals of the serpent-handling tradition*.

The basis for the following analysis of these fundamentals is a group of 16 personal interviews conducted with serpent handlers by Williamson (2000) from 1998 to 1999.[4] The interviewees were active religious serpent handlers from five different congregations in Alabama, Georgia, Kentucky, and West Virginia. Among these 16 participants, 8 were preachers, and 4 of the group were female. The youngest participant was 24 years of age; the oldest was 66 years. Their experience within the serpent-handling tradition ranged from 3 to 38 years. The nature of each interview was nondirective, except for the first question, which asked participants to reflect on any of their serpent-handling experiences and to describe them in detail. The only follow-up questioning in the process involved requests for clarification of any details that seemed ambiguous. For approximately 1½ hours, each handler gave detailed descriptions of such experiences, including his or her personal meanings for these—always in the context of the Bible.

As might be expected, a range of idiosyncratic meanings and Bible-referenced beliefs emerged from these descriptions of serpent-handling experiences. However, an analysis of these text-based beliefs found that four of them were common across all 16 transcribed protocols. Each of these fundamentals is rooted in an understanding of the Bible that has emerged from tradition as believers have engaged the text and struggled to make sense of their personal experiences. According to participants, these four fundamentals of serpent handling are (1) a mandate to handle, (2) power to handle, (3) danger in handling, and (4) confirmation of blessing on believers. All these fundamentals were linked with the sacred text by either explicit or implicit reference. The following discussion includes brief excerpts from protocols that provide support for these fundamentals of religious serpent handling.

A Mandate to Handle (Mark 16:17–18)

Not surprisingly, all 16 participants referred to understanding Mark 16 as an imperative that true believers will take up serpents. Although each knew that the perceived mandate was a traditional one (i.e., a historical practice that preceded their own time in serpent handling), each had to come to terms with the mandate for him- or herself by taking up the text for dialogue and struggling to know its intent from God on a personal level. One handler, new to the tradition, recalled his first concern with coming to an understanding of the Mark 16 text:

> Jesus said, . . . "In my name, you shall cast out devils, thou shall speak with new tongues, thou shall take up serpents, and if you drink any deadly thing, it won't harm you, and you'll lay hands on the sick, and they'll recover." So the Holiness-background-type churches that I'd visited pretty much practice three signs. They'll go about casting out devils. . . . They speak in tongues. . . . And they lay hands on the sick. . . . But these other two . . . those scriptures just started gnawing at me inside. And I started questioning the Lord, asking him, "What did this mean about taking up serpents?" . . . I'd probably read it [before] I don't know how many times, but the scripture just never hit me in the spirit or pulled me . . . it just didn't grab me . . . and I started saying, "Lord, what does this mean?" . . . And I started asking different ministers, "What did the signs mean about these serpents?" And they'd say, "Oh, that's a spiritual thing. It means a spiritual serpent—not a physical one." . . . So it just kept bothering me, and I couldn't buy any explanation any minister or pastor or man of God could [give me]. They just

couldn't satisfy me with an explanation of this scripture on this sign. . . .
So I started asking. (P2)[5]

This believer continued asking until he was given directions to a church that practiced serpent handling. During his very first visit, he "followed [his] feet" (a self-description of feeling the Spirit move) and took up his first serpent as an obedient believer—but not until after he had struggled with the text himself for understanding.

A young preacher who had recently converted to the tradition described his own experience of coming to terms with the text in a similar way:

> I remember reading the signs one night—the actual scripture, Mark 16:18. . . . And I remember it was like all through my sleep that night. I was quoting that scripture, "They shall take up serpents. They shall take up serpents. And if they drink any deadly thing, it shall not harm them." And when I woke up that morning, I was quoting that scripture. . . . And then, it wasn't long. . . . I had a made-up mind that I was going to do that. So I did. (P4)

As handlers come to take up the text for themselves, they also bring other passages into dialogue with Mark 16. For example, P1 found evidence in the text that Jesus himself (whom the handler believes is God) had handled serpents as an example: "In Job, the 26th chapter and 13th verse, he said, 'His spirit had garnished the heavens. His *hands* formed the crooked serpent.' He did this too. I mean, he wouldn't be a just God to tell us to do something he wouldn't do himself." As did others, one participant made reference to this and other passages when refuting the criticism that the mandate stood only in Mark: "It's in the whole Word of God. Back in Moses' day, that staff turned into a snake and the Lord told Moses, 'Take it by the tail.' God handled serpents 'cause he formed them with his hand. It said in the whole Bible they did signs and wonders" (P9).

Clearly, the mandate is a fact of obedience for believers, derived from an intratextual dialogue that takes the text as authoritative and sufficient for interpretation in and of itself. As we have seen here (and will continue to see), this fundamental is based not only on the 16th chapter of Mark, but also on other passages of text that enter into the search for revelation of truth and meaning. Contrary to popular belief, most serpent handlers are aware of the argument that the latter portion of Mark 16 in the King James Version is not an authentic rendering of the original manuscript. They typically have two responses to this criticism. First, the truth of serpent handling is not contained exclusively in

Mark 16; other passages also support the practice. Second, however the course of argument may go, the passage in Mark 16 is ultimately believed to be inspired because of divine providence; God simply moved someone at a later date to include it according to his divine will. Hence the principle of intratextuality allows the mandate of serpent handling to emerge as an objective reality infused with meaning for contemporary believers.

Power to Handle (Luke 10:19)

All participants described their handling experiences in terms of an ability that was not their own. Although some had many years of experience within the tradition, none referred to this ability as a skill that was acquired over time; rather, they described it as an enablement granted to the obedient believer by God. Referring to the basis of this belief, one handler stated, "There's a scripture, and it says you can tread upon [serpents]" (P5). Perhaps one of the most explicit references to the text concerning this power emerged in a description offered by a new convert:

> Well, in Luke, Chapter 10, verse 19, it says he'll give us power to tread upon serpents and scorpions and over all the powers of the enemy. . . . God gives power from heaven. It's a spiritual power. It's not a fleshly power. It's not something we can do with our carnal minds. It has to be a spiritual thing. It's just a power that he gives us to where the devil can't hurt us. He cannot touch us. We're not his to touch. (P9)

Despite the fact that this young believer later described an experience of receiving a harmful serpent bite, he had taken up the text of Luke 10 and brought it into dialogue with Mark 16 in such a way as to understand the objective truth that God would grant the power necessary to accomplish the mandate.

This power to handle is usually perceived as the anointing of God. In describing one of her serpent-handling experiences, one female handler declared, "That serpent was bound by the Holy Ghost, by the anointing" (P8). It was the demonstration of this power that first appealed to another believer before his conversion: "I wanted to learn about those people. How they lived. How they had this power of God. How they could take up these serpents. And I sat back, and I watched, and I observed" (P13). Still another believer described how the truth of this ability was experienced in the act of handling:

> The power of God began to move upon me, and I thought that there was no harm. I began to just look up and let God take my mind, blocked

everything out from all around me, and said, "God, here I am. Just whatever you want me to do, God. Ever how you want to move on me, here I am." . . . I began to handle that serpent, and like I said, that began to come from another world—something that I can't explain. (P14)

Believing the truth of the text, obedient believers take up serpents in faith that God will supply the power necessary for the serpents to be handled. On the other hand, becoming excited by such power can pave the way for pride among contemporary handlers, said one believer, just as it did for the 70 disciples of Jesus in the passage of Luke: "When they came back, they were bragging how the spirits were subject to them, and . . . sometimes maybe we get to bragging about what we can do. But we never need to brag about what we can do" (P11). Although a major fundamental of the tradition is that God will grant to believers whatever power is needed for carrying out the signs, it must be remembered that the power of God, and not the believer's power, is what makes such manifestations possible. To think otherwise can be costly.

Danger in Handling (Ecclesiastes 10:8)

Although believers in this study described encounters in which they experienced what they felt to be God's power when handling serpents, they also told of handlings in which they either experienced for themselves or observed in others personal injury as an outcome. Of the 16 interviewed, the serpent had struck 11—3 of whom gave detailed descriptions of what they thought at the time were fatal bites. All participants acknowledged personal acquaintance with at least one individual who had died from serpent bite when practicing the sign (3 participants had family members who had done so), whereas half (8) described their experience of being at actual services in which individuals were fatally bitten. Three participants, in fact, had handled the very same serpent that delivered a lethal bite; one handler even did so after the death of his own sister. Another interviewee solemnly described the service in which he had provided the serpent that fatally bit a renowned serpent-handling minister of yesteryear. Still another told of handling a serpent at the graveside of a close friend who himself had died of a serpent bite. From their reflections on their experiences, it seems clear that believers are keenly aware of the risk involved with handling serpents. As one believer metaphorically put it, "It's like you take up death in your arms and just hold it there" (P1).

Although believers affirm the power of God for serpent handling, based on their understanding of the Bible, they also have derived truth from between its covers concerning the danger experienced in handling serpents. A major text relied on to provide context and meaning to this danger was referenced by one participant who claimed to have experienced serpent bites at least 125 times:

> When it [the anointing] gets higher, I just get to feeling more like I'm ready for it—ready for taking up serpents. That gives you the feeling that they're not going to do nothing. They're not going to strike, bite, or nothing. . . . You feel protected. . . . [But] I know the Bible did say this in the old scripture [Ecclesiastes 10:8]. He said, "If you break a hedge, a serpent will surely bite you." . . . You can break the hedge. (P12)

This believer described experiencing the power (or anointing) of God to such an extent that he felt perfect safety when handling a serpent. At the same time, however, he observed that a danger remains in that "a hedge can be broken" (i.e., there is a loss of God's protection), which renders the believer vulnerable to the venomous serpent.

Another handler described in more explicit terms what he believed was the meaning of this Biblical "hedge" when serpent bite occurs:

> All I know [when a believer gets bit] is just what the Bible said. The Bible said, "He that breaketh the hedge, him a serpent will bite." And I believe that hedge is the spirit of God. If God put that hedge around you, and it's there, I don't believe they can bite you. That's just the way I believe. (P10)

Based on the text of Ecclesiastes 10:8, all participants specifically described God's power as some type of protection, hedge, or shield; moreover, each expressed the same concern that such defense was not always a guarantee when taking up serpents. To account for this realized danger when obeying God's mandate, believers have taken up the text and brought Ecclesiastes 10 into dialogue with Mark 16. The truth arising from such intratextual dialogue allows them to continue with the command of Jesus for true believers, even in the face of potential injury or even death. Based on the sacred text, the absolute truth is that if believers handle serpents, the hedge will sometimes be broken, allowing the serpents to injure them. That handlers fundamentally believe this truth is expressed in the words of one female handler: "You really have to have your life in order when you go in that box—or you better have—because that could be instant death" (P16). This belief serves as an incentive to promote right living among believers, especially since the next handling could be their last.

Since all participants expressed belief that events happen only if God allows them, why is it that God allows the hedge to be broken?

Why does God allow injury and even death from serpent bites among those who seem earnestly concerned with obeying the words of Jesus? Here again, believers take up the text in a struggle to find meaning for such experiences. Although any individual serpent handler might give a variety of reasons for why a bite occurs, an analysis across all 16 protocols found that only 3 were consistently related to the text. First, the occurrence of a bite could be a *sign to unbelievers*, which might be understood in either of two conditions: If a handler was bitten and unharmed, it would be testimony of God's power; if a handler was bitten and harmed, it would be necessary refutation of the age-old criticism that serpents are defanged or "milked" before handling.[6]

As an example of the first type of sign to unbelievers, one female handler saw a fellow believer receive a bite during an Easter service at which unbelievers also were present, and claimed that the handler experienced no suffering as a sign of God's healing power:

> People, you know, will say, "Well, the reason it didn't hurt you is because it was a dry bite. The snake didn't put venom in you." Well, I think the Lord let the unbelievers see it because of the hand swelling, so that means the snake did put the venom in there. The hand did swell up, but there was no pain. No sickness. When you get snake-bit, you get sick. You get weak. You hurt extremely. It's an excruciating pain. But he enjoyed church—enjoyed the Easter dinner. . . . I think that was strictly done for a sign to the people that wanted to know more about the serpent handling. (P3)

In their interviews, all participants gave meaning to similar experiences in the context of Acts 28:3–5, which describes the experience (role) of the Apostle Paul who, when bitten by a deadly viper, suffered no harm and thus manifested a sign for convincing unbelievers.

As examples of the second type of sign to unbelievers, believers described experiences of bites in which harm and suffering were apparent, but convinced the unbelievers that the serpents were real and dangerous. For instance, one believer had a skeptical friend who accompanied him to a meeting where someone had brought a "bad snake." The believer was moved to handle the serpent and experienced a serious bite that resulted in immediate swelling and pain in his arm. Upon observing the serious effects of the bite, his friend later said, "I didn't believe it before I came, but I believe it now" (P1). For the friend (who afterward became a regular attendee), the injury was a persuasive sign of the believer's willingness to be an obedient disciple of Jesus, regardless of the cost. "You know, if I get bit, and if it helps somebody, hey, that's good. If that makes somebody believe, that's all right with me" (P1). The meaning of an event such as this is derived from the text in Mark 16, which simply states that "they shall take up serpents" as a sign; it does *not* say that "they shall not suffer bite nor harm." In this understanding of the text, both harmless and harmful bites may serve as persuasive signs to unbelievers.

Participants have also taken up the text to find a second meaning for experiencing serpent bites: *disobedience and sin.* As P12 explained, "Maybe you got out of the will of God. You see, God's the hedge, and maybe we moved out of the will of God. . . . There can be sin there." The sins of pride and haughtiness can result in disapproval from God, according to P11, for "when he moves his hand back [in such cases] and the hedge is broke, serpents *will* bite." Sometimes believers enjoy the blessing of serpent handling so well that they fail to heed God's warning that the time has come for returning the serpent to the box. Such was the case for one handler in the presence of elderly female visitors who had not witnessed the sign in several decades:

> I was handling it, and I was testifying, and its head was laying in my hand. Had good victory, and the Lord said, "Put it up." But I thought I was living good enough that I could handle it, and these women needed to see it just for a little longer . . . and it bit me right there [on the finger] and got me with one fang. As soon as it did, I felt my fingers began to roll where it was already beginning to work on the nerves. . . . [While suffering, he told his uncle:] "Have them pray for me, and then take me on up the road [to the house]." He said, "Why?" I said, "This one's going to last a while. I'm going to suffer." (P15)

Serpent handlers take up a variety of passages in the text to understand the relation of disobedience and sin to the affliction of a serpent bite. A few passages commonly used to provide such a context of meaning are 1 Samuel 15:22–23, Luke 12:47, and Colossians 3:5–6.

The third meaning of a serpent bite is more general and indiscriminant, in that other meanings have failed to provide satisfactory understanding. If the bite was understood neither as a sign (no unbelievers were present) nor as chastisement for sin, participants ultimately came to understand it in terms of the *unknown will of God.* Concerning the death of a friend who was the same age as herself, one young handler said:

> You know, when somebody dies like that from a snake bite, I don't know why. And you know it's only human nature to wonder about something like that, but . . . I believe she had a lot of faith. . . . She trusted the Lord for a lot of things. To me, I just look at it like, "Well, it was her time to go." (P6)

Also searching for meaning, another believer who witnessed a lethal bite concluded, "I don't know. I honestly don't know, because I don't know what the boy had in his mind when he went to the box to get it, or what went through his mind when it bit him" (P7). P13 was resolved that "if you are a Christian and you do the signs and you get bit, that's just part of [God's] plan." Despite knowing that some critics would take her understanding of serpent bites and death as naïve or shallow, P16 reasoned, "I know it's a pat answer, but it was the Lord's will. . . . I just think that's the way the Lord wanted to take them out of the world, as opposed to a car wreck, or a cancer, or whatever." All serpent handlers (as well as all other Christians, for that matter) admit to not always understanding why God allows certain things to happen—that is, why God allows what we think are "bad things" to happen to "good people." When all other explanations fail believers, psychological closure to such perplexities is often found in the Bible, which allows for an ultimate interpretation that the sovereign God does all things well.

The danger in serpent handling is a fundamental aspect of the tradition's objective reality. Simply believing that the obedient are supernaturally empowered to handle dangerous serpents does not displace their awareness of the fact that the potential for death is always present. Believers clearly understand that injury or death is a possibility any time serpents are handled. What moves them to continue, despite this reality, is their trust in the text after they reconcile their own experiences with truth as perceived from their dialogue with the text. To make sense of an inherent danger that accompanies an explicit command of a loving Jesus, such passages as Ecclesiastes 10 and Acts 28 are brought into the interpretive process with Mark 16. The truth that emerges from the dialogue is that believers sometimes can and will be hurt as they obediently take up serpents. As Jesus suffered for his obedience, so will his disciples at times. It remains a fundamental truth of the text that no serpent handler will deny.

Confirmation of Blessing on Believers (Mark 16:20, Acts 28:3–6)

All participants described their serpent-handling experiences as a confirmation of God's power and blessing on obedient believers. The sign is understood not only as a blessing for the believer who manifests it, but also as a wonderment for others who look on. Pointing out this aspect, one handler made reference to the last verse in Mark 16: "And then after he ascended up to heaven, they went forth preaching everywhere with signs following. They manifested every bit of it. . . . Like the Apostle Paul . . . [it] was for a sign" (P1).

Other believers described the effect that observing serpent handling had on their own conversions:

> You could just see these people. You could see the expression on their face that they were really getting a hold of something. And I said, "Lord, how *great* that must feel." It wasn't the idea of handling a serpent. I wanted to feel what those people were feeling. (P5)

> Unbelievers can see the Lord moving on you, and they know that there's something there. That's really how I got to believing, you know, got to believing in this. 'Cause I saw something or other move on people that I knew was real, and I wanted it. (P10)

From a believer's perspective, this type of confirmation has a far-reaching effect on unbelievers as a witness for God. For example, a female handler said:

> We have letters from all over the United States—and probably some foreign countries—when they've seen us, like in an interview, on TV, or a news clip, or a documentary, whatever. You would be amazed at the people that will actually call if they can get a hold of your number. . . . People in other countries will actually call the visiting center in your state—the state welcome center—and see if they can get in touch with you. . . . They will write letters and ask you to pray for them because they know you have got a hold of something. . . . They see that there's something [to it]. (P16)

As suggested by this excerpt, the handling of serpents can be an effective confirmation to some people that believers are genuine people of God. They can be seen as disciples who have a special connection to God by virtue of their faith and complete obedience to his commands. None of the participants in this study described their status as believers in condescending ways; rather, they depicted themselves as Christians who had been enlightened as to the truth of the Bible signs—a truth that, once lived out, can have a forcible impact on others who also are open to this truth.

For participants, the truth of serpent handling as a confirmation of believers is explicit in Mark 16:20 and other passages (e.g., Exodus 7:9, 15 and Acts 28:3–6); it is implicit in still other passages (Acts 2:43, 5:12, 8:13). As believers reflected on their own conversion experiences, what they perceived as the power of God on handlers they had observed for themselves became a profound influence on their own lives. It is in taking up the text that such believers find intratextual justification and meaning for the amazement experienced by unbelievers who look on their ritual. What emerges from such intratextual dialogues among passages is a fundamental truth: confirmation of God's blessing on genuine disciples, which rings true for both believers and many unbelievers alike each time a serpent is taken up—a sign of wonderment and awe.

CONCLUSION

Using our intratextual model, we have shown in this chapter that certain beliefs of serpent handling are interconnected and emerge from dialogue with the sacred text as fundamentals that enlarge the worldview of the tradition and afford it meaning. Other nuances of beliefs exist at the individual level, but Williamson's (2000) study has revealed that at least 16, if not all, serpent handlers have embraced four core beliefs as objective facts of the tradition. Attempting to make sense of their own experiences, they have taken up the text, struggled with it for revelation and meaning, and interpreted truths that for them have become objective facts of reality maintained by the tradition. In addition to a worldview characterized by the most basic of certainties shared by all Protestant fundamentalists, SHSs also are convinced of a Biblical mandate to handle venomous serpents as obedient believers; they are convinced of the availability of supernatural power that makes such handling possible; they are convinced of the inherent danger in handling venomous serpents, which makes necessary the connection with supernatural power; and they are convinced that what they do confirms their blessing in the eyes of God and others as true believers of Jesus. Such objective facts have become established as fundamentals of serpent handling that help believers to structure their experiences and interpret their world with meaning. As we have discussed in earlier chapters, religion can serve as a focal point for constructing a psychological worldview of meaning and purpose. For members of SHSs, their religion affords them a way in which to understand themselves as true believers, who are distinguished as such by full obedience to an intratextually derived command of Jesus. For them, this is both their religion and their world. There are believers, and there are unbelievers; there is no middle ground between these two groups. The reality of this dichotomous world is certain for those who take Mark 16 literally and embrace the fundamental truths of serpent handling—so real, in fact, that true believers are willing not only to live, but also to die by them.

CHAPTER SIX

Fundamentalism among the Amish

> In the Amish case, the message of the sectarian society is exemplary. A way of living is more important than communicating it in words. The ultimate message is the life. An Amish person will have no doubt about his convictions, his view of meaning and purpose of life, but he cannot explain it except through the conduct of his life.
>
> —HOSTETLER (1993, p. 8)

In this chapter, we apply the intratextual model of fundamentalism to the Amish.[1] The Amish are an extraordinary group of people with a rich heritage dating back to the Protestant Reformation. Their society is sectarian, in that it stresses the necessity of absolute separation from all other religious and civic loyalties. This has resulted in a style of living that clearly flies in the face of contemporary American culture, with "quaint" buggies, styles of dress, and one-room schoolhouses, and with a tendency to eschew modern conveniences. Many secular Americans romanticize the apparent simplicity of Amish life from afar, with a touch of nostalgia. For others, Amish society is a puzzling community with silly customs and countless contradictions. Yet as one author (Kraybill, 1989) has put it, perhaps the most intriguing puzzle of all is the secret of Amish survival through the 20th century (and now into the 21st). What one discovers on taking a closer look is that beneath the surface of simplicity and unusual customs is a hard yet purposeful existence based firmly on scriptural convictions. The result? A uniquely coherent set of beliefs that, despite attack from the larger culture, provides a resilient social framework—one that has remained remarkably unchanged from the 16th and 17th centuries.

CHARACTERISTICS OF THE AMISH

It is easy to spot Amish people. They look different; they travel in unusual modes; their houses are strikingly simple and without many modern conveniences; and their forms of entertainment are often different from those to which most of us are accustomed. To the outsider, characteristics such as these are perhaps what define this now not-so-small band of people, numbering more about 145,000 (up from an estimated 5,000 at the beginning of the 20th century). Such growth is all the more amazing, given that the Amish (with a few isolated exceptions) do not seek new converts, and therefore few outsiders join. Amish growth is largely the result of a high birth rate (with a lower-than-expected infant mortality rate), averaging almost seven children per family; a low attrition rate (10% to 15%) among its youth; and increasing longevity (Hostetler, 1993; Kraybill, 1998).

The Amish themselves, however, are not likely to use the same markers as their defining characteristics.[2] Certainly the Amish are aware of their differences from the dominant culture—tourists' curiosity and frequent comments on how "quaint" they look are constant reminders—but those differences are understood by the Amish to be indicators of a far deeper and more meaningful religious structure. Why do they separate themselves from the modern world? How do they regulate social change? Why do most Amish children remain Amish?

Religion as a Primary Meaning System

To answer questions such as these, it is crucial to understand that the Amish are culturally rooted in a religious belief system that takes the Bible as objective truth revealed, recorded, and preserved, and therefore to be trusted as the authoritative word of God. Thus Amish beliefs reflect a meaning system through the basic tenets of the Christian faith, though those tenets are understood and demonstrated in considerably different ways from those of most other Christian fundamentalist groups. In fact, some Amish beliefs appear, at face value, downright inconsistent with orthodox Christianity. For example, the Amish discourage individuals from reading the Bible in private or from forming small Bible study groups (common staples for other conservative Protestants). Rather, the Amish understanding of the text is mediated through the community—not because individuals are not capable of study on their own, but because it is feared that individual study will lead to varying interpretations, which may undermine community authority and stability. Similarly, though the Amish believe that theirs is a unique and redemptive community called to be separate from the world, it is inappropriate for the Amish to boldly claim their own salvation to the exclusion of others. Such behaviors, including underlying attitudes, do not reflect the proper spirit of humility. Thus, unlike many other fundamentalist groups, the Amish are not concerned with propagating the gospel by insisting that others conform to their beliefs or practices. Instead, salvation is found through a community that withdraws from involvement in the larger society. For this reason, the Amish are characterized by Wilson (1970) as an "introversionist" Christian sect, as opposed to the far more common "conversionist" groups.

In fact, such characteristics as introspection and submissiveness, which outsiders might think of as introversion, are precisely what are understood by the Amish as authentic virtues of a meaningful life. Therefore, only within this context should such needs for making meaning as purpose, value, efficacy, and self-worth (Baumeister, 1991; Hill, 2002) be interpreted and conceptualized. This introversionist tendency is perhaps also the reason why the Amish are rarely considered fundamentalists, for it does not match the stereotype of fundamentalists as militant. However, if one conceptualizes fundamentalism in terms of intratextuality, then the Amish have much in common with other fundamentalist groups.

The Charter and *Ordnung*

The organizing principle of Amish life is the charter (Hostetler, 1993). The charter, which contains the fundamental beliefs and values as recognized and accepted by the people, and the accompanying *Ordnung* (the charter's behavioral code, acted on by consensus of leaders at semiannual meetings), are oral narratives and teachings through which a young Amish child's understanding of the world is established and categorized. The body of wisdom and tradition that the charter comprises guides the everyday lives of the Amish people. The charter is so powerful and effective in passing its wisdom from generation to generation that it need not be written, but it is finely crafted through carefully examined experiences of tradition. In part, of course, the effectiveness of this orally communicated and experientially lived charter relies upon the coherency of its constituents—yet the respect that the charter commands creates further adhesion. This does not mean that the Bible is disregarded; rather, the Bible is supplemented, since the charter is an expression of Biblical beliefs for everyday life. This also does not mean that the Amish do not rely on written words. Indeed, they recognize the necessity of the written word of the Bible, and also refer to a text called the *Martyrs' Mirror* for documentation of the 16th-century persecution of Anabaptists in Europe (though the latter is not regarded as sacred in quite the same sense as the

Bible is sacred). It does mean, however, that the work of theological scholars is diminished in the Amish tradition, for the charter is not the work of great theological sophistication (which would draw attention to the work of individuals, and thus would not cultivate the valued personal characteristic of humility). Rather, it is something that becomes understood through the wisdom accumulated over generations from the experience of the community. This accumulated wisdom has no doubt been influenced by centuries of struggle for survival, conflict with society, and an "intimate agrarian experience" (Hostetler, 1993, p. 10) that brings the Amish close to nature.

Thus certainly one of the striking features of Amish life is its oral tradition, which gives it an informal and nonrational character, with heavy reliance on a collective memory to transmit its values (Kraybill, 2001). It is in this context, then, that religion becomes highly patterned and tradition-laden through a distinctive group consciousness, in which the oral tradition of the charter speaks with the same clarity and authority as the Bible itself.

At first glance, it may seem that the case of the Amish does not fit the intratextual model, since oral tradition and a collective consciousness are given the same authority as the Biblical text. Yet for the Amish, the charter must at least implicitly conform to Biblical teaching. Thus there is ultimately just one coherent set of beliefs and practices, rooted in the sacred text through which meaning is interpreted and afforded. Indeed, conformity to the meanings found in the sacred text is what legitimates the charter and the *Ordnung*.

Through a number of communal safeguards, the Amish believe that life's principles are best articulated not by abstract theological doctrines, but by the relational acts of living in community. The *Ordnung*, as the Amish "blueprint for expected behavior" or "grammar of order" (Kraybill, 2001, p. 112), is the orally communicated code of conduct; as such, it is the behavioral expression of the Biblically based charter. As Kraybill notes, the *Ordnung* is an "understanding" that does not require a set of systematic rules. The Amish claim that people simply know it and know when they have violated it. It is through their understanding of the *Ordnung* that the Amish express religious rituals and symbols. It is the understood regulator of all behavior, whether ceremonial, public, or private. It is a practical, lived-out interpretation of what the Bible teaches as God's will for his people—both collectively as the church, and individually as responsive members of the church—and is therefore capable of providing a complete sense of redemptive meaning and purpose. The *Ordnung* is the corporately defined application of the sacred text in contemporary life. Thus, though the typical Amish person is not likely to read or have access to outside scholarship on the meaning of religion, the Amish fully comprehend through their oral tradition the meaning of religious symbols.

However, the ultimate source of the truth for the charter and the *Ordnung* remains the Biblical text. Though outside influences (e.g., practical and economic considerations) may affect its collective wisdom, the fundamental principles underlying the *Ordnung* always remain loyal to the Biblical text, even if only in the form of not intentionally violating scriptural standards. Though some of the *Ordnung's* regulations are not directly related to specific passages of scripture, the overriding concern is with worldliness—a Biblical concept that stands in contrast to God's plan for righteousness.

The intratextual model of fundamentalism therefore applies well to the case of the Amish: Again, the process and structure of the beliefs, rather than the content of the beliefs, are crucially important in understanding fundamentalism. The Amish will agree with other conservative Protestants about, for example, the divinity of Christ and the centrality of Christ's atonement for the salvation of sins. However, their particular interpretive stance on what the text itself says about how people are to live their lives—and, more importantly, on the powerful role of the unwritten charter (i.e., *how* the text makes itself known)—is uniquely Amish.

Though the Amish, like the Church of God (Chapter 4) and serpent-handling sects (Chapter 5), have historically had strong leaders (most notably their namesake, Jakob Ammann), the sect itself is less defined by the personalities of individuals than by their collective identity. This is not surprising, given their collectivist culture. Hence, unlike the psycho-historical accounts in Chapters 4 and 5 of key leaders such as A. J. Tomlinson and George Went Hensley, the approach here is more sociohistorical. That is, to understand the societal structure and belief system of the Amish, we must first be aware of their unique history. As we shall see, the very issues of central importance to the Amish today can be traced back to the years of the Protestant Reformation. Indeed, in many ways, contemporary Amish life resembles the existence of centuries past far more than it does 21st-century America.

THE ANABAPTIST TRADITION: A BRIEF HISTORY[3]

The Amish are part of the Anabaptist tradition. The word "Anabaptist" means "rebaptized" or "twice baptized" and can be traced back to the 16th-century Protestant Reformation. Individuals of that day who had been baptized as infants in the Catholic Church were believed to be required, based on the teachings of Scripture, to be rebaptized as adult believers. Adult (i.e., "believer") baptism remains to this day one of several distinctive characteristics of Anabaptist belief. Though the Anabaptists are today a diverse group with many denominations and sects, other general markers of the tradition include a strong sense of community, pacifism, and relatively autonomous congregations with minimal influence from a church hierarchy. However, virtually all of these characteristics are rooted in an understanding of Scripture centered on the life of Christ and Christ's spiritual teachings, particularly those from the Sermon on the Mount (Matthew 5 through 7).

Anabaptists emerged in Switzerland in 1525 as a radical branch of the Protestant Reformation, which challenged the historic alliance between civil government and the Catholic Church. Like other Reformation groups—but perhaps even more so because of their explicit dissension through mass rebaptisms (especially one notable occasion in Zurich on January 25, 1525, which marked the formation of a church apart from the state)—the Anabaptists were treated with great harshness. This "etched a sharp distinction between the church and the larger world in the Anabaptist mind" (Kraybill, 2001, p. 6). The persecution of what was seen in Zurich as a socially subversive group was well documented in the almost 1,500-page *Martyrs' Mirror* that can still be found in many Amish homes today (Nolt, 1992). To escape persecution, Anabaptists retreated into the Swiss mountains; later, when the persecution temporarily subsided, they established farming communities in rural Switzerland.

It was during this period that a Catholic priest, Menno Simons, torn between the traditions of the Catholic Church and the teachings of scripture, found the Anabaptist interpretation of scripture most convincing and became a powerful leader with a large following. In fact, by the mid-1500s, the Swiss Anabaptists in the north were so influenced by Menno Simons's leadership that they became known as "Mennonites."

The Birth of the Amish

The latter half of the 17th century witnessed renewed persecution of the Anabaptists near Bern, Switzerland, and along the south Rhine River. By the 1690s, many Swiss Anabaptists had migrated north along the Rhine; some moved into the Alsace region, which was governed by religiously tolerant French aristocrats. Whether in Switzerland or Alsace (or also the Palatinate region of Germany, where more Mennonites settled), the Anabaptist Mennonites found helpful neighbors. The sympathizers became known among the Mennonites as "Half-Anabaptists" or "True-Hearted People"—names that Nolt (1992) suggests indicated a degree of ambivalence toward the sympathizers among the Mennonites. The issue of how to relate to the sympathizers—especially during an era where suspicions between churches ran high, and where the Mennonites were making strong and exclusive statements about the necessity of adult baptism—became a divisive issue.

On one side of the issue were largely the Swiss Mennonites, who were the primary beneficiaries of the True-Hearted People's kindness. The Anabaptists had now lived long enough in Switzerland for extended family connections with the True-Hearted People to develop, and official state-supported opposition and persecution were most extreme there. On the other side were the Alsace Mennonites, whose benefit from these helpful neighbors was less direct, and who therefore maintained a lesser sense of obligation. Concern was rapidly growing among the Alsace Mennonites that accepting the aid of the True-Hearted People reflected an increasing compromise with larger society, and thereby violated the strict Anabaptist teaching of separation from the world.

One of the Swiss Mennonite leaders who moved to the Alsace region at the end of the 17th century was Jakob Ammann. Sensing a weakening of Mennonite resolve, Ammann called for a number of reforms, including adding a second annual communion service (thereby encouraging members to be more diligent as they examined their lives closely in preparation for communion). Another Mennonite leader, Elder Hans Reist, resisted Ammann's call for a second communion service, and the stage was set for a series of disagreements between the two men that resulted in two distinct groupings: the larger and better-established Mennonite community, led by Reist, and the reformed faction, led by Ammann. Though the second communion service was the catalyst for division, subsequent efforts at reconciliation broke down largely over the issue of "shunning" (i.e., social avoidance of members excommunicated from the church).

Reist supported associating with the True-Hearted People and even entertained the possibility that they might be part of Christ's church. Though he did exclude those who left the church from participating in the (once-a-year) communion service, he did not engage in the practice of shunning. Arguing that Christ himself was pure, though he had social connections with sinners, Reist believed that the Church could remain pure while still interacting with the outside world—including those who had consciously left the Mennonite church or who had not confessed their sins.

For Ammann, Reist's position was a compromise of what the early Anabaptist reformers had fought for; to him, indeed, Reist and his followers represented a church that was becoming more and more like the sinful mainstream culture. Ammann's concern was that the church would become so acculturated that it would be hardly distinguishable from a society so foreign to the teachings of Christ. To distance themselves from their more liberal cousins, Ammann and other leaders of the reformed faction insisted that Anabaptist meekness and simplicity be demonstrated outwardly through such indicators as simple dress (e.g., hooks rather than frivolous buttons, untrimmed beards), among other things.

Nolt (1992) contends that both the Reist-led Mennonites and the followers of Ammann were concerned about their communal identity as Christ's true church. The Mennonites interpreted this identity in terms of an inner piety represented by righteous attitudes and personal character, and not by strict boundaries that provided an isolated physical and social reality. For Ammann, such boundaries were necessary for a personal commitment and the enforcement of strict discipline, which he saw as vital for church renewal. To this day, the Amish see the true church of Christ as a redeemed community called out and separated from the larger church, which has fallen from what God had originally intended.

Coming to America

By the beginning of the 18th century, Anabaptist groups had settled in a number of European countries; though different settlements had different experiences, their nonconforming ways rarely led to recognized legal religious status. The primary lands where the Mennonites and Amish had settled (particularly Switzerland and the German Palatinate) were in political and economic turmoil, with rampant persecution of the nonconformist Anabaptist groups. For example, the Swiss government formed a secret police force of Anabaptist hunters, imprisoning many and confiscating their property. Soon the prisons were full, and allowing emigration (or deportation) was an attractive option for the civil authorities. The German Palatinate was a region beset with major wars during the middle and late 17th century, and the only recognized churches were Catholic, Reformed, and Lutheran. Many members of the other "sectarian" religions, including the Anabaptist groups, were removed from their lands and either imprisoned or driven from the country, despite their value as skillful and productive farmers. The harsh German winters and the devastation of war and continued persecution made the New World especially appealing to the Mennonites, the Amish, and other religious groups.

This was the situation when William Penn traveled the Rhine River early in the 1700s, welcoming the religiously oppressed to Pennsylvania. In 1711, after continued negotiations with the Mennonite-influenced Dutch government, the Swiss government in Bern established a policy of general amnesty (including prison release, full proceeds from the sale of their properties, and no departure tax). Anabaptists were allowed to emigrate to their choice of Holland or Prussia—both friendlier confines. It is not clear how many of these early emigrants eventually came to the New World, but the important point is that a pattern of emigration was established.

However, the Amish in particular were reluctant to leave their homeland (in fact, many who emigrated to Holland quickly returned to Switzerland), causing one scholar (Hostetler, 1993) to speculate that perhaps the first ones who eventually came to America were the least religiously committed and most opportunistic. Because the Amish tend not to keep extensive records, it is unclear exactly when they started coming to America, but it is well documented that in 1737, a ship with numerous Amish aboard arrived in Philadelphia.

American Settlement

Many of the Anabaptist groups (including the Amish) initially settled in the southeastern quadrant of Pennsylvania, but by 1800 Amish settlements were established as far west as Somerset County in the southwestern part of the state. The early years for the Amish settlements, where several Amish families would live in contiguous relationship, were fraught with difficulties on many fronts. The settlements were small[4] and dispersed with problems both external (conflicts with other denominations, assaults by Indians, and harsh winters) and internal (disputes both within and between settlements). Also, some Amish were being tempted by American "good living"—hardly prosperous by contemporary American standards, but far better than the persecuted life in Europe. The principle of nonresistance meant that the Revolutionary War brought its own set of difficulties, to the point that many Amish were imprisoned with the charge of treason; their unwillingness to engage in conflict was interpreted by many authorities as siding with the British.

The 19th-century Amish migrated west—particularly to Ohio, Indiana, and Illinois, but also to Iowa, Missouri, and even Ontario, Canada. The reasons for such migrations were numerous, but they often involved troubles in church life, which frequently centered around issues of Biblical interpretation and cultural accommodation. For example, Nolt (1992) reports that in the 1840s, a conflict surfaced in Indiana between the more conservative recent migrants from Pennsylvania and those close by who had resettled from Ohio. The latter group tolerated more extensive and formal education, as well as "fancy" clothing—suggesting to the Pennsylvania migrants that they no longer valued the virtues of humility and simplicity. Those who moved west often did so either to maintain a more traditional church and family lifestyle or to challenge this tradition. Though others migrated primarily for economic reasons (often to obtain better farmland), it was clear that reasons for migration were mixed and often resulted in further tension between communities.

The Amish custom of local, decentralized government in the form of community decision making further accented community differences. By 1862, a national gathering of Amish ministers (a *Diener-Versammlung*) was established for the purpose of setting a course for unity in Amish belief and practice. Though it would appear to outsiders that the differences were relatively minor and that some unity was restored, by 1865 it was apparent to many Amish leaders that the differences were so substantial that any hope for reconciliation was impossible. The more traditional-minded became known as the "Old Order Amish," while the more progressive, change-minded Amish became known as "Amish Mennonites"—a distinction never bridged to this day. Further divisions continued, especially among the Amish Mennonites, who differed on the types of changes that could be allowed; at the heart of each division was the issue of selective change versus maintaining tradition. Following the great division of the *Diener-Versammlung*, which no longer met after 1878, it was apparent that some Amish would opt for spiritual renewal through the order of the community, while others would seek such renewal through an individual spirituality—including, for some, a new vision of Christian commitment exemplified by a broad-mindedness and tolerance that were no longer true to historic Amish identity (Nolt, 1992). During the late 19th and early 20th centuries, many of this latter group merged with the Mennonite church (in one of its multiple forms), which today reflects few distinguishing characteristics of the Amish.

Further divisions and splits have continued among the Amish (e.g., the 1927 establishment of the Beachy Amish in Somerset County, Pennsylvania, even allowed the use of automobiles and electricity). As recently as 1972, "New Order" Amish communities have risen in Ohio and Pennsylvania that favor the use of telephones, power-driven generators, and tractor-driven farm machinery, but not automobiles. Indeed, one accounting of Amish history is that it is best characterized in terms of tensions and fragmentation,[5] and perhaps such differences should be expected among groups who treat the text with such reverence. However, such a view is probably simplistic and does not account for perhaps the greatest of all attributes of the Amish—how they have resisted the onslaught of a dominant American culture that operates in such contrast to their religious values and worldviews.

MAINTAINING AMISH BELIEFS AND LIFE

A social structure that reflects society's underlying values is necessary for those values to survive. Thus, in a highly individualistic culture, a social structure fostering individual freedom is necessary. In a collectivistic culture, such as that of the Amish, the social structure must reflect the sense of corporate identity and meaning as well as a willingness to yield to collective wisdom. From the psychological perspective employed in this text, these rituals help define a unifying philosophy of life through which personal meaning and purpose are understood. Though the Amish may tend to downplay the necessity of personal meaning, nevertheless personal needs for meaning are met in the Amish way of life. For example, purpose, value, and self-worth are all understood in terms of contribution to the welfare of the community. Even a sense of efficacy is communally embedded, in that personal efficacy is understood only in terms of interdependent relationships with others in the community. Thus the establishment of good character is not a complete goal in itself; it is a goal only so that it can be used to the betterment of the community. For the Amish, personal needs for meaning are met only through service to others, and this understanding of personal meaning is what best expresses the true Biblical message.

Such an understanding of personal meaning requires a strong social structure. For the Amish, the strength of the social structure is its reliance on religious beliefs manifested through an elaborate system of rituals—a system that effectively maintains cultural boundaries. As Kraybill (2001) points out, "Amish rituals are not hollow. From common meals to singing, from silent prayer to excommunication, the rites are filled with redemptive meanings. As sacred rituals, they retell holy stories, recharge group solidarity, and usher individuals into divine presence" (p. 112).

What are some of these sacred rituals, and how are they so effective in maintaining the Amish way of life? What is the Amish reasoning behind what seems to be an inordinately complex maze of rules? Again, from the perspective of our intratextual model, we must answer these questions not through analytical social-scientific models and theories, but through the perspective of the Amish themselves—in this case, through the Amish charter and *Ordnung*, or the textually affirming language of order itself. The fundamental purpose of the *Ordnung* is to protect the purity of the church (i.e., the community) and the development of personal character consistent with this understanding of collective purity. For the Amish, then, it is this collective sense of coherence (Antonovsky, 1987) or purpose through which the text is interpreted and applied. With the Amish, all practices are evaluated within the context of this primary purpose—a purpose defined through the sacred Biblical text.

Separation from the World

The collective wisdom of the *Ordnung* clarifies, through both prescriptions and proscriptions, what is righteous and what is sinful or worldly. It is not necessarily the behaviors themselves that are right or wrong, but what those behaviors *represent* and what they can lead to (in the case of proscribed behaviors) if left unchecked. Thus practices prohibited by the *Ordnung* (central heating in homes, wearing jewelry and makeup, owning computers or televisions, entering military service, driving in automobiles or flying in airplanes, etc.) are sinful because they represent refusals to bend to the collective wisdom and order of the community— and ultimately to the very will of God, since the foundation of the *Ordnung* is the sacred text. Similarly, faithful obedience to the will of God through a yielding to the collective wisdom is exemplified by such prescribed practices as wearing certain colors and styles of clothing, using horses in the field, following a specified order in corporate worship, continuing to use Pennsylvania German, and so forth.

Some practices are prohibited simply because they are so foreign to the Amish way (e.g., divorce or the use of genetic enhancements for dairy cows) that they are clearly a violation of the *Ordnung*. Such violations of core understandings require little if any enforcement. Other practices may test the periphery of the *Ordnung*, particularly in light of changes within the dominant culture. When new issues arise, they are discussed by the ordained leaders, and any consensus (if reached) will become part of the *Ordnung*. The key in determining whether a practice should be prohibited or not is whether it contributes to an erosion of a clearly definable cultural boundary—a boundary that is consistent with (though not necessarily prescribed by) the text. If a new practice is seen as harmless to the textually affirming community standard, it will probably be allowed. As Kraybill (2001) notes, barbecue grills or trampolines, for example, are acceptable. The wisdom of the *Ordnung* maintains that such devices are not "worldly," and therefore their use is acceptable. Ultimately, the concern is that the *Ordnung* remain a sacred order that allows for unity from within but separation from without. As one minister put it, "A *respected* [emphasis in original] Ordnung generates peace, love, contentment, equality, and unity. . . . It creates a desire for togetherness and fellowship. It binds marriages, it strengthens family ties, to love together, to work together, and to commune secluded from the world" (Beiler, 1982, p. 382, as quoted in Kraybill, 2001, p. 115).

Character Virtues

"'Tis better to remain quiet and let people think you are dumb, than to speak and remove all doubt."[6] This humorous motto reflects well the spirit of meekness so valued in the Amish community. Humility and self-surrender in submission to the *Ordnung* are primary character virtues that underlie many sacred religious rituals and symbols. The Amish believe that these characteristics were most prominently modeled by the life of Christ—in other words, that the redemptive power of Christ was found in his humility and submission to the will of God. It is thus these characteristics that should be cultivated in the true church. For the Amish, to be humble means to use selflessly what God has given them for the benefit of others. This is precisely, according to the Amish, what God did through Christ when Christ left heaven to come and be part of a sinful world. A favorite scriptural passage among the Amish is found in the Apostle Paul's letter to the Philippians:

> Let nothing be done through strife or vainglory; but in lowliness of mind let each esteem other better than themselves. Look not every man on his own things, but every man also on the things of others. Let this mind be in you, which was also in Christ Jesus: Who, being in the form of God, thought it not robbery to be equal with God: But made himself of no reputation, and took upon him the form of a servant, and was made in the likeness of men: And being found in fashion as a man, he humbled himself, and became obedient unto death, even the death of the cross. (Philippians 2:3–8)

For the Amish, such scriptural passages profoundly define ultimate meaning and purpose.

Though reactive to traditional church rituals and icons, the Amish maintain a sophisticated set of practical rituals, symbols, and behavioral guidelines to facilitate the development and expression of such Christian virtues as humility. For example, the Amish stress a posture of kneeling as a symbol of humility when one is praying in public, confessing sins, washing the feet of others, or being baptized or ordained. The Amish also have a humble theology and, unlike other conservative Protestant groups, do not assume that they are in the position to make bold claims regarding any person's eternal destiny. This privileged responsibility belongs to God alone as the final judge. Rather, the Amish simply believe that God communicates through the sacred text what is expected of them; their responsibility is to obey the text faithfully and humbly, and then allow the rest to remain in God's hands. This obedience is the essence of the Amish faith.

Humility as the "hallmark of Amish ideals" (Kraybill, 1998, p. 27) has important and intentional implications for Amish life practices. For example, elaborate home decorations, the use of gaudy colors for possessions, and ceremonial recognitions of achievement are discouraged, as they can readily lead to an enhanced sense or expression of the self. Rather, one's home décor should remain simple, and one's personal achievements should be recognized quietly and with a sense of humble gratitude to God for granted abilities. The pursuit of material possessions beyond basic necessities is discouraged, for such possessions can easily become status symbols that foster an inflated sense of self. Possessions of necessity, such as clothing or transportation, are standardized to eliminate individual expression. Jewelry, makeup, fashionable clothing, or "souped-up" buggies do not befit a humble spirit. Personal photos are also not allowed, because they are considered "graven images" of the self.

FOUR MARKERS OF AMISH LIFE

We consider four basic characteristics of Amish life[7] that reflect their understanding of the purpose and meaning of the "true-hearted" church: church discipline and shunning, child rearing, occupation, and modern conveniences. This is, of course, only a sampling of distinctive Amish practices. We believe, however, that it is a representative sampling and is enough to show that what seems from an outside perspective like a slavish preoccupation with regulation and ritual provides instead a "firm ethnic identity" and a "secure emotional home" (Kraybill, 1998, p. 30), through a larger sense of community rooted in the teachings of the sacred text and maintained through a highly effective oral tradition. Thus the Amish perhaps represent the ideal type of Wuthnow's (1998) conception of "dwelling" spirituality.

Church Discipline and Shunning

The practice of shunning can be traced back to the founding of the Amish church and was the basis for one of the fundamental schisms between the Amish under the leadership of Jakob Ammann and the Mennonites led by Hans Reist. It is important to understand that in most Amish communities, shunning is not frequently or widely practiced. It is, however, a practice with great symbolic meaning that is clearly communicated in the charter and enforced through the *Ordnung*. The practice of shunning both symbolizes and enforces the church's need to remain uncontaminated by the world. Thus, though shunning as a practice is not explicitly prescribed in the Bible, it is based upon a Biblical passage

(Matthew 18:15–18) about discipline, and it has become an Amish practice to maintain Biblical standards regarding the purity of the church.

Though meekness and humility are cardinal traits to be developed, the Amish maintain that they must be tempered with an awareness of Christ's teaching of church discipline (recorded in Matthew 18:15–18) that may require decisive action. If a baptized member of the church lives in unrepentant sin, he or she is to be approached privately about the sinful practice. If the person remains unrepentant, he or she should be confronted with a small group of witnesses. If the person still refuses to repent, the church should provide a public warning, after which the unrepentant individual must be excommunicated from the church and socially avoided, or shunned, by all church members (including the person's family). The shunned individual will be left out of conversations at social gatherings or during work. At meals, especially at extended family gatherings, the person must sit at a table isolated from the others. The individual is not allowed to engage in corporate worship until he or she repents of the disobedience. Given that the typical Amish person has few (if any) close friendships and little social support beyond the Amish community, and given the importance of social connectedness in the Amish way of life, shunning appears to be an unusually strict and harsh method of discipline—one that does not convey the spirit of love and humility cherished by the Amish.

How can such gentle and peace-loving people be so harsh? To answer this question, as with all the riddles of Amish life, one must place this practice within the context of the textually affirming *Ordnung*—and both Kraybill (1998, 2001) and Hostetler (1993) remind us that several key points must be kept in mind.

1. The purity of the church, as it is defined intratextually and applied through the *Ordnung*, is the highest social value that must be protected. To allow willful disobedience to the *Ordnung* is to allow a cancerous growth within the social order. Thus social avoidance is understood as a mechanism (and experience has proven it to be an effective one) to maintain Biblical standards. Though shunning stigmatizes the disobedient person, this is not its purpose. The cost to the individual, no matter how great, is small compared to the importance of maintaining the social order.

2. Shunning signifies the importance of baptism (which typically occurs during late adolescence) as a lifelong vow to the *Ordnung* (Kraybill, 1998). Only baptized members who have been disobedient are to be socially avoided. Children, youth, and nonbaptized adults do not face social avoidance.

3. Shunning is an effective form of prevention and is used as an ex-

ample to teach the young. Being the object of social avoidance is painful to anyone, but perhaps even more so for the collective, yet separatist, Amish. To be shunned means losing all that a person has, for all that the person has is understood in the context of social relationships within the community. Young children who see a person shunned may vow never to practice anything that may bring such shame on themselves.

4. Though shunning is a powerful form of social leverage, it is not meant to be a direct and overt display of power. Rather, even the implementation and enforcement of shunning are meant to be done with a spirit of humility and love. The decision to shun a person is made reluctantly, and sometimes as much as a 6-month period of grace will be allowed for the individual to repent and change his or her ways (especially if it involves a practical matter, such as selling a piece of equipment). Again, the intention is to maintain the purity of the community by providing a moral compass, not to punish the disobedience of the individual.

Child Rearing and Education

Having large families is considered a virtuous practice that fosters humility and obedience. Amish are discouraged from practicing birth control; rather, they view children as a gift from God, and the number of children that God blesses a family with is based on God's will alone. To interfere intentionally with God's will is prohibited by the *Ordnung*. Also, a large family teaches cooperation and the necessity of yielding to others among siblings—and, indeed, the social order applies to family life every bit as much as it applies to the larger community. The principles of the charter and *Ordnung* are first observed within the context of the family and such principles are less vulnerable to distortions in larger families. It is feared that children in smaller families, especially if there is only one child, are more likely to get their own way and therefore become "spoiled." Extended family members, who for practical reasons may live under the same roof, are also highly valued and often play a key role in teaching the young.

Educating the young is viewed as a family responsibility. Home schooling is an option for the Amish, and it is practiced more in some communities than in others. However, even when children are sent to school, their families are highly involved. Amish children are typically taught in one-room schoolhouses, and Amish teachers are hired not for their expertise or on the basis of their credentials, but for their Christian character and the ability to exemplify the values of the redemptive community (Kraybill, 2001). The educational system of the Amish was not recognized until a 1972 U.S. Supreme Court decision ruled in their favor following a 35-year battle with the forces of progress—specifically, the practice of closing one-room schoolhouses in favor of larger, consolidated schools. Until the 1930s, the Amish had sent their children to public schools, but the consolidation plan caused Amish leaders to fear that their children would be led away from the community. The legal battle was highly complex (see Kraybill, 2001, pp. 161–177, for a more thorough discussion), but underlying the Amish resolve was a fear that the very future of the church was potentially at stake, and on this point they refused to budge. The bottom line was that the Amish wished to maintain control of their children's education. For them, the Bible teaches that it is the parents' responsibility to train their children, and the inability to maintain control over their local school systems where families were intricately involved in education decisions was a violation of Biblical standards.

Anything beyond an eighth-grade education is deemed unnecessary in Amish society. Education is not a virtue in and of itself, for education is viewed in practical terms. Being "well educated" means being able to read and write sufficiently well to serve the community and to provide or care for a family. Education beyond this level can only make one proud and is therefore discouraged as worldly.

Occupation

The nature and meaning of work for the Amish are perhaps among their most distinguishing characteristics. "We feel our occupation should be home and community centered. Our occupation should do at least four things: 1. Provide some useful service or product. 2. Provide an opportunity for children to work with parents. 3. Permit the father to be at home most of the time. 4. Provide an income" ("Letter," 3-80, from Igou, 1999, p. 120). Farming remains the primary occupation for the Amish, in part because it meets the four criteria just listed as well as or better than most occupations.

Two primary reasons are generally given for why farming is the dominant occupation in Amish society. Both reasons are likely to be quite true, though scholars and other outsiders might attribute primary causation to one, while the Amish might see the alternative as far more important. These different perceptions of the primacy of farming as occupational choice provide yet another illustration of Amish peculiarity that eludes secular understanding. Outsiders, for example, might rightfully point to an agricultural heritage that goes back to the 17th-century European Anabaptists. It was during those years of disenfranchisement that the Anabaptists developed finely tuned skills as farmers, turning dry and sterile lands into productive and beautiful pastures (Seguy, 1973).

The Amish learned to improve the soil through the use of mineral fertilizers, manure, and a healthy 3-year crop rotation. The Amish recognize this great heritage and are grateful. Within the proper spirit of humility, they recognize that it is something they do well.

But the Amish also see a far greater significance to a life close to the soil. The Amish believe that they have a sacred obligation as God's stewards of the land—that they are placed on earth as managers of God's domestic affairs. Being a faithful steward is a Biblical concept of central importance to the Amish. As such, good stewardship includes these recognitions: All possessions belong to God (Exodus 19:5, Psalms 24:1); God is the source of everything, including wealth (1 Corinthians 4:7), personal talents (Romans 12:3, 6), and ability to work (Deuteronomy 8:17–18); talents must be used in a faithful manner (Matthew 25:14–27) to serve others (Romans 14:9) and to glorify God (Romans 14:7–8); the basic attitude toward wealth and possessions must include faith that God will provide (Matthew 6:24–35); people are to be content with what they have (Philippians 4:11–12); and people cannot take personal credit for what they have (1 Corinthians 4:7). Nowhere are these principles of stewardship better enacted than in care for the land:

> Soil has for the Amish a spiritual significance. As in the Hebrew account of Creation, the Amish hold that man's first duty is to dress the garden. That is, he is to till it, manage it, presumably for pleasure and fulfillment (Gen. 2:15). Second, man is to keep the garden, protecting it from harm through the use of his labor and oversight. Ownership is God's (Ps. 24, "the earth is the Lord's . . . "), while man's function is looking after it in behalf of God. . . . This view of land implies not only sustenance but to a certain extent pleasantness, attractiveness, and orderliness. Man has limited dominion. He has power over animals and vegetation, but land must also receive proper toil, nourishment, and rest. If treated violently or exploited selfishly, it will yield poorly, leaving mankind in poverty. The Amish view contrasts sharply with the so-called western view, which sees man's role as an exploiter of nature for personal advancement and progress. To damage the earth is to disregard one's offspring. (Hostetler, 1993, p. 114)

This sacred love for the land fits well with the life of simplicity. For the Amish, one does not farm to live, but lives to farm. Thus many Amish will save money and live frugally (even by Amish standards) to faithfully obey God's command to be good stewards of the land. The ideal life for many Amish is to support themselves and their families off the land, with minimal worldly interference.

Yet this dream is becoming increasingly difficult for the younger generations of Amish. The Amish are not immune to the financial plight of all farmers in the United States today; indeed, because they do not utilize much modern machinery, they are at an even greater disadvantage than non-Amish farmers. Furthermore, as the Amish population grows and as real estate prices soar (particularly in Lancaster County, Pennsylvania), it is increasingly difficult for Amish families to support themselves fully by farming alone. Thus, over the past several decades, other occupations—particularly those entailing closeness to the land—have become popular. For example, many Amish today are engaged in such occupations as furniture making or construction. These not only require sophisticated woodworking skills, but also (at least as practiced by the Amish) involve a great respect for the land, with which there is a special sense of spiritual connectedness.

Modern Conveniences

A story reported in the Amish *Family Life* magazine communicates well the underlying concern of Amish toward many modern inventions. An Amishman was asked by a group of 52 churchgoing tourists what it means to be Amish. After some thought, the Amishman asked his own question:

> 'How many of you have TV in your homes?' Fifty-two hands went up. 'Now, how many of you feel that perhaps you would be better off without TV in your homes?' Again, fifty-two hands went up. 'All right, Now how many of you are going to go home and get rid of your TV?' Not one hand went up! Now that is what it means to be Amish. As a church, if we see or experience something that is not good for us spiritually, we will discipline ourselves to do without. The world in general does not know what it is to do without. (Monroe L. Beachy, Sugarcreek, Ohio, 9/8-92, from Igou, 1999, p. 62)

It is impossible in this brief application of the intratextual model of religion to the Amish to cover all the nuances of Amish attitudes and practices regarding the use of modern conveniences. In fact, the complex maze of rules and principles would require a full book for explanation; fortunately, Kraybill (1998, 2001), Hostetler (1993), and others have provided insightful analyses. However, a few examples are discussed here as the final of the four markers used to represent and understand the Amish way of life in light of the intratextual model.

Once again, the foundational principle in understanding Amish reasoning is whether the use of a modern convenience has the ability (or potential) to disrupt the boundary of righteousness of the redemptive community, as modeled in scripture and interpreted and enforced through the charter and *Ordnung*. The general model is that if there is a possibility of such disruption, the modern practice or convenience is prohibited. But there has also been a pressure, perhaps heightened by increased financial pressures in recent decades, that call for compromise with the modern world. It can hardly be said that the Amish are not practical, and at least one scholar (Kraybill, 1998) believes that such pragmatism is a secret of their success and bodes well for their continued survival in the midst of a hostile culture. Consider, for example, the case of automobile usage. There may be no clearer threat to the Amish sense of community than the automobile—an invention that typifies the spirit of individualistic modernity, providing a degree of mobility, freedom, and speed not known to the common person before. Of concern to the Amish is that people, particularly young people, can be seduced by the automobile's worldly charm. As one Amish person put it, "How many sixteen-year-olds do you know who own a car? Is it not usually that the car *owns them?*" (Pa., *Family Life*, 7-89, from Igou, 1999, p. 159). Yet it is also increasingly true that Amish businesses could benefit from the use of the automobile. For example, many Amish construction crews build houses far away from their own settlements, and a car is necessary for transportation to and from the work site. Thus a distinction has been made between automobile ownership and simple use as passengers in someone else's automobile.

A similar compromise has been reached with regard to telephone usage. A mainstay of community behavior in the collective consciousness of the Amish is face-to-face interaction, in which the complete image of each person in an interaction (how the person is meant to be known) is available. Nonverbal cues carry much meaning in Amish society, and the use of the telephone is thought to limit the degree of personal interaction so necessary in a collective culture. On the other hand, the telephone is useful for Amish businesses and perhaps necessary for those businesses in competition with the non-Amish. So, again, a compromise has been reached. The Amish are forbidden to *own* phones in their homes or places of business (though some settlements allow phones in business settings), but are permitted to use "community phones" (or what we might call "pay phones"). Indeed, community phones have been established in many Amish settlements, and individuals are encouraged to use them for emergencies, but not "small talk."

The final example we consider here is the use of electricity. Electricity's economic impact and the ways it has changed daily living in the host culture have created a number of hurdles for the Amish. Once again, compromise without violating the sacred text has the been the prescription for success. An outsider is hard pressed to come up with a rationale that allows batteries and 12-volt motors for applications not only in shops, but also in homes and barns, yet does not allow 110-volt current. For the Amish, however, the reasoning is really quite simple. Using 110-volt alternating current would lead to a potential avalanche of unnecessary modern gadgets (radios, televisions, computers, modern kitchen appliances, etc.), which would violate the boundary of separation from the world. Furthermore, such electricity requires electrical lines installed from public utilities, which serve as both literal and figurative symbols of a spiritually unhealthy connection with the outside world. By contrast, batteries and 12-volt motors as sources of electricity are under local control and therefore separate from the world. Once again, therefore, the guiding principle is theological, and the reasoning (though unusual from the modern perspective) is both logical and coherent. To the Amish, it simply works.

CONCLUSION

Are the Amish fundamentalists? For many, the Amish do not at all fit the classic stereotype. Though they are separatist, rural, and not highly educated by modernist standards, their image does not fit well in other respects with many other stereotypical characteristics of fundamentalists, as erroneous as such stereotypes are: confrontive, militantly defensive, Bible-thumping, soul-saving evangelists with an apocalyptic message designed to transform culture. Calling an Amish person this kind of fundamentalist is easily seen as inaccurate, even by one with little knowledge of Amish ways. In fact, the Amish are prototypes of nonconfrontational passivism. Though they stand firm on what they believe and can confront fellow Amish in the form of shunning, it is their spirit of meekness that ironically has an almost charmingly persuasive effect on the larger culture. Thus the Amish, though tax-paying American citizens, have been able to maintain local control of many customs, including those that violate many current laws (e.g., requiring no more than an eighth-grade education). They understand that their culture as a redeemed community is unique, and therefore they are not evangelistic. Their purpose and their understanding of meaning as communicated through the text is not to transform culture, but rather to withdraw from it; the request they make of the larger culture is simply that they be allowed to continue their ways without interference. Other Protestant fundamentalists adopt the slogan that they are to be "in the world, but not of the world." The Amish believe that they are to be neither in nor of the world. They choose not to speculate about the future or end times, for that belongs to the providence of God alone.

Yet we have contended that the Amish are intratextualists, and thus that they are indeed fundamentalists, for theirs is but a simple faith that calls for a humble obedience to the text. This does not mean, however, that their faith is at all simplistic. It is, in fact, a sophisticated faith with powerful meanings through rituals and symbols. In this admittedly cursory overview of the Amish, we have made the case that the Amish defy typical social-scientific explanation. Rather, solving "the puzzles the Amish life," to borrow a phrase from Kraybill (1998), requires understanding and appreciating the Amish on their own terms—that is, taking seriously their commitment to the authority of the text.

CHAPTER SEVEN

Fundamentalist Islam

Why do I fear Mahound? For that: one one one, his
terrifying singularity. Whereas I am always divided, always
two or three or fifteen.
—RUSHDIE (1989, p. 102)

Where there is no belief, there is no blasphemy.
—RUSHDIE (1989, p. 380)

Islam is properly identified as one of the major revealed faith
traditions intimately linked to the legacy of Abraham, along with Judaism and Christianity (Feiler, 2002). These three great faith traditions fulfill the personal need for meaning for many people worldwide, as they
provide clarity with respect to behavioral regulations (Baumeister, 1991;
Wuthnow, 1998). Fundamentalist Islam, perhaps even more than other
expressions of the Islamic faith, provides a strong sense of coherence for
the believer (Antonovsky, 1987). It argues that the Quran[1] contains
Allah's final revelation, given to the Prophet Muhammad through the
Angel Gabriel. Muhammad spoke what was revealed to him over the
23-year period of the revelation. The spoken words were written down
by scribes and constitute Islam's sacred text. As Tehranian (1993b) emphasizes, "Muslims consider the Quran as the Word of God, the Revelation itself, a veritable Miracle, a book of unsurpassed eloquence in classical Arabic, revealed by God to an unlettered Prophet" (p. 342).

The two major branches of Islam are Sunni (constituting the vast
majority of Islam) and Shia (no more than 10% of Islam and a powerful
majority only in one country, Iran). The distinction between Sunni and
Shia emerged historically, with the Sunni favoring succession of the
Prophet via election, while the Shia support succession via inheritance
(Adil, 2002; Choueiri, 1990). We are less concerned with the complexities of this historical distinction than with the current fact that the Shia,

more than the Sunni, focus upon reading the Quran in terms of the apparent or literal meaning (al-dhaher). Thus Shia Islam is the focus of our concern in this chapter. This is the version of Islam that the West most commonly calls "fundamentalist" (usually with the word "militant" attached), and properly so in terms of our model. As Denny (1994) notes, "If in Christianity the 'Word became flesh,' in Islam it became a book" (p. 144).

The Shia Muslims are caricatured in the Western mass media as a religion "of the ferocious Ayatollahs, of suicide bombings and hostage-taking" (Ahsan & Kidwai, 1993, p. 77). This stereotype, accentuated after 9/11, persists despite the fact that Muslims primarily based in Saudi Arabia—not the fundamentalist Shia of Iran or Iraq—were involved in the 9/11 plane crashes. However, instead of focusing upon acts of violence (both terrorist and retaliatory) that currently occupy the Western media's attention and the current political scene, we focus in this chapter upon a case study in which the faith of those committed to Islam was challenged by a widely respected novelist in an affair that Western intellectuals find less frightening than acts of terrorism, but perhaps more puzzling. This case study exemplifies the type of ideological split between secular and religious orientations that provides the framework for conflicts between individuals.

Religiosity has repeatedly been shown to be related to traditional values (Schwartz, 1992). Religious individuals have a different ordering of values that secular individuals may not pursue (e.g., salvation) and these values have been shown to be related to high levels of life satisfaction (Emmons, in press; Rokeach, 1969). To the extent that the pursuits of ultimate concerns (Emmons, 1999, in press) within secular and religious ideologies clash, individuals protecting different ultimate concerns may be placed in conflict (Roccas, in press). Thus in this chapter we use the intratextual model in a unique methodological fashion: We provide the context illuminating a clash between intratextuality and intertextuality— a clash that is less rooted in personality than in the defense of ultimate concerns that placed fundamentalist Islam and the secular West at odds.

It is not accidental that the question of blasphemy in the novel *The Satanic Verses* (hereafter referred to as *SV*; Rushdie, 1989) resulted in a *fatwa* (legal opinion) of Ayatollah Khomeini,[2] who ruled in Iran, the only country where Shia is clearly the dominant expression of Islam. To understand the Shia support of a death sentence issued from Iran for a book published in England by an Indian author is to go a long way toward understanding the importance of intratextuality in Islamic fundamentalism.

We divide our discussion into three sections. First, we describe the novel and the *fatwa* that followed its publication. We use our intratextual model to understand the justification for the *fatwa*, as well as re-actions to it both within and outside Islam. Second, we focus upon the role of the Quran and its unique status in providing a normative system of meaning and a normative guide for action for Shia Muslims. Finally, we present selections from a published discussion between a defender of Rushdie's controversial novel and a fundamentalist Muslim whose reaction to *SV* is an example of intratextuality.

THE NOVEL, THE OFFENSE, AND THE *FATWA*

The Novel

A description of Salman Rushdie, the author of *SV*, as an accomplished novelist, essayist, and critic is neither disputed nor our concern in this chapter. Our focus is on a single work of his, *SV*, and on the reasons why fundamentalist Islam reacted to it with such force. How could a novelist be guilty of blasphemy by writing a fictional account in which the pro-tagonist is both paranoid and presents his view of Muhammad in a se-quence of dreams?

SV is just under 550 pages long. It is a complex text, written in the centuries-old Western tradition of Cervantes and Voltaire, and in the more recent tradition of Latin American writers such as Gabriel García Márquez and Jorge Luis Borges. The latter tradition is one of "magical realism," which is perhaps the single best characterization of *SV*, even though Rushdie himself does not like this identification. Still, *SV* utilizes a subversion of the narrative form with mixtures of fact and fantasy that characterize the genre of magical realism.

More than one scholar has noted that *SV* is really two texts in one. One text is the story of Gibreel Farishta and Saladin Chamcha, their ex-ploits in England, and their eventual return to India. The novel begins in true magical-realism fashion with their survival from a fall from a jumbo jet. Their story, a surrealistic mixture of fact and fantasy, comprises the majority of *SV* (Chs. 1, 3, 5, 7, 9).

The second text can be divided into two stories, each carefully crafted on the basis of actual historical events. One (Chs. 4 and 8) is the story of the Hawkes Bay incident. The other (Chs. 2 and 6) is the story of the revelations to the Prophet Muhammad. Both stories reveal Rushdie's extensive knowledge of Islamic history and culture.

The Hawkes Bay incident is an event held sacred to Shia Muslims but ridiculed by Sunni. Thirty-eight Shia Muslims followed Willayat Shah into the Arabian Sea at Karachi, Pakistan, expecting it to part and provide a safe passage to Basra, and from there to a holy city in Iraq, Karbala. Eighteen perished in the sea. It is applauded by Shia Muslims as a sacrifice confirming not only devotion, but also assurance of paradise for those who perished. The relatively recent occurrence of this event (February 1983), and the clear documentation of its facts (see Ahmed, 1986), leave little doubt that Rushdie's treatment of this incident is a deliberate use and transformation of historical facts through the genre of magical realism. The event occurred in a town where Rushdie's family has a home. Although the chapters describing this incident have not been the focus of concern in Islam, Rushdie's employment of a real historical event is consistent with his considerable knowledge of Islamic history.

In fact, the second part of Rushdie's history tripos (final honors examination) at Cambridge University was entitled "Muhammad, Islam and the Rise of the Caliph" (Weatherby, 1990, p. 26). Rushdie also clearly utilized standard works on Muhammad, such as Martin Ling's (1983) *Life of Muhammad Based on Early Sources* in *SV*. Moreover, he relied heavily on a translation of the Quran by N. J. Dawood and Muhammad Ali, with a "few touches" of his own (Pipes, 1990, p. 57). Finally, it is worth noting that the noted scholar Edward Said (see the later discussion of "Orientalism") read *SV* in typescript before its publication and warned Rushdie that it would disturb Muslims (cited in Weatherby, 1990, p. 102). Rushdie clearly utilized his knowledge of Islam to forge a particular view of the Prophet Muhammad and the Quran that became of immense concern to Islamic fundamentalists. Furthermore, he was probably aware (and unquestionably became aware after *SV* was published) that his use of the privileged status of the novel in Western literature clearly did not apply in Islamic lands: "The use of fiction was a way of creating distance from actuality that I felt would prevent offense from being taken. I was wrong" (Rushdie, quoted in Weatherby, 1990, p. 223).

The second specific historical aspect of this second text in *SV* (Chs. 2 and 6) is the story of the revelations to the Prophet Muhammad. Again, there is little doubt that Rushdie carefully utilized historical facts and the genre of magical realism to produce a modified history of the Prophet that offends Islamic fundamentalists. According to scholars, fundamentalist Islam perceives *SV* to be a kind of anti-Quran (Brennan, 1989). This is but a particular claim illustrating the general fact that what most fundamentalisms share is an antisecular stance (Tehranian, 1993a, p. 313).

Several scholars have noted that the two texts (and, we add, the historical events of the second text) of *SV* have very little to do with one another. Pipes (1990, pp. 53–54) claims that Rushdie merged two separate novels into *SV*. That is, Rushdie mixed a novel about migration set in the West (the magical-realism story of the actual and fantastical wandering of Farishta and Chamcha) with a historically based study of Islamic fundamentalism, in which he used magical realism to explore the revelations of the Prophet Muhammad and the Hawkes Bay case. Few who opposed *SV* read the entire novel. Excerpts from the historical chapters dealing with the revelations of the Prophet (i.e., only two chapters, or less than 15% of the novel's length) were what resulted in charges of blasphemy and the eventual issuing of a *fatwa* by Ayatollah Khomeini on February 14, 1989. Although it can be argued that excerpts out of context distort the meaning of the text, fundamentalist Islam found the excerpts offensive enough in their own right to refuse to place them in any context that would justify them. Excerpts were sufficient for Ayatollah Khomeini to declare Rushdie a *murtadd*—a born Muslim who had abandoned his faith and was supporting the enemies of Islam (Weatherby, 1990, p. 155). He also identified Rushdie and those involved in the publication of *SV* as *madhur el dam,* meaning "those whose blood is forfeited," and hence no longer enjoy the protection of authorities and may be killed without penalty (Pipes, 1990, p. 87). Many Muslims did not publicly support the *fatwa*, but probably privately agreed with it, even if they did not want it carried out. In addition, fundamentalist Islam claimed that the refusal of many Sunni Muslims to endorse the *fatwa* simply indicated that they had sold out to America and that Shia Muslims were the true defenders of Islam. Though one need not accept this claim uncritically, one also must accept the reality of the genuine religious motives of a widely respected Imam who simply was responding appropriately within an intratextual understanding of Islam. Pipes (1990, pp. 95–105) has documented the claim that the weakness of Imam Khomeini's political case for the *fatwa* is more than matched by the strength of his religious case. As we have done with Rushdie, we do not explore the motives of the fundamentalist Islamic participants in this issue; instead, we focus upon the clash between intertextual and intratextual perspectives inherent in the *SV* incident.

The Offense

Obviously, the offense taken by Islamic fundamentalists over *SV* is linked to the historical material that defames the Prophet. Yet even the major characters' names in the novel are disturbing, as Rushdie carefully crafts each from real historical characters. "Gibreel Farishta" alludes to the Angel Gabriel, who brought the Quran from God to Muhammad. "Saladin Chamcha" alludes to the champion of medieval Islam who brought Sunni Islam to Egypt (Ruthven, 1991, p. 16). However, most offensive in terms of names is Rushdie's use of the term "Mahound" for the Prophet Muhammad. Mahound and its variants (such as Macon, Mahum, and Machound) are medieval versions of Muhammad, who Christians claimed was worshipped as a counter to Christ. Christians accused Muhammad of being variously a charlatan or a madman (Ruthven, 1991, p. 36). To fundamentalist Muslims, Rushdie's use of "Mahound" indicates support of the Christian viewpoint. Obviously, the undermining of Muhammad is the essential offense of *SV*, and it is done through the use of a discredited history.

In a dream sequence of a narrator who is undergoing a psychotic breakdown, Rushdie skillfully explores the central tenet of Islamic faith—that the Quran is God's revelation via the Angel Gabriel to Muhammad.[3] Although fundamentalist Muslims may question all aspects of Islam and its leaders, including the Prophet's own political conduct, they may not question the authenticity of the Quran. To do so is an act of apostasy (Pipes, 1990, p. 56).

Muhammad brought the Quran to a culture that was the center of Arabic polytheism, Mecca. The Quran's strict monotheism flew in the face of the powerful people of Mecca, who were sympathetic to the polytheism of the time. In *SV*, Rushdie (1989) states: "There is a god here called Allah (means simply, the god). Ask the Jahilians and they'll acknowledge this fellow has some sort of overall authority, but he isn't very popular: an all-rounder in an age of specialist's statues" (p. 99).

In a historical event now thoroughly discredited by fundamentalist Islam, it was suggested that one passage of the Quran made reference to three prominent goddesses in Mecca: Uzza, Manat, and Lat. Rushdie makes the mother-goddess, the highest of the three, Allah's equal. In *SV* he notes, "Ilat they called her here, or more frequently, Al-Lat. *The goddess*: Even her name makes her Allah's opposite and equal" (Rushdie, 1989, p. 100). The passage is quoted by Rushdie (1989) as follows: "Have you thought upon Lat and Uzza, and Manat, the third, the other? These are the exalted birds, and their intercession is desired indeed" (p. 114). It is the last two verses (the last sentence of Rushdie's version) that are historically identified as the "Satanic Verses," as it was claimed Satan caused the Angel Gabriel to utter these words, confusing Muhammad, who believed they came from Allah. These verses are not, of course, in the Quran. Their historical authenticity has been rejected, and in *SV*, Rushdie's claim is that the prophet abrogated these lines. Rushdie's (1989) version of the "abrogation" is as follows: " 'Shall he have daughters and you sons?' Mahound recites. 'That would be a fine division' " (p. 124).

The abrogated "Satanic Verses" do not appear in the Quran. The Quran passage reads as follows:

Have ye seen
Lāt and Uzzā
And another,
The third (goddess), Manāt?
Shall he have daughters and you sons?
What for you
The male sex,
And for him, the female?
Behold, such would be
Indeed a division
Most unfair!
They are nothing but names
Which ye have devised,
Ye and your fathers,
For which Allah has sent
Down no authority (whatever)
They follow nothing but
Conjecture and what
The souls desire!—
Even though there has already
Come to them Guidance
From their Lord! (Surah 53:19–23)

Fundamentalist Islamic historians have thoroughly explored the story of the "Satanic Verses" and deny their authenticity. Western scholars suggest that Muhammad probably recited these verses at one time, but do not attribute devious motives or "satanic" influences to their abrogation. The most reasonable explanation is that Muhammad may have recited these verses to indicate that worship of Allah was acceptable in each of the three shrines associated with Lat, Uzza, and Manat. As the power of Muhammad rose, these three shrines were destroyed (see Watt, 1953, pp. 100–109). What is of interest to us is how Rushdie uses this history and transforms it into the central thesis of one of his two texts—doubt. As Weatherby (1990, p. 27) notes, Rushdie's own personal journey has been from faith to doubt. He also would take others with him on that journey. In his own words, "One of the things that has happened to us in the twentieth century as a human race is to learn how certainty crumbles in your hand. You cannot any longer have a fixed view of anything" (quoted in Weatherby, 1990, p. 20). From an intertextual perspective, this is entirely appropriate; from the intratextual perspective of fundamentalist Islam, it is blasphemy.

As noted earlier, Rushdie rejects identification with magical realism. However, on many occasions he has said that the major influence on him has been his own cultural classic: *Arabian Nights*.[4] Ruthven (1991,

p. 11) notes that Rushdie once said in a radio interview that he would choose *Arabian Nights* to be marooned with on an atoll. Elsewhere, in response to the *SV* affair, he has noted that the fantastic stories of carpets and horses that could fly were never thought true: "And in spite of that blatant untruth, they reached for a deeper truth. So I grew up in a world where it was understood that fiction was a lie—and the paradox was that the lie told the truth" (quoted in Weatherby, 1990, p. 99). Rushdie then notes that *SV* is about the origin of a religion and about questions of temptation and compromise. Others have argued that Rushdie's *SV* applies broadly to all revealed religions. As Weatherby (1990), for instance, has said, "The ideas about religious faith and the nature of religious experience and also the political implications of religious extremeness are applicable with a few variations to just about any religion" (p. 93). Rushdie claims that he is not concerned in *SV* with historical truth, but clearly he has carefully crafted his novel in terms of historical facts, as noted above. However, what truly offends fundamentalist Islam is that *SV* is about the Prophet's going to the mountain and not being able to tell the difference between the Angel Gabriel and the devil (Weatherby, 1990, pp. 94–95). Rushdie says that he used a novel to explore an essentially psychological issue: "What is the nature of mystical experience? Given that we accept it happens, and we also don't believe in God or archangels. That's what I tried to write about" (quoted in Weatherby, 1990, p. 96). *How* he wrote about it is precisely the issue. As Van den Veer (1989) has noted, Rushdie's use of fiction to assault what is essential to fundamentalist Islam was matched by fundamentalist Islam's assault on that fiction. Fundamentalist Islam views *SV* as a counter to the Quran and an assault upon Muhammad—something unacceptable and beyond the protection of freedom of speech.

In the second chapter of *SV* devoted to the Prophet (Ch. 6), "Return to Jahilia," Rushdie uses a term, *Jahilia*, that in Islam refers to the "realm of ignorance." *Jahilia* originally referred to the period of ignorance before Islam, but fundamentalist Islam applies the word to contemporary cultures (Islamic ones included) that have drifted from the teaching of the Prophet (Ruthven, 1991, p. 41). In this chapter Rushdie again carefully crafts a magical-realism account of actual historical facts to present alternative views of the Prophet. Ironically, Rushdie uses his own name in *SV*, as Muhammad's scribe is named Salman. This scribe introduces minor alterations in the text and finds that the Prophet does not notice them. Rushdie (1989) has him note:

> Little things at first. If Mahound recited a verse in which God was described as *all hearing, all-knowing*, I would write, *all-hearing, all-wise*. Here's the point: Mahound did not notice the alterations. So there I was,

actually writing the Book, or re-writing, anyway, polluting the word of God with my own language. But, good heavens, if my poor words could not be distinguished from the Revelation by God's own Messenger, then what did that mean? (p. 367)

The answer, of course is obvious in Rushdie's eyes: The Prophet is not as Islamic fundamentalists recognize him to be, nor is the Quran the absolute revealed word of God. The allusion is not simply obtuse, but relates directly to a historical event. A Meccan convert to Islam named Ibn Abi Sarh served as one of Muhammad's scribes. On occasions he introduced variations into the text and noticed that Muhammad did not recognize the changes. This caused him to apostatize and flee to Medina (Pipes, 1990, p. 63). Islamic fundamentalists believed that if SV was allowed to stand as an exploration of the psychology of prophecy applied to Muhammad, then Ibn Abi Sarh's actions might be widely imitated within contemporary Islam.

In a second assault on the Prophet in Ch. 6 of SV, Rushdie explores the possible psychology of human interest in the Prophet's various regulations. The scribe Salman now is able to understand not only that the Prophet cannot recognize alterations in the text (deliberately introduced by his scribe as a "test"), but also that the Prophet's integrity is now at stake. " 'The closer you are to a conjurer,' Salman bitterly replied, 'the easier to spot the trick' " (Rushdie, 1989, p. 363).

If the charge of "Orientalism" (to be discussed below) has any merit, it is most credible when classic charges of licentiousness are applied to the Prophet. Perhaps the passage of SV most widely cited by fundamentalist Islamic critics is the discussion of a brothel. Twelve prostitutes, each named for one of Muhammad's wives, practice their craft behind "The Curtain" (an English translation of al-hitja, the Arabic term for the veil Islamic women use to cover their faces [Pipes, 1990, p. 65]). In SV Rushdie has the men of Jahilia flock to The Curtain, and the reader is told that business increases 300%. And in a final insult, an essential Islamic fundamentalist ritual is profaned:

For obvious reasons it was not polite to form a queue in the street, and on so many days a line of men curled around the innermost courtyard of the brothel, rotating about its centrally placed Fountain of Love, much as pilgrims rotated for other reasons around the ancient Black Stone. (Rushdie, 1989, p. 381)

The attack on the motivation of the Prophet continues in a variety of forms. Perhaps most offensive is the reply put by Rushdie in the mouth of one of the Prophet's favorite (both in SV and in historical fact) wives, Ayesha: "Your God certainly jumps to it when you need him to fix things up for you" (p. 386). The reply is in the context of what Islamic fundamentalists have found doubly offensive—the claims about the licentiousness of the Prophet, expressed in language that itself is unacceptable: "Finally he went into—what else?—one of his trances, and he came out with a message from the archangel. Gibreel had recited verses giving him full divine support. God's permission to fuck as many women as he liked" (p. 386).

Not only was and is the language immensely offensive to fundamentalists, it is especially offensive when used in conjunction with the Prophet Muhammad. Mazrui (1993, p. 217) has tried to capture the extent of this offensiveness for Christian readers by suggesting a parallel in which Jesus Christ is fictionalized as the bastard child of a prostitute (the Virgin Mary) eating his Last Supper with his homosexual lovers. Later we claim that perhaps "religious pornography" is an appropriate phrase for Islamic fundamentalists' concern about SV. Surely few Protestant fundamentalists would care to read a book, attend a play, or see a movie if they were given this description.[5]

The *Fatwa*

It is not our intent to present a detailed history of the various Islamic responses to the publication of SV. An excellent summary of the sequence of events—including riots, deaths, and the banning of SV in several Islamic countries—is provided in Ahsan and Kidwai (1993, pp. 9–24). Here we simply note that the first ban of SV was in Rushdie's native India, leading him to claim that the government had given in to those "whom I do not hesitate to call extremists, even fundamentalists" (quoted in Weatherby, 1990, p. 128). Our purpose is limited to understanding how it is possible for fundamentalists not simply to be offended by a text, but to feel compelled by their own sacred text to react in a fashion many outsiders find inexplicable, if not simply inappropriate.

We have already noted that fundamentalist Islam cannot permit the blasphemy of its Prophet, nor can it allow its sacred text to be challenged. Thus, from an intratextual perspective, it is clear that Rushdie was challenging all that fundamentalist Islam holds to be essential. In the simplest sense, one would anticipate the Muslim community to be offended by this novel. As one Muslim put the case,

> Should not the Muslim community have the right to condemn this man for blasphemy because he is using a thin veil of fiction in order to vilify the Prophet and all they hold dear to him? As the author is not interested in presenting his own realization of any truth, as he is preaching anti-

Islamic theory in the guise of a novel, his liberty as a writer ends and he should be treated as anyone producing blasphemous writing is treated. (Ashraf, 1993, p. 314)

It would be naïve to think that Islam is united as one entity and speaks with a single voice on any issue, just as it would be to think this about Christianity. Furthermore, a clear distinction can be made between lands where Islam is dominant and those where it is only another minority faith. However, it was in Iran, under Ayatollah Khomeini, that we have the most recent historical instance of Shia Islam ruled by an Imam—a person of extreme stature in fundamentalist Islam. As Imam, Ayatollah Ruhollah Musavi Khomeini was widely accepted as the Expected One (al Mahdi), the bringer of peace and justice to the world (Nasr, 1987, pp. 112–113). Not surprisingly, then, it was in Iran that the fatwa, which earned substantial international publicity, was issued. It is important to note the differing views of fatwa in Islam. Fatwa is a legal ruling, typically in response to a query. It is not universally accepted in Islam, and there are wide variations in how it is interpreted. Some argue that it must follow a trial; others argue that the accused must be given the right to repent. Thus Ayatollah Khomeini's fatwa was far from universally accepted, even in Islamic countries. Again, it is important to note the great diversity within Islam, even its fundamentalist forms. Intratextuality does not imply unanimity or ease of a single interpretation in Islam any more than it does in Protestantism. It simply assures the ultimate criteria by which exploration and understanding must be guided—in a word, intratextuality.

Ayatollah Khomeini's fatwa was issued on February 14, 1989. It stated:

I would like to inform all intrepid Muslims in the world that the author of the book entitled The Satanic Verses, which has been compiled, printed and published in opposition to Islam, the prophet and the Quran, as well as those publishers who were aware of its contents, have been declared madhur el dam (i.e., those whose blood must be shed). I call on all zealous Muslims to execute them quickly, wherever they find them, so that no one will dare insult Islam again. Whoever is killed in this path will be regarded as a martyr. (cited in Ruthven, 1991, p. 112)

It is within this context—where a novelist may be ordered killed for his fictionalized account of a religion's origins—that perhaps we can better understand why, for example, on 9/11, some Islamic fundamentalists were willing to sacrifice their own and others' lives for their faith.

Rushdie did release a formal apology in response to the fatwa:[6]

As author of *The Satanic Verses* I recognize that Muslims in many parts of the world are genuinely distressed by the publication of my novel. I strongly regret the distress that publication has occasioned to the sincere followers of Islam. Living as we do in a world of many faiths, this experience has served to remind us that we must all be conscious of the sensibilities of others. (Rushdie, cited in Appignanesi & Maitland, 1989, p. 120)

Despite the apology, the *fatwa* stood and was never withdrawn by Ayatollah Khomeini during his lifetime. Technically, it remains in effect, and that is where we wish to leave the issue. Our concern is simply to note that within Islamic fundamentalism, there is a firm tradition that makes what is so prized by the West anathema to fundamentalist thought. This is why Sardar and Davies (1990) can rightly state, "The Rushdie affair has a long history, and emotionally charged present, and could, unfortunately, have a devastatingly long future" (p. 3). Before his death, Ayatollah Khomeini was quoted from Radio Tehran as claiming, "God wanted the blasphemous book of *The Satanic Verses* to be published now, so that the world of conceit and ignorance, arrogance and barbarism would bare its true face in its long-held enmity to Islam" (quoted in Weatherby, 1990, p. 15).

In the present discussion, the fact that Ayatollah Khomeini's *fatwa* was and remains a threat to Rushdie's life is a serious matter—but it also dramatically called attention, prior to 9/11, to the intensity of insult the fundamentalist Islamic community can feel in the face of what otherwise are valued Western ideals of freedom of expression. Islam, as diverse and varied as any great faith tradition, reminds us by the *fatwa* of only one of its many voices. Fundamentalists—those who are informed by and committed to their scared text—have a history and a tradition that cannot be properly explored from the perspective dominating Western academic discourse—that of uncritical acceptance of intertextual views.

The absolutism so vociferously expressed in the *fatwa* is, in fact, countered by the negative absolutism suggested by the intertextual tradition of a more liberal West, whether "Orientalist" (again, see below) or not. This negative absolutism privileges no text, while privileging its own history of intertextuality. In a long passage worth quoting, one Muslim has stated the case well:

We are the truth, all else is falsehood. This is the basic premise of the civilization that dominates the world—the Western civilization. It is the driving force of its history, its organizing principle (secularism, and all literary products). What it actually means is that Western perception is used as a yardstick to measure reality: Western culture becomes *the* culture into which all other cultures must be subsumed; Western history becomes the history. The histories of all other people, cultures and civilization are only a pre-modern version of European history and therefore only a small segment of the Grand history of Western Civilization; secularism becomes the value of a society to which other values must refer; and Western art and literature present the apex of human experience in front of which all else pales into insignificance. (Sardar, 1993, p. 277)

If there is a lesson to be learned from *SV*, it is in the outrage of many Muslims, and the extreme reaction of one community in a culture where Shia Islam is dominant. The fundamentalists in Islam have reacted with an insight we risk failing to appreciate if we fail to understand not only Islamic fundamentalism in particular, but fundamentalism as a form of expression of any great faith tradition. In fundamentalism in this latter sense, a text defends itself from within and refuses to authoritatively accept methods and procedures associated with intertextuality, which would destroy its faith. Fundamentalists of all traditions seem to understand this well. Those of us who study fundamentalism "from the outside in" find this hard to comprehend, but it may be as much our limitation as we think it something lacking in the fundamentalists we study. This is perhaps our error: The issue is not so much fundamentalism as it is fundamentalism's intratextual imperative, which creates a coherent meaning within its own framework once a text is acknowledged as sacred. How this occurs is a challenge to those of us who would study fundamentalism fairly. What Weller (1965) said of Appalachian mountaineers is true of Islamic fundamentalists as well: It is unlikely that anyone who is willing to read this text on fundamentalism qualifies to be a fundamentalist. Thus we turn now to explore the Quran from within a fundamentalist view to contextualize our discussion.

THE QURAN AND ISLAM

The Quran Itself

Fundamentalist Islam emphasizes that the revelations contained in the Quran comprehensively encompass all areas of life and are fully binding on all believers (Tehranian, 1993b, p. 342). Scholars attempt to distinguish orthodox or traditional Islam from fundamentalist Islam. However, as in American Protestantism, the overlap between the two forms is substantial. As Nasr (1987) has noted, "Needless to say, that which is branded as 'fundamentalism' includes a wide spectrum, part of which is close to traditional Islam" (p. 13). In terms of our concern with intratextuality as a major criterion of fundamentalism, it is crucial to note that the Quran is both read and recited. The text itself references a powerful oral tradition. It is said that the first word addressed to the Prophet by the Angel Gabriel was *Iqra,* which means not simply "to read," but also "to recite" (Ruthven, 1991, p. 147). Thus fundamentalist Islam demands respect for both orality and reading. As Sardar and Davies (1990) have noted,

> For Muslims the Quran *is* the word of God. It was revealed through the angel Gibreel (Gabriel) to the Prophet Muhammad over the course of twenty-three years, from 609 to 631 CE [Christian Era]. An essential article of belief for a Muslim is to accept the Quran as a direct, literal narration of God's word. (p. 144; emphasis in original)

As the literal narration of God's word, the Quran cannot be translated: "It is the actual Word of Allah; not created but revealed for the benefit of all mankind" (*The Holy Qur-ān,* 1410 A.H. [After the Hegira]/1989, Preface, p. iv). The Quran is both recited and read in silence. The recitation of the unique Arabic-language form of the Quran is diminished in translation. Any translation, whether read or recited, of its 114 "chapters" (each "chapter" is called a *surah*) is identified as an interpretation, because it is not the original Arabic in which Allah made the revelation. Both the fundamentalist Shia and the orthodox Sunni recite the Quran in the original language of the revelation, never in translation. To assure that the Quran is read correctly, it (unlike other Arabic texts) is always printed with short vowel sounds (Nelson, 1985). As Sardar (1993) has said,

> At any one time–space co-ordinate, it is in the hearts, minds and memories, cover to cover, of millions of people who can recite all of it, or any part from anywhere to anywhere. A poem whose segments are recited and have been recited for fourteen hundred years, five times a day by most devout Muslims. (p. 286)

However, the tradition of recitation does not diminish the centrality of the physical text. Islamic fundamentalism, like Christian fundamentalism, is inherently an intratextual enterprise. In both traditions, revelation is textually preserved. This textual preservation is what makes it reasonable to apply a phenomenon originally designated to Protestantism to cultures as different as those dominated by Islam. The distinctions between varieties of Christian and Islamic fundamentalisms are immense and worthy of empirical exploration. Yet these differences should not mask the crucial fact of intratextuality that lies at the core of our model of fundamentalism. Sardar (1993) admits this fact while apparently rejecting any true similarities between various fundamentalisms. As he puts it,

The distinction is to be found in the adjective Christian and Islamic. Both "isms" arise from different roots, are founded on different texts, history of ideas and institutional and philosophic worlds of thought and action. Neither are simplistic movements and both contain many diverse shades of opinions and interpretative stances. *The crucial point is both fundamentalisms are interpretative even though their approach is literal in the self-evident meaning of their founding texts.* (p. 305; emphasis added)

It is important to emphasize that Islamic fundamentalists take their text no more literally than Christian fundamentalists. Again, literality is not the defining characteristic of fundamentalism. As we have emphasized in Chapter 2, no fundamentalist reads every word of his or her sacred text literally. The text declares how words are to be read. The Quran itself notes explicitly that only parts of the revelation are clear, and that ultimately only Allah knows the true meaning of certain passages in the Quran:

> He it is Who has set down
> To thee the book;
> In it are verses
> Basic or fundamental
> Clear (in meaning);
> They are the foundation
> Of the Book: others
> Are not entirely clear. But those
> In whose hearts is perversity follow
> The part thereof that is not entirely clear.
> Seeking discord, and searching for its interpretation,
> But no one knows
> Its true meanings except Allah. (Surah 3:7)

Literality does apply to the text's declaring itself to be absolute, but within the text interpretations must be made, including when the text literally says that what it means is not to be taken literally. As noted earlier, Shia Islam accepts *al-dhaher,* or the reading of the Quran in terms of a plain understanding of what its words convey. As in Protestant fundamentalism, literalism is rejected within the sacred text itself. Ironically, this can only be conveyed if the text is read "literally"—that is, in terms of a simple meaning conveyed by the words of the text.

Unlike the King James Version of the Bible, the Quran affirms itself in a unique challenge: The reader who doubts the text to be Allah's revelation to an unlettered prophet is challenged to produce even one line equivalent to the beauty of the Quran. Of course, the language of the

Quran is the absolute standard of beauty, against which all deviations are necessarily judged as faulty. Hence the text announces in rhetorical fashion what necessarily cannot be done:

> Or do they say,
> "He forged it"?
> Say: "Bring then
> A Surah like unto it,
> And call (to your aid)
> Anyone you can,
> Besides Allah, if it be
> Ye speak the truth!" (Surah 10:38)

As Ruthven (1991) has noted, "Since the Quran became the absolute standard of literary excellence, its claims were [and are] self validating" (p. 41). Given the beauty of the language of the original revelation, Islamic fundamentalists and orthodox believers alike discourage any translation of the text (Gibb, 1963).[7]

If the centrality of the text in Islam as the final revelation to humankind is what defines Islam, it remains to explore the role of the Prophet Muhammad in Islam to understand the issues raised when the sacred text of Islam was challenged by an intertextual tradition of the West— that is, what many people outside Islam saw as merely a novelist exercising his right to free speech.

The *Hadith*

Fundamentalist Islam accepts not only the Quran, but the *hadith* as well. The *hadith* contains narratives associated with the life of the Prophet. Not all lives of the Prophet are canonical. Scribes recorded the revelations given to Muhammad over the 23 years of their deliverance, and numerous others reported on the actions of the Prophet. *Hadith* collectors checked the contents and origins of all such reports for their authenticity. Of crucial concern has always been a focus upon these reports' chain of transmission. That is, stories of the Prophet told by individuals at increasing removes from Muhammad himself are thought to provide narratives of decreasing degrees of authenticity; as one recent Islamic biographer of Muhammad has put it, the authenticity is believed to range from "good" through "fair" to "weak" (Adil, 2002, p. xiii) as the distance of the reporters from the Prophet increases. All *hadith* narrations are concrete examples of the Prophet's application of the revelations of the Quran to worldly experience. Largely concerned with guaranteeing the chain of transmission of reports from reliable sources, the *hadith* is central in Islam, as it contains actual examples from Muhammad's life of how the principles found in the Quran are to be applied.

Furthermore, it is essential that only authenticated examples from the life of the Prophet be used for guidance. The *hadith* is thus what is traditionally authentic and hence authoritative. However, its authority derives from the Quran, and no *hadith* narrative can contradict what is in this sacred text. Again, the principle of intratextuality applies to *hadith* narratives, whose peripherality feeds back into authentic historical applications of the principles of the Quran in the actual life of its messenger. Tales and stories of the Prophet that are not accepted as historically accurate—or, even worse, narratives that present a fictionalized life of the Prophet—risk blasphemy. This is an offense that violates boundaries set by Allah (a *hadd* offense) and cannot be settled by compensation, as, for instance, murder can be (Nasr, 1987). Westerners may find it curious that murder is an offense that can be resolved by compensation, but blasphemy is not. However, as we shall see, this demonstrates a difference in values between cultures, defined by the nature of the texts they hold sacred. According to a famous Islamic scholar, Taymiyya (cited in Nasr, 1987, p. 51), anyone who defames the Prophet *must* be executed, whether Muslim or not.[8]

A common Western error is to identify Muslims who follow Muhammad as being "Muhammedans," as if "Muhammedanism" was a term parallel to "Christianity" (followers of Christ readily identify themselves as "Christians"). This insults Muslims, who know the Prophet to be fully man, not a god. This distinction most clearly separates what Christians believe of Christ and what Muslims believe of their Prophet. The Prophet states, "I but follow what is revealed to me" (Surah 6:50).

Unlike Christ, Muhammad was heavily involved in secular enterprises and was himself a warrior (see Watt, 1953, 1956). In his consideration of the 100 most influential persons in history, Hart (1987) has listed Muhammad as the single most influential, precisely because of his "unparallelled combination of secular and religious influence" (p. 40). He has ranked Jesus Christ third, arguing that Muhammad had a more central role in creating the religion of Islam than Jesus Christ did in creating the religion of Christianity. Because Muhammad is recognized within Islam as humankind's final Prophet, the relationship between the messenger of Allah and Allah's message is integral (Sacranie, 1993, p. 328). No assault upon Muhammad can be permitted by the devout, for whom the Prophet is an archetype or essential role model (Ruthven, 1991, p. 35). The Quran explicitly lists execution as one possible punishment for those who blaspheme Allah or his messenger (Surah 5:33).

Despite the extreme punishment possible for blasphemy, fundamentalist Islam is not opposed to freedom of expression. The issue is in the *meaning* of "freedom of expression" in Islam versus the West. In Islam one is free to criticize, but not to mock or ridicule, the Prophet. Furthermore, not only is it illegal and inappropriate to vilify the Prophet; Islamic law also provides punishment in many instances for an attack on the honor of *any* person, whether the person is generally perceived to be honorable or not (Sardar & Davies, 1990, p. 92). Both fundamentalists and orthodox Muslims link the Quran and the *hadith* together, consistent with an intratextual reading. They also accept the *Shariah*.

The *Shariah*

The *Shariah* is the law of Islam. Unlike other traditions, Islam does not distinguish between religion and the state. The *Shariah* must be within the scope of the Quran, and as such is both revealed and canonical. Classical jurists in Islam distinguish between *Dar al Islam* and *Dar al Harb*. The former is the realm of Islam, where Allah's laws apply in their totality (*Shariah*). All must obey these laws fully. *Dar al Harb* is the realm where the *Shariah* either has been abandoned or has not yet been applied. The claim of Islamic fundamentalists that eventually the entire world will become *Dar al Islam* is crucial (Nasr, 1987, pp. 51–52). Indeed, Pipes (1990, p. 24) essentially defines Islamic fundamentalists as those Muslims who seek the application of Islamic law in every detail. Extending this law to the entire world is one goal of fundamentalist Islam. This can be achieved by a holy war (*jihad*). There is a social context for *jihad* (waged outwardly against others), as well as a psychological context for *jihad* (waged inwardly against one's own failure to comply with the *Shariah*).

It is crucial to an understanding of Islamic fundamentalism that one not treat the relationships between *Dar al Islam* and *Dar al Harb* as if they, like Islam itself, were simply "ideologies" in the sense that Western social scientists use the concept. Fundamentalist Muslims do not view Islam as simply another "religion," nor do they view it as one possible organization of beliefs and values (i.e., one set of "ideologies"). Guillane (1987) has stated the case forcefully:

> The Quran does not claim that Islam is the true compendium of rites and rituals and metaphysical beliefs and concepts, or that it is the proper form of religious (as the word is nowadays understood in Western terminology) attitude and thought for the individual. Nor does it say that Islam is the true way of life for the people of Arabia, or for the people of any particular country, or for the people proceeding any particular age (say the Industrial Revolution). No! Very explicitly for the entire human

race, there is only one-way of life, which is right in the eyes of God and that is al-Islam. (p. 69)

The intratextual map of fundamentalist Islam refuses to relegate religion to a personal preference, a matter of conscience, or a choice. Taking the intratextual claims as seriously as fundamentalist Islam does not only courts being out of step with modern times, but also appears "quite abnormal" to Westerners (Sardar & Davies, 1990, p. 3).

Fundamentalist Islam and the Western Intertextual Tradition

One risks being identified as an apologist for a perspective when one tries to present the issue in terms that would be accepted by those whose perspective is distant from one's own. Elsewhere, Hood (1983) has argued that much of the social-scientific literature on fundamentalism in general suffers from the social distance between those who study fundamentalism and those who practice it. Voll (1989) has specifically noted that any sympathetic treatment of Imam Khomeini and Shia Islam is likely to be misperceived by Westerners as advocacy. We risk this perception here in order to describe fully the radical oppositional stance that Islamic fundamentalism takes in the face of some aspects of modernity. In regard to the SV affair, the deep anger and offense fundamentalist Muslims feel over the blasphemy they perceive in SV have been framed by the West as an issue of freedom of speech versus censorship, and this framing has placed Islamic fundamentalism decisively on the defensive (Ahsan & Kidwai, 1993, p. 25). Indeed, the West's interpretation is an excellent example of its post-Enlightenment concerns with intertextuality. Van Doren (1991, p. 127–167) reminds us that there is a long tradition in Renaissance and post-Enlightenment thought of using satire and criticism to undermine both religion and culture—from Erasmus to Cervantes to Voltaire, to name only a few figures to whom Rushdie has been compared. Literature and literary criticism are inherently intertextual enterprises. By their very nature, they undermine a sacred text. Brians (2002b, p. 3) rightly notes that Western fiction has become an alternative to religion. Although Brians clearly admires and defends Rushdie's right to explore religious themes in SV, he also recognizes the reason for fundamentalist Islam's offense:

> To a conservative Muslim, Islam is not just a religion in the sense most Westerners use the term, a private faith which provides hope and consolation within a secular world. Islam is a way of life, a body of law, an all-embracing cultural framework within which novels are distinctively

unimportant and potentially troublesome. *That a mere novelist would dare to satirize fundamental religious beliefs is intolerable.* (p. 1; emphasis added)

However, to defend literature's right to express opposition freely to the absolute of religious freedom is also, ironically, an opposition to freedom of expression (Kuortti, 1997). Thus, at the extremes, Islamic fundamentalism forces us to consider the clash of two absolutes—one intratextual and the other intertextual. The intertextual absolute includes both freedom of expression and the assumption of multiple perspectives. Furthermore, in Wittgenstein's sense, each absolute supports a form of life. For fundamentalist Islam, the Quran demands not simply a religious interpretation but, as Guillane (1987) claims, "a whole form of life" (p. 15). Intertextual criticisms risk the charge of "Orientalism" (Kuortti, 1997, p. 19) when they elevate intertextual understandings above intratextual ones by fiat. The long history of Orientalism anticipates Said's (1979) coining of the term. At a minimum, it refers to the fact that the study of Islam has long been dominated in the West by non-Muslims who have little respect for Islamic cultures and even less for Islamic fundamentalism. Thus Orientalism is a style of thought that elevates Western epistemological and ontological claims in a manner that restructures, dominates, and assures authority of the West or "Occident" over the East or "Orient" (Said, 1979, pp. 2–3). In this sense, the debate the *SV* affair engendered in the West over criticisms of Islam, the Prophet, and even the right to blasphemy under the guise of "freedom of speech" is as Sardar (1993) claims, "only a residual of the Orientalist tradition" (p. 298).

Intratextual Islamic Fundamentalism versus Intertextual Secular Knowledge

Perhaps in the debate over freedom of expression and the right of literature to challenge religion, the value of an intratextual model of fundamentalist thought is obvious—even more so, given that fundamentalism was first identified as a Protestant phenomenon. As we have noted in Chapter 3, Protestant fundamentalists had to oppose post-Enlightenment thought, insofar as it utilized methods that undermined the claims of its sacred text to absolute authority. Post-Enlightenment thought is inherently intertextual (Van Doren, 1991). The parallel with Islam is inexact, as Islamic cultures did not undergo an Enlightenment; nor have methods of "higher criticism" been adapted to the Quran, at least not until quite recently (Brians, 2002b, p. 4). Some have gone so far as to claim that Islam is "a religion yet to experience its Reformation" (Pipes, 1990,

p. 244). Although we do not subscribe to such claims, which suggest Orientalism, we do accept the fact that the privileges claimed for literature in the West are heresy when seen through the intratextual eyes of Islamic fundamentalism (Stern, 1989, p. 21). Furthermore, Choueiri (1990, p. 16) has aptly noted that the Quran, in its metaphysical claims, alleges to correct false scriptures in Judaism and Christianity and to restore Abrahamic monotheism to its pure origins. As such, fundamentalist Islam affirms what intratextually is a timeless reality, rooted in the continual affirmation of Allah's permanent laws as revealed to his final messenger.

Islamic scholars defend three issues central to an intratextual understanding of fundamentalism. Each can be briefly noted in turn to set the stage for at least an appreciation of how a *fatwa,* demanding death as punishment for what to many Western minds is simply an unusual form of artistic expression, can be viewed with approval by many devout Muslims.

First, it is ironic that from the Orientalist perspective, Islam is often ridiculed relative to its intellectual merits. However, Islam has a long history of cultivating science and other forms of knowledge, without fear that they will contradict what is revealed in the Quran. Thus the *hakim,* or sage, has always been important in Islamic civilization (Nasr, 1987, p. 41). Likewise, books are widely recognized as central to Islam, and indeed are divinely sanctioned as basic vehicles for the expression of a wide variety of knowledge. This acceptance is based upon the belief that all beings in the world are Muslim, or as Nasr (1987) explains, "surrendered to the Divine will" (p. 23). Thus no knowledge can contradict the Quran (this idea is equivalent to the Protestant notion of "all truth is God's truth"); nor does the Quran reveal all that can be known. Sardar and Davies (1990) have stated the case succinctly:

> The idea of the book, or *kitab*, is fundamental to Islam; it is fundamental not only in the sense [that] as a religious and metaphysical worldview Islam is based on the Book of God, the Quran, but also in the sense that the book is a basic tool for discourse, a vehicle for dissemination of thought and ideas, a prime instrument of criticisms and counter-criticism, and a basic means of intellectual and literary expression. (p. 92)

In fundamentalist Islam, the centering of the argument must respect the Quran and the Prophet. Ridicule and mockery are inappropriate, but disputes and claims to truth are always open. It would behoove the reader to note that in Chapter 3 we have emphasized the wide range of differing opinions among those who authored *The Fundamentals,* despite that all were what we now identify as fundamentalists. Islamic fundamentalists differ among themselves as well, but, like Protestant fundamentalists, they accept the absolute authority of the text that frames the very possibility of their debates.

Second, even within the West, freedom of expression is far from absolute. More than one scholar has noted that fundamentalist Islam's outrage over *SV* was and still is hard for many Westerners to understand—even more so when many Muslims who opposed *SV* admitted that they did not read the text, but only read or heard excerpts.[9] Such Westerners are bewildered largely because the notion of a religious absolute is a victim of post-Enlightenment thought, along with the claim that there can be a form of life based upon that absolute. Yet we have seen (in cases like those of the serpent handlers in Chapter 5 and the Amish in Chapter 6) that appeals to absolutes, associated with a resistance to selected aspects of modernity, have a residual existence even in the most modern (or postmodern) of cultures.

If religion cannot be perceived as an absolute deserving protection in the West, perhaps some of the closest parallels to the fundamentalist Islam concern with blasphemy can be seen in current concerns with gender and race in secular works of the West. Few publishers would permit blatantly offensive language about women or minorities in modern texts. There are sensitive "subcultures of outrage" ready to defend their honor in such cases. An even stronger parallel may be the issue of pornography, especially child pornography. If America has any mirror image of fundamentalist Islam outrage over blasphemy, it is in its controls on various expressions of sexuality—often under the rubric of "pornography," which, unlike blasphemy, continues to be a focus of legal restrictions (Heins, 1998). Few think they would have to see every picture in a pornographic book to know that the book offends them. Perhaps then, if we coin a phrase such as "religious pornography," it might suggest how fundamentalist Islam could so quickly respond with outrage to a work of fiction, even if it is widely known only for a few selected excerpts and is seldom fully read by the fundamentalists most offended by the text.

Third, the appeal of intertextual models is by definition a more liberal perspective—one that weighs differing claims to truth and that privileges no single text. Perhaps the best example in the West is the value placed upon literature and literary criticism. Importantly, no text is immune from the devastating power of the modern secular novel. Islamic fundamentalists quickly recognized *SV* as an attack on the religion of Islam and the Prophet, carefully crafted in terms of historical claims. It is precisely as an alternative historical reading in the form of a novel that *SV* can be seen as blasphemous. The privileged position of the novel in the West has no parallel in lands where Islam rules. As noted above, the novel is not simply restricted to a critique of religion; it has largely supplanted religion in the West (Brians, 2002a). However, this does not make it immune from attacks in lands where the novel is not privileged. The issue of freedom of expression cannot carry the case from an intratextual perspective, and this perspective is what Islamic fundamentalism demands. The Protestant fundamentalist concern with "higher criticism," noted in Chapter 3, has come full circle. Inherently intertextual, "higher criticism" is prejudiced against the sacred text it claims to illuminate. Yet it must do so from some claim to truth, whether historical or hermeneutical. Yet as we shall note shortly, *SV* is more appropriately a *post*modern novel in which *any* claim to certainty is suspect. *SV* is less about disbelief as the opposite of faith than about doubt. Even disbelief is too assertive a claim.

> Question: What is the opposite of faith?
> Not disbelief. Too final, certain, closed. Itself a kind of belief.
> Doubt. (Rushdie, 1989, p. 92)

Rushdie's casting doubt as to the truth of the revelation is a direct assault upon the text that asserts: "This is the Book: In it is guidance sure, without doubt to those who fear Allah" (Surah 1:2).

More than one Western reviewer welcomed *SV*'s power to "punch holes in fundamentalist faith" (cited in LaPorte, 1999, p. 46). However, this novel's postmodern decentering punches holes not simply in fundamentalist faith, but in any claim to certainty. As Rushdie has said, "One of the things that has happened to us in the 20th century as a human race is to learn how certainty crumbles in your hand" (quoted in Appignanesi & Maitland, 1989, p. 30). Thus *SV* cannot be seen as simply undermining fundamentalist faith in general and Islamic fundamentalism in particular. Rather, it is an exemplar of postmodern and deconstructionst views—which leave all authoritative texts ravished, whether they are expressions of science or of faith. As we shall see, Rushdie's careful attention to historical fact is transformed by means of magical realism into a novel that fundamentalist Islam immediately recognized as blasphemous.

In a phrase closely paralleling "Orientalism," Sardar and Davies (1990) have suggested that a clash of worldviews is what lies behind the debate over *SV*. The phrase they use is the title of their book, *Distorted Imagination*. Though they are far from being supporters of Islamic fundamentalism, they nevertheless note that the uncritical support of *SV* in the West elicited outrage from a people whose historical legacy, collective history, and all they hold sacred is demeaned in this novel (Sardar & Davies, 1990, p. 279). If fundamentalist Islam is ridiculed for its intratextual view—its "terrifying singularity" (Rushdie, 1989, p. 102)—

then the intertextual secular model common to literature can be viewed in turn by Muslims as problematic. As Sardar and Davies (1990) note,

> While the Rushdie affair has been perceived as a clash of worldviews, the true protagonists have not been identified. They are [the proponents of] militant, dogmatic secularism which claims the realm of literature as its new religion, an absolute where unlimited freedom should be executed by the high priests of modern culture, the artists. On the other side, there is the religious worldview wherein freedom of thought and expression arises from the existence of the sacred and the ideas of respect, sanctity, tolerance for others and responsibility in the exercise of freedom. (p. 268)

In this clash between intra- and intertextual models, fundamentalist Islam gives us a clear understanding of the difference between the two. Kuortti (1997) puts the case precisely: "The Western principle is founded on the liberal 'text' of the Enlightenment whereas the Muslim principle rests on the status of the Quran as the infallible word of God, the ultimate text" (p. 22). Of course, the issue is not simply cultural—the East or "Orient" versus the West or "Occident." Rather, it is one of intratextual models in both cultures, associated with sacred texts that confront a world whose knowledge claims are increasingly intertextual. In this sense, the issues in fundamentalism are linked with ontological and epistemological assumptions and with an attempt to privilege one language over another. If that charge has been leveled against fundamentalists who would privilege their supposed "literalism," it is no less true of what Sardar (1993) calls "the child of militant secularism," the postmodern novel. As he says, "It seeks to privilege the language of secularism" (p. 292).

Finally, an intratextual understanding of fundamentalism focuses upon process, but not to the exclusion of content, as we have noted in the Introduction to this book. Within an intratextual model, the crucial question to ask is always "What does the text say?" In our intratextual model, the text with supreme authority is the sacred text, which in Islam is the Quran. This text comments on key figures within Judaism and Christianity and clarifies their sacred texts. With respect to a Western understanding of Christianity, it denies the divinity of Christ. Therefore, from the beginning, Western scholars, heavily influenced by Christianity, had to undermine the Quran and hence the Prophet. Nasr (1987, pp. 47–48) has compared what he terms the *Imitatio Christi* with *Imitatio Muhammad*. He rightly notes that often Christians value suffering and can claim a higher moral ground by avoiding violence (turning the other cheek). However, Islam is different, because Muhammad gained power and ruled during a bloody period of Arabic history. The concept of *jihad* not only permits but demands retaliation for some acts. Thus, Nasr argues, Islam provides a divine mandate—including the divinely inspired behavior of its Prophet, which was sometimes violent—to be emulated. This is not to say that Islam is inherently violent, but that its violence (as with Christian violence) is to be judged intratextually. Even the most pious biographies of Muhammad from within Islam explore his violent acts (Adil, 2002). This is crucial since, as noted above, blasphemy is an offense against the Prophet that cannot be forgiven. Again, as we have already noted, the intimate linkage between the Quran and the Prophet explains why fundamentalist Islam refuses to let offenses against the Prophet go unchallenged. In the case of the *SV* affair, the fact that the offenses originated in a work of fiction makes little difference. The reading of the entire novel is considered unnecessary; for fundamentalist Islam, the title and a few select passages are offensive enough. To illustrate this, we shall end this chapter with some simple comments from a published conversation with a believer whose schema for being offended by *SV* is mirrored in our discussion above.

AN OFFENDED BELIEVER AND HIS INTRATEXTUAL RESPONSE

Ruthven's (1991) exploration of the *SV* affair led him to interview an Islamic fundamentalist, Anwar, who attended a conference held to discuss *SV* at a community college in England. The college was located in a city (Bradford) where the vociferous Muslim reaction to *SV* had resulted in violence and deaths. As Ruthven reports much of his conversation with Anwar, he distances both himself and the reader from Anwar's intratextual understanding of his faith. Anwar's responses to Ruthven's queries (Ruthven, 1991, pp. 131–149) constitute a useful empirical example of intratextuality clashing with intertextuality, without the need to impugn the motives or denigrate the personalities of those engaged in the conversation.

Anwar is a teacher of biology in a secondary school. He was born in Pakistan, but migrated to Great Britain. As sympathetic as Ruthven (1991) is to Anwar, he seems to fail to grasp the depth of Anwar's fundamentalism. Ruthven questions Anwar primarily about his reaction to *SV* in the light of Anwar's own fundamentalist commitment to Islam. A few examples from this conversation will vividly illustrate the issues we have discussed above.

A common ploy by outsiders is to select a few politically incorrect passages from a sacred text and ask a believer to defend them. Ruthven does this to Anwar by asking how he can believe certain requirements of the Quran (with respect to women) that are far from politically correct in the Western secular world. Anwar's reply is to reject the challenge: "God decrees what he pleases. We have to accept it, that's the scandal of faith. God's commands sometimes seem impossible; but we are duty bound to obey" (p. 128). Furthermore, Anwar refuses to separate the sacred from the secular: "There is no separation in Islam. It's all just One. You can't be God-conscious some of the time and then unconscious" (p. 134). Anwar uses the Islamic term "*Al din wa al dunya*" to refuse the separation between secular and sacred (p. 134). In response to Ruthven's claim that the incident giving rise to the original *Satanic Verses* was discussed by early Islamic historians, Anwar defends his faith (as all fundamentalists must) intratextually. He knows both Islamic history and the Quran.

> Yes [acknowledging the historical discussion of the "Satanic Verses"], but the lives of the Prophets are not canonical. The story has no authentic basis. There is nothing in the text [i.e., the Quran] that could authenticate the story. To imply that even one verse of the Quran could have been inspired by the devil undermines all the rest. If a single word can be proved to be other than divine origin, the Quran is not the Quran—it is not what it says it is, the utterance of God. (p. 140)

Ruthven insists from his own intertextual perspective that it does not matter if some parts of the Quran are seen as interpolations. However, Anwar refuses to accept an intertextual view: "It matters because the text has to live up to the criteria it establishes for itself. The text has gone out of the way to tell you, 'I am beyond corruption.' If a single word has been added or subtracted, the whole edifice collapses" (p. 142).

Finally, when Ruthven argues that the text came from an oral tradition and hence we cannot be certain that it is written as it was initially recited, Anwar responds from what can only be substantiated intratextually: "The one thing Muslims can be certain of is that the Quranic text has been preserved in its perfection" (p. 142).

Anwar's comments are useful as empirical data, indicating how one fundamentalist refuses the move into intertextuality that would challenge what can be sustained only intratextually. That Ruthven, as a nonfundamentalist, cannot accept such claims is as intertextually valid as it is intratextually impotent. The discourse that surrounds *SV* is less an issue of the personalities of the participants than, as Hirschman (1991) rightly notes, "the imperatives of argument, almost regardless of the desires, character or convictions of the participants" (p. x). This is to be expected when intra- and intertextual models collide.

In this sense, fundamentalism is a reaction to advances in secular knowledge that make intratextuality a self-limiting enterprise, sustained only at the cost of refusing the intellectual enlightenment. But as Akhtur (1993) notes, "In all its manifestations, from born-again Christianity to Ayatollahism, fundamentalism is a direct creation of secularism. It is the last refuge from the abuse and ridicule of the secular mind, a declaration that man is much more than a manikin" (p. 317). These words echo those of another novelist struggling with issues of religious faith. In *Notes from Underground*, Dostoevsky (1864/1956) states that even if it can be proven by secular means that a man is nothing but a piano key, even then he will not become merely reasonable: "He will launch a curse upon the world, and as only man can curse—maybe by his curse alone he will attain his object—that is, convince himself that he is a man and not a piano-key" (Dostoevsky, 1864/1956, p. 75).

CONCLUSION

It is said that all explanations must end somewhere, but surely their end must not be contained in a prejudicial description of what they claim to illuminate. Our task in describing the *SV* incident has been to present a description based on our model of intratextuality that indicates why, without reference to motives or personalities, those of fundamentalist faith can find a novel blasphemous. The threat posed by intertextuality on methodological grounds is the one great challenge that all fundamentalisms recognize, and their resistance to this threat is the source of their apparent anti-intellectualism and opposition to modern epistemologies. That there are wise, even sophisticated fundamentalists is certain, but their approach is intratextual and geared to protecting and advancing a form of life. In terms of our intratextual model, their sacred text forbids elevating other texts to a position of privilege. Neither explanation nor illumination can come from outside the text.

Differences in sacred texts are what make particular fundamentalisms of interest. Paradoxically, these differences are also the reason why fundamentalist faiths are pitted against one another. If there is an irony here, it is that "fundamentalism," as a term judged by some to be appropriate only to American Protestantism, may have come full circle. As noted in Chapter 1, Bob Jones University has publicly repudiated its identification as a "fundamentalist" school in order to distance itself from Islamic fundamentalism. Although the intertextual tradition that seeks to tear fundamentalists from an absolute reliance on their sacred text is reasonable, perhaps its major flaw is that it is merely reasonable. As Kuortti (1997, p. 19) notes in regard to the entire *SV* debate, if we have done little but to pit "fundamentalists" on one side against "Orientalists" on the other, the issues of definition and the methods that follow from such definitions are crucial. But then this might be less an ideological than a methodological insight into the entire debate over not simply Islamic fundamentalism, but fundamentalist religion in general.

CHAPTER EIGHT

Intratextuality, Stereotyping, and Quasi-Fundamentalisms

From its historical origin, the problem of hermeneutics goes
beyond the limits that the concept of method sets to
modern science. The understanding and interpretation of
texts is not merely a concern of science, but is obviously
part of the total human experience of the world.
—GADAMER (1975/1982, p. xi)

The approach we have taken to understanding religious fundamentalism focuses upon the authority of the sacred text and suggests
that all fundamentalisms be approached from within the framework of
their own first principles. The sacred text, we have argued, is in itself
sufficient for fundamentalists as a source of life's meaning and purpose.
The textual narrative provides fundamentalists with a worldview that allows comprehensibility and manageability to an otherwise fragmented
existence, thus contributing to what Antonovsky (1987) calls a sense of
coherence as a generalized resistance resource. Textual authority, for
fundamentalists, provides moral certainty and stability. Thus we have
suggested that from a psychological perspective, there are legitimate reasons why a person might choose to be a fundamentalist. We have also
contended that for psychological science to be true to its own first principles, it must provide accurate description and must therefore approach
its object of study—fundamentalism, in this case—within the framework
of that object's own first principles.

Our approach is not a new one, but it has seldom been taken seriously by social scientists who study fundamentalism. Most social scientists have avoided any serious consideration of fundamentalism in terms
of its foundational principles (Packer, 1958). This is why the social-
scientific literature on fundamentalism has been so skewed. Even social

scientists who are sympathetic to religion have suggested that fundamentalism is what gives religion a negative connotation. However, much of what passes for social-scientific knowledge about fundamentalism is better viewed as a stereotyping of fundamentalism. Accordingly, we now consider some assumptions associated with intratextuality that would permit a less stereotypical understanding of fundamentalism, before we investigate (and question) some common stereotypes themselves.

ASSUMPTIONS OF INTRATEXTUALITY

Richard Gorsuch (2002) has argued that the task of integrating psychology and spirituality hinges precisely on crucial assumptions that prevent psychology from being inherently reductionistic. If one assumes that there is no God, revelation must be understood outside the parameters of the text that reveals the revelation. Consider, as an example, the case of Christianity: Once one accepts that the Bible might be true, then the internal evidence from within the text provides its own testimony to the truth of revelation (via the principle of intratextuality). However, this can occur only if one assumes—at least provisionally—that the Bible is God's revelation (Gorsuch, 2002, p. 71). This principle holds true for any sacred text. If a science or hermeneutic rejects the possibility that a sacred text is revelatory, it is intratextually rejected by the very text that is being intertextually analyzed. This is the aspect of modernism that conservative American Protestants rejected at the beginning of the 20th century, and for which (as we have noted in Chapter 3) they were tagged with the label "fundamentalists." We contend that this label can now be appropriately extended to a religious group in any culture, as long as the group's sacred text rejects the intertextual commitment of modernity, which denies the possibility of a God or of revelation. As Lechner (1989) notes, analytical definitions of fundamentalism focus upon one type of antimodernism characterized by what he terms "value-oriented dedifferentiation" (p. 197). Protestant fundamentalists, as we have noted in Chapter 3, are *in* the world but not *of* the world. Our discussions of the serpent handlers in Chapter 5 and the Amish in Chapter 6 illustrate how dedifferentiation isolates fundamentalists as it protects a system of meaning and a style of living that devalues many aspects of modernity. In contrast, Shia Islam, as we have discussed in Chapter 7, seeks to bring the entire world under its sacred umbrella, so that eventually the law of Islam will prevail globally (*Dar al Islam*).

Once a sacred text is accepted intratextually, it becomes the revelation of God, Allah, or some other deity, and provides a frame by which opposition to the world is both meaningful and normative. Fundamentalists' value-oriented dedifferentiation is not simply oppositional; it positively articulates an alternative system of meaning. Thus, insofar as fundamentalism provides a total *Weltanschauung* (i.e., a worldview), it must be understood on its own first principles, and this demands an intratextual model. Although others have argued for a fundamentalist or evangelical mindset, they have done so in a prejudiced fashion, denying the possibility that a fundamentalist or evangelical mindset can be other than an instance of mind control (see Cohen, 1988).[1] Our model simply asserts that intratextuality is a form of cognition controlled by a sacred text, just as other modes of thought are controlled by realities they themselves acknowledge.

Perhaps a parallel to the fundamentalists' defense of intratextuality is the defense of statistical analysis by social scientists committed to measurement. Paralleling Protestant fundamentalists' claim that "you can find whatever you want in the Bible" is social scientists' claim that "you can use statistics to confirm whatever you want." However, as anyone trained in statistics knows, statistics do not lie; they simply describe (descriptive statistics) or provide means to predict measured phenomena (inferential statistics). Although one can select statistics to reflect a particular bias (e.g., even though unemployment is up, the rate of unemployment is decreasing), such statements are in no sense contradictory. The skillful manipulation of statistics to support a bias is easily uncovered by those who understand statistics (Huff, 1982). In a parallel fashion, those unsympathetic to intratextual models can claim that one can make the Bible or the Quran (or any other sacred text) support whatever one wants. Yet fundamentalists trained in intratextuality are no more accepting of selective use of isolated quotes or manipulation of meanings than are social scientists trained in statistics, who react with similar offense to a student or layperson who claims, "You can make statistics say anything you want." We do not mean to equate statistics with a sacred text, but rather to emphasize that statistics must be employed properly to describe or predict the criteria from within this language form. To refuse numbers is to be unable to judge what they can properly say (Best, 2001). Fundamentalist communities do not blindly accept the words as they see them; instead, they struggle with their text to reach a consensus on a correct understanding of it, just as statisticians must abide by certain rules with their numbers.

The irony is that statistics, with their associated probabilities, are more acceptable to modernism (and postmodernism) than an appeal to a text that claims not probabilities but certainties. The fact that a single text can carry so much weight and have such absolute authority defies the logic of modernism (and now postmodernism). Probabilistic statistics are most acceptable to those educated in what we have called post-Enlightenment thought. The careful understanding of the historical and cultural emergence of all texts, sacred texts included, is the very essence of scholarship and often serves to undermine the claims from within a text itself. The diverse authors of *The Fundamentals* recognized this as a danger, as discussed in Chapter 3. The issue was never a proper understanding of the text. All agreed then, as now, that this is essential. The issue was, and still is, the means by which a proper understanding of the text can be achieved. What fundamentalists most oppose is the use of methods or the application of theories of interpretation that a priori rule out the possibility of revelation, absolutes, or the possibility of transcending the recognized reality of historical and cultural limitations. Indeed, the examples in this text reveal extreme diversity among fundamentalists—including, for example, those who collectively attempt to shun modern culture (the Amish); those who once courted but now oppose the handling of serpents (the Church of God [COG]); and those who continue the handling of serpents today, in the "renegade churches of God" in contemporary Appalachia (the serpent-handling sects [SHSs]). These groups, as is the case with all fundamentalists, do not doubt their text even as they doubt one another's understanding of the text.

Part of the psychological task that remains is to explore the myriad possibilities that various understandings of a sacred text provide. How communities of faith construct their orthodoxies is not well understood. It does require paying attention to the culture and the history of particular fundamentalist groups, as we have done in this text. We are reminded that Ayatollah Khomeini's *fatwa* was never universally accepted in Islam, even among Islamic fundamentalists. However, the debate was never couched in terms that would suggest that the Quran does not prohibit the blasphemy of its messenger. Diverse opinions were expressed only over the proper enforcement of the *fatwa* and whether it could be applied outside Islam. Efforts in the West to attack Ayatollah Khomeini as if his motivations could have been only personal or political fail to enter into the reality of the varieties of fundamentalist Islam, as rooted in an intratextual approach to its sacred text. As noted in Chapter 1, both social support and cultural stability are key aspects of Antonovsky's generalized resistance resources. Thus, not surprisingly, the *fatwa* came from the leader of a country in which Shia Islam is both socially and culturally the dominant force.

The rise of postmodern thought has actually been somewhat helpful by placing the shoe on the other foot, so to speak: In its most extreme forms, postmodernism denies to science and schools of literary criticism what modernism denied to fundamentalists. No knowledge claim is privileged. Although we are not arguing in favor of the more extreme forms of postmodernism (see Sandage & Hill, 2001), we simply note that as a revolutionary approach to the study of society, postmodernism has challenged the privileged position of science, as well as objective claims to truth (see Rosenau, 1992). Fundamentalists all over the world reject the "higher criticisms," whether from science or hermeneutics, that have precluded the possibility of God and revelation (Brasher, 2001). Fundamentalists often see intertextuality as a web of speculative hypotheses, ungrounded in the realities they recognize. Ironically, many contemporary social scientists find postmodernism unacceptable for similar reasons: It both precludes social-scientific claims to a "higher, objective" knowledge and undermines the claims of modern science to be an objective modeling of reality, mathematically expressed. As we have noted in Chapter 3, Protestant fundamentalists were challenged to defend their beliefs in the face of intertextual models, whereas now both the fundamentalists and the social scientists who study them can no longer accept simply being held by their beliefs, but must now defend *how* they hold their beliefs (Geertz, 1968). Veling (1996) has introduced the useful concept of "intentional communities" to focus attention upon the processes by which individuals struggle to maintain a tradition, even as they change it. Fundamentalism is not static, even as it strives for an intratextual understanding of the world. Fundamentalists, regardless of their faith tradition, demand that meaningful knowledge be intratextual. In this sense, their knowledge claims are tautological, but the tautology encircles all reality and changes as that reality does. From a postmodern perspective, scientists fare little better: They rest their faith in methods that, without adequate philosophical defense, are simply implemented into a form of life that defines people as scientists. In this sense, judgments of all modes of thought are suspect when they become detached from communities for whom either texts or methods have both existential and normative importance (Veling, 1996). As systems of meaning, fundamentalisms have a dynamic and a history that cannot be ignored.

A SUMMARY OF FUNDAMENTALISM AS A MEANING SYSTEM

We have argued that the believability of fundamentalism accounts in part for its robust survival—even in extreme expressions such as those of the SHSs, discussed in Chapter 5. Believability is possible insofar as fundamentalism is a system of meaning, as we have discussed in Chapter 2. Here it may be useful to summarize how fundamentalism functions as a system of meaning for the various religious groups we have explored— that is, how it provides a unifying philosophy of life, furnishes a sense of coherence, and meets personal needs for meaning.

A Unifying Philosophy of Life

The crafting of their lives in terms of intratextuality is possible for fundamentalists because they have a sacred text. The text itself provides a revelation from God on how to live and what is true. It is thus normative in the sense of providing assurance about what is the case and what ought to be. For example, for members of the COG, the assurance that one can and ought to be filled ("baptized") with the Holy Spirit provides the setting within which all of life can be lived and understood in terms of cosmic forces at war with each other.

The SHSs also participate in this drama with perhaps an even more forceful mandate, as they wait upon the anointing to handle serpents and even drink the "deadly thing." The fact that a central ritual of their faith could lead to death at any moment requires believers to be sure that they are living in complete obedience to God.

The Amish, a stable community, are not simply constrained by the *Ordnung*; they are also liberated from many of the concerns that trouble the outside world. The collective nature of the life lived in obedience to God relieves individuals from the anguish of many decisions they would otherwise have to face. As trivial as it might sound, the Amish know how to dress at all times, and are freed from much of the market consumerism that drives the outside world.

Islamic fundamentalism is perhaps even more extreme. No distinction is made between secular and sacred. The question of whether life is meaningful and has a purpose never arises. One need only read the Quran to know that obedience is less a burden than a recognition that life is infused with meaning, which comes directly from the revelation of the Angel Gabriel to the Prophet Muhammad.

A Sense of Coherence

Fundamentalists' adherence to the principle of intratextuality assures a sense of coherence. A sacred text can be confusing to merely mortal minds, but the text itself cannot be confusing; it cannot be in error, nor can it contradict itself. Thus coherence lies within the text, and it becomes the proper focus of ultimate concern. In this sense, all fundamentalists share the same ultimate concern—to be obedient to their Divine Being. Even when the fundamentalist groups we have discussed appear to outsiders to be grasping at straws, the concern is obedience to God or Allah. Thus members of the SHSs refuse to abandon Mark 16 as they handle deadly serpents with the firm belief that they are being obedient to God. As one handler said, though near death from an ultimately fatal bite, "It's still the word." Likewise, less lethal concerns such as wearing jewelry, attending movies, or drinking alcohol have occupied the COG at various times, but always in light of what is most obedient to God.

The Amish have the advantage of a redemptive community (the church) in which normative guidelines (the *Ordnung*) assure coherence that is not simply overtly indicated by dress, but also supported by a diminished range of alternatives in all aspects of life. However, instead of being confining, such constraints assure a coherent pattern to life—freed from the sins and temptations of an outside and hopelessly fallen world. Here the parallel is with the fundamentalists of Islam, who refuse to accept a distinction between the secular and the sacred. All must live in accordance with the Quran. Islamic fundamentalism accepts no apostasy, nor will it allow what the West perceives as "religious freedom." In matters of faith there is no choice, but rather a recognition of the truth as revealed to the Prophet Muhammad and contained in the sacred text of Islam, the Quran.

Personal Needs for Meaning

As we have discussed in Chapter 1, personal needs for meaning include purpose, value, efficacy, and self-worth. Clearly these are provided by religious fundamentalism. Both the COG and its "renegade" offshoots, the SHSs, find purpose in the Bible. Although less "open to experience" in the sense of consulting a multitude of texts, they are open to exploring what purpose God has for them, both collectively and individually, as revealed in the text. The text also indicates what ought to be, providing a rich source where evaluation can be absolute. A popular quip that most Protestant fundamentalists readily accept is "The Bible says it; I believe it; that settles it." Of course it settles it, because the purposes of God for humankind are seen as good for them as well. In a similar fashion, both COG and SHS fundamentalisms provide efficacy in that, regardless of outcomes, obedience to God assures success. God is always in charge. Apparent failures can be reframed as obvious successes. As the father of a fatally bitten serpent handler said as he took up a serpent at his son's funeral, "God has called him home." Problematic deaths, whether from accidents, disease, or human acts, are all ultimately in "God's hand." The power of religious surrender based upon knowing that God is "in charge" transforms apparent helplessness into a faithful surrender, which is efficacious for those who believe.

Among the Amish, the power of belonging to a redemptive community (*Gemeinde*) shifts the focus from personal achievement to obedience to the *Ordnung* as a Biblically based guide for the protection of all. Amish legal victories with respect to protecting their children from a purely secular education were predicated on the fact that the Amish have a right to educate their children in what is efficacious for their collective form of life. The Amish rejection of much of modernity is predicated on the acceptance into a redemptive community of believers; much of what is perceived as efficacious from a more secular or liberal religious perspective would be destructive to the shared values of the Amish community.

Fundamentalist Islam seeks to foster efficacy among its believers by assuring that secular values cannot contradict the Quran. Fundamentalist Islam seeks Islamic laws, rooted in the Quran. The ideal situation is a theocentric state as perhaps best illustrated by contemporary Iran. As we have noted in Chapter 7, the notion that freedom of speech could protect a literary work perceived to blaspheme the Prophet is unacceptable to fundamentalist Islam. Efficacy cannot be defined independently of the cultural or community context. The parallel perhaps most acceptable to more secular and liberal minds in the West is to pornography. The pattern allows community standards to define what is acceptable. Fundamentalist Islam supports an Islamic state, where the community standard that applies is the Quran.

Finally, it is obvious that all fundamentalist groups we have discussed in this text provide a sense of self-worth for their believers. Even when the emphasis is upon sin and damnation, means of salvation are available. Protestant fundamentalists believe that God loves the sinner but hates the sin. What might appear oppressive and exploitative to outsiders can be accepted by believers as normative and as a provider of dignity. For example, women, who cannot be ordained in the COG, can be licensed as ministers to preach and administer the sacraments. Similarly, women may not be allowed to preach in SHSs, but they can nevertheless testify. Amish dress liberates both men and women from concerns of the flesh and of consumerism. The much-maligned veiling of women in fundamentalist Islam is paralleled by the similarly conservative dress required of males. Having self-worth means knowing that one is made in the image of God, obedient to his commands, and assured of eternal salvation. The discriminations and exploitations outsiders see are framed otherwise within fundamentalist groups and are not unrelated to common stereotypes of fundamentalists, to which we now turn.

SEVEN MAJOR STEREOTYPES
CONCERNING FUNDAMENTALISM

Kressel (1996) reminds us that "nearly everyone thinks with stereotypes some of the time, even those who are predominately unprejudiced" (p. 232). Social scientists are no exception. Insofar as stereotypes identify individuals as belonging to particular types, they attribute traits of the types to the individuals. Scientists simply claim to have empirically identified the traits that differentiate various groups and can be applied to most individuals within a group. The resulting typologies share common efforts to generalize these traits to "most" members of the group, and thus risk stereotyping what they propose to study if the traits are not empirically valid or if there are numerous individual exceptions (statistically lumped into the "error term"). When traits are inappropriately applied to individuals identified as belonging to a type or are false about the general type, we can properly speak of stereotypes in a negative sense. Social scientists are more apt to see themselves as studying stereotypes than as fostering them. Yet stereotypes can be fostered by collecting data in a biased or limited fashion, or by simply defining groups according to criteria that prejudge what are better left as open empirical issues. We suggest that much of what passes for scientific knowledge about fundamentalists is more stereotypical than appropriately descriptive of them (Bruce, 2000; Hood, 1983; Kressel, 1996). We now discuss seven major stereotypes of fundamentalism perpetuated by social scientists.

Stereotype 1: "Fundamentalism Is a Religion."

Fundamentalism has roots deep in religious history (Hunter, 1983; Marsden, 1980; Sandeen, 1970). However, it is not itself a religion. It is best seen as a logical possibility inherent in any faith tradition that has a text believed to provide unique revelation.[2] It is only when the text containing the revelation is challenged by external factors that fundamentalism can emerge. Its emergence is dependent upon whether the sacred text is defended against such challenges; how it emerges is dependent upon its adherents' reactions in the face of particular oppositions. Fundamentalism itself is not a unitary religious tradition, nor can it be understood apart from the particular religious tradition from which it derives its unique content characteristics (Harris, 1994).[3] Thus, as Nielsen (1993) has observed, "Even if fundamentalism is not a religion, it has its own coherence as a phenomenon in most religions of the world" (p. vii). Likewise, Gasper (1963, p. 2) has suggested that there is a "latent fundamentalism" not only in Protestantism, but in other faith traditions as well, including Judaism and Catholicism. All fundamentalists are forced to defend a particular text elevated to distinctiveness as *the* sacred text containing *the* revelation from *the* Supreme Being. That there is only one sacred text is the claim from within each specific fundamentalism. From the outside, there are many sacred texts, allowing us to speak of various "fundamentalisms." But to do so is to be keenly aware that one has moved into a study of the *structure and process* of fundamentalist belief and away from a study of the *content* of fundamentalist belief, which we have noted in Chapter 1 is best viewed as orthodoxy. Orthodoxy is by definition tradition-specific; it provides a meaningful frame that allows a clear sense of coherence, and a clear normative frame that specifies what is to be valued as it specifies what is ultimately real. As Chesterton (1908/1995) said in defense of the Apostles' Creed, "We need to value the world [so] as to combine an idea of wonder and an idea of welcome. We need to be happy in this wonderland and without being merely comfortable" (p. 15). Furthermore, any orthodoxy has a history that social psychologists ignore at their own peril (Belzen, 2000).

Stereotype 2: "Fundamentalists Are Literalists."

Because fundamentalism is linked with revelation, it is inherently dialogic rather than monologic with respect to person–other relationships (Sampson, 2000).[4] In its purest form, the dialogic relationship includes a Supreme Being whose self-disclosure is recorded in a sacred text. More correctly stated, the sacred text is itself the revelation. In its Protestant version, one can speak of "verbal inspiration," meaning that the words of the Bible are in fact the thoughts of God (Machen, 1923). Similarly, as Denny (1994) notes in regard to Islam, "There is almost a sacramental quality to the recitation of the Quran, in that God's presence is made apparent and all else is hushed before it" (p. 144). A crucial assumption of fundamentalism is that one need not "interpret" the words in the sense that modern and postmodern literary critics explore. Indeed, these "interpretations" are what fundamentalists reject as "higher criticism" or forms of intertextual criticism that are themselves fallible commentaries on an infallible text.

A sacred text is true and complete in itself. It guides its own interpretation. The issue for fundamentalists is more correctly one of inerrancy, not one of literality (Barr, 1977, p. 51; Hawley & Proudfoot, 1994, p. 13). Both Protestant and Muslim fundamentalists have long argued that scripture teaches its own inerrancy.[5] Furthermore, inerrancy is crucial, since finding an error *within* the text can only be claimed on the basis of criteria *outside* the text. Since fundamentalists note that God or Allah cannot contradict himself, the negation of any claim within a sacred text can only come from outside the sacred text (intertextually). Something known to be true by other than intratextual means would not be considered as a judge of the sacred text. If any part of the sacred text is allowed to be shown in error by such means, the entire text loses authority, as many scholars both in sympathy with and in opposition to fundamentalism have noted.[6] The primary task of fundamentalist thought is simply one of objective understanding of the text, perceived as a dialogic relationship between a Supreme Being and a believer. The absurdity of this claim from modern and postmodern perspectives reveals the outsider's failure to understand fundamentalism or to accept what is considered the paradigmatic basis of the structure of fundamentalist thought. As Henry (1979) has said, "No fact of contemporary Western life is more evident than its questioning of any sure word" (p. 17).

Claims to an infallible text as essentially a dialogic relationship between a Supreme Being and individuals requires understanding of what literary criticism refers to as "authorial intent" or "consciousness" (Hirsch, 1967). Attempting to understand authorial intent is an approach that both modern and postmodern literary criticisms argue is limited at best, and ultimately not achievable. Whether concerned with psychoanalysis, Marxism, or deconstruction, postmodern textual criticism assumes that one can bring an *outside* theoretical perspective to the interpretation of any text—a perspective that overrides any claim to have understood the author's own intent (Rosenau, 1992). Sacred texts are not exempt from interpretation, but rather are to be illuminated in terms of historical and other processes that have established their privileged status within a given culture in time. That any text, much less a sacred text, can plainly and simply reveal the consciousness and purpose of its author is rejected by most forms of modern and postmodern literary criticism. Yet, as noted in Chapter 3, it was precisely "authorial consciousness" that the authors of *The Fundamentals* rightly defended when they refused to submit God's word to a "higher criticism"—particularly if this criticism assumed that God did not exist.[7]

It is misleading to think that the fundamentalist support of authorial intent requires a sacred text to be interpreted only literally. The wisdom of fundamentalism is that to lose the objectivity of the sacred text as a revelation from a Divine Being is to lose its authority altogether (Barnhart, 1986; Boone, 1989; Hunter, 1987; Schaeffer, 1975). It is this objective claim to truth that fundamentalists insist on. It does not demand a consistent literalism for all that is said in a sacred text. In fact, an objective understanding of the text requires an appreciation for when it is and when it is not appropriate to treat the text "literally." Fundamentalists only insist that discernment must come from intratextual considerations. In other words, the text itself reveals when it is and is not appropriate to take it literally.

Any theory of literary criticism that supports a determinant theory of meaning, such as authorial intent, must guard against a too-subjective rendering of interpretation that focuses more on the reader than on the author's intent. For instance, Hirsch (1967) distinguishes between a text's "meaning" (what the author objectively intends) and its "significance" (what the reader finds meaningful or significant in the text). We suggest that the focus upon objective meaning minimizes personality factors (subjectivity), which more properly are major factors in the significance of a text. Fundamentalism not only assumes, but also is virtually defined by, the continual presence of and submission to the author's intent in and through its sacred text. The author's intent is both revelatory and objectively meaningful; it is inherently dialogic. Thus the act of reading a sacred text, for fundamentalists, is not simply a person–text encounter, but rather a disclosure from the Divine Being through the text to the reader. It is in this sense that the words are thoughts, and that the interpretation is simply to understand what is being said as intended by the Divine Being. Such interpretation is only "literal" when intended. For instance, both the Bible and the Quran contain allegory, symbolism, and allusion—even within a literal reading of the texts. The point is simply that a sacred text reveals when it is literal and when it is not. Hence all interpretation or understanding is to be intratextual; this requires staying within the text, or, to put it another way, listening only to the revelation that the text contains.[8]

In this sense, fundamentalism is a subset of what scholars identify as "revealed religions." Stark (1999) provides a succinct definition: "Revelations are communications believed to come from a divine being" (p. 289). Obviously a general social-psychological analysis, such as proposed by Stark, allows for a subclass of fundamentalists who lay claim to a divine revelation contained within a sacred text. Revelation is intratextual for fundamentalists. However, as Stark also notes, it is a general social-psychological axiom that as religions become successful, they attempt to curtail new or novel revelations. What makes fundamentalism unique is that the revelation—in terms of the authored text itself—is complete and final, and can be used to invalidate any claim to new or novel revelations. Novel revelations, if successful, would result in their own sacred texts. As Stark (1999) notes, successful new sacred texts often build upon previous ones; Christianity extends the Jewish texts, as the Quran clarifies the Christian text. However, it is only when this sacred text emerges and is understood as sufficient in itself, and as the ultimate criterion of truth, that fundamentalism emerges—not as a religion, but as a way or process of being religious within a given faith tradition. Thus fundamentalist Muslims do not read the Bible, nor do fundamentalist Jews read the New Testament.

Stereotype 3: "Fundamentalists Are Militant."

Although fundamentalism may be a latent potential within all faith traditions, the consensus of historians is that it emerges "first and foremost" as a defensive reaction to forces of modernity (Nielsen, 1993, p. 3). As Marty and Appleby (1992) have noted, fundamentalism is a "religious way of being that manifests itself as a strategy by which beleaguered believers attempt to preserve their distinctive identity as a people or group" (p. 34). This description is useful, as it suggests that social scientists ought to focus on how fundamentalists try to preserve a distinctive identity and way of life in the face of opposition. Without opposition, fundamentalism simply does not emerge as a self-reflective movement. However, it is misleading to suggest that fundamentalists must defend themselves militantly against opposition. Indeed, if there is a misleading claim that dominates the literature on fundamentalism, it is not that they have a faith to defend, but that fundamentalists are mired in malice and are militant in their defense of their faith (Kepel, 1991/1994; Marsden, 1971, 1990; Marty & Appleby, 1991). In the Western popular press, fundamentalist Islam is tagged not simply as "militant," but as "terrorist." However, as Kressel (1996) cautions in his study of Muslim extremists in New York, "The fundamentalist, or revivalist, strand of Islam itself constitutes a multitude of ideologies which differ significantly in their level of militancy" (p. 54). Likewise, insofar as there is a relationship between terrorism and religion, it is complex and is not restricted to fundamentalists (Juergensmeyer, 2003). Not all terrorists are fundamentalists, and few fundamentalists are terrorists. But because it does not include militancy as a necessary criterion of fundamentalism, our model permits the empirical study of the conditions under which some fundamentalisms become militant.

Many scholars have argued that an essential defining criterion of fundamentalism is some degree of militant opposition to modernity. The "User's Guide" to the Fundamentalism Project (Marty & Appleby, 1991) states: "It is no insult to fundamentalists to see them as militant, whether in the use of words and ideas, or ballots or, in extreme cases, bullets" (p. ix). Perhaps this is true for some fundamentalist groups, but for others it is offensive. It is partly why sympathetic scholars such as Packer (1958, p. 8) reject the label "fundamentalism" as a prejudicial term. "Evangelicalism" is the label most Christians would prefer over "fundamentalism"; it is more tempered and restrained in its defense of the means and methods used in safeguarding their religious identity and lifestyle against opposition from the modern culture. Boone (1989, p. 8) observes that among self-identified evangelicals, "fundamentalism" is a term of derision, connoting "extremism." It is but a short step from "extremism" to "fanaticism" and to a definition that serves not only to caricaturize and stereotype a group, but also to suggest that its members are in need of special psychological or sociological explanation (Hood, 1983).

Although it is true that some fundamentalists may be militant, it ought not to be their defining characteristic, lest we foreclose the interesting empirical issue of exploring under what conditions they may or may not be militant. It has become popular to note that "fundamentalists are evangelicals with an attitude" or that "evangelicals are fundamentalists with manners," but whatever truth there may be in such quips, it is not one that ought to define a difference between these groups. As Ammerman (1987) has noted, it seems easy to recognize that Fuller Theological Seminary is "evangelical" while Bob Jones University is "fundamentalist," and that Jerry Falwell is a "fundamentalist" while Billy Graham is an "evangelical." However, precisely why this distinction is made is more complex than much of the literature now accepts.[9] Indeed, as Ammerman (1987) has observed, "Fundamentalists simply do not accept either the cultural pluralism or the institutional differentiation that have come to be assumed in the modern world" (p. 3).

However, this rejection of cultural pluralism can take a variety of forms and need not be militant. As we have observed in Chapter 6, some fundamentalists, such as the Amish, quietly separate themselves and ask only to be left alone. Interesting empirical studies can focus on the conditions under which fundamentalists may or may not become militant in the defense of their faith, but only if militancy is not included as a necessary defining criterion of fundamentalism. Hofstadter (1962), in his general discussion of anti-intellectualism in American life, reminds us that "There are both serene and militant fundamentalists; and it is hard to say which group is the more numerous" (p. 118). This is partly due to the obvious fact that few social scientists have even identified "serene" fundamentalists, given their unfortunate confounding of fundamentalism with militancy. Our inclusion of the Amish in this book was partly motivated by the desire to look at "serene" rather than "militant" fundamentalists.

Rejecting militancy as a defining criterion of fundamentalism places us in opposition to many scholars who have made significant contributions to the study of various fundamentalisms—but, ironically, only to those whose idea of militancy has come to characterize fundamentalisms in the popular culture. Hofstadter's (1962) "serene" fundamentalists remain unstudied. However, as we have observed, they do exist; along with their more militant brothers and sisters, they continue to reject the cultural pluralism that so many modernists and postmodernists applaud.

Stereotype 4: "Fundamentalism Is Not Modern."

Although the roots of fundamentalism are deep, its Protestant flowering in the 20th century was a defensive reaction to many of the tenets of modernism, as we have noted in Chapter 3. Ironically, fundamentalism is a modern expression of antimodern views.[10] Fundamentalism emerges as a defensive reaction to what modernity (and now, even postmodernity) claims as its own enlightenment. We think that any model of fundamentalism must account for the defensive nature of fundamentalism without making the prejudicial assumption that what is being opposed is "better" or "more true." If modernism is conceptualized to include such notions as change—defined in terms of "progress," the favoring of pluralism over monism, the elevation of quantity over quality, and the encouragement of individual autonomy based on reason (Lawrence, 1989, p. 57)—then fundamentalists are modern without being modernists. It is modernity that modern fundamentalists oppose, and in turn, it is fundamentalism that modernity opposes.

As Harding (2000, p. 270) has noted, fundamentalists are among those whose rejection help give "shape and substance" to modernity. Fundamentalists both represent and enact what modernity is not. Thus they actually help produce modernity and maintain its distinctiveness as modernity claims to make "progress" toward a more appropriate understanding of reality. One of the ironies is that as fundamentalists reject cultural pluralism, they are dependent upon this pluralism for their acceptance as a subgroup within the larger culture. The Amish are a successful example of such accommodation, whereas the serpent handlers are less so. The same culture that interpreted the law to defend the Amish lifestyle interpreted the law to oppose that of the serpent handlers of Appalachia. Thus, as Lechner (1998, p. 200) notes, the future of fundamentalism (we would add, in the West) is intimately linked with the future of liberal modernity. Both Boone (1989) and Harding (2000) remind us that fundamentalists and modernists both recognize the distinctiveness of the clash between modernity and its opponents. Even pejorative terms, such as "the Bible belt" or "Bible bangers" for Protestant fundamentalism, indicate that in some cases a single text defines reality and identifies for modernists and fundamentalists alike what divides them and makes each camp possible. Fundamentalists, like many scientists, are universalists. Each identifies a process that elevates understanding above mere historical and cultural contingencies. However, whereas the scientists applaud a single *method* (the scientific method), the fundamentalists elevate a single *text*. For the latter, the text itself is what structures reality and informs its readers, via the principle of intratextuality. Accordingly, it is a mistake to think that fundamentalists lack a methodology for understanding textual reality as some have suggested (e.g., Tracey, 1978). Boone (1989, p. 13) has rightly observed that to understand fundamentalists, one cannot simply read their text; one must read their text *with* them as they read it. We agree and have presented a model that requires the reader to enter into the text, not simply to explore the text from without.

Although we have identified the sense in which fundamentalists are modern in their rejection of modernity, Latour (1993) has appropriately observed that "we are not modern" is a response defiantly asserted by those fundamentalists who refuse to see themselves in the discourse of a modernity that has created caricatures of others not conducive to its agenda. Thus, as Harding (2000, p. 270) notes, "peasants" are created from those who reject industrial and corporate agriculture, and "tribes" and "ethnic groups" are created from those who do not participate in national polities. Likewise, believers in a single text as the revealed word of God become for the first time "fundamentalists." The irony is that fundamentalists are in fact always modern while in distinct opposition to modernity (Latour, 1993; Lawrence, 1989; Harding, 2000).

Stereotype 5: "Fundamentalism is an American Protestant Religious Phenomenon."

Among contemporary scholars, Ammerman (1987) has argued that much of the research on fundamentalism has tended to confuse characteristics of the host culture with those of fundamentalism. Likewise, Hood (1983) has elsewhere argued that many of the characteristics assumed to describe fundamentalism are purely contingent characteristics of the subcultures in which fundamentalists are dominant. Thus the demographic characteristics of fundamentalists are less useful in distinguishing them than descriptions of their participation in an all-encompassing social and ideological world (Ammerman, 1987, p. 39). Lawrence (1989) has gone so far as to claim that "Fundamentalism is an ideology rather than a theology" (p. x).

Viewing fundamentalism as an ideology does not mean that we must focus only on the content of fundamentalist beliefs. Not only is fundamentalism a viable system of belief (i.e., ideology), but the process of believing, rather than the personality of the believer or the content of belief, may be what is crucial.[11] Moving the study of fundamentalism away from a focus on belief content to a focus on the process of believing is part of what we think is needed. As Marty and Appleby (1992) have noted, "Like traditionalists and orthodox people, moderates and liberals, fundamentalists come in many personality styles and wear many guises" (p. 10). Fundamentalists are distinct enough in their own right that the criteria by which we define them are the only necessary criteria for distinguishing them from others. Fundamentalists may be wrong, but if so, the criteria of truth by which their error is revealed cannot be assumed nonproblematically. Fundamentalist scholars have made significant contributions to many fields, including that of Biblical studies. As one prominent Biblical scholar—clearly *not* committed to fundamentalism— has nevertheless observed, "the particular drives and interests of fundamentalist scholarship have at times led it to discern and identify things that no one else would have noticed or evaluated properly" (Barr, 1983, p. 113).

As noted above, to deny fundamentalism its modern nature is to stereotype it, as well as to restrict it to its American Protestant expression. Fundamentalism is a possibility in any modern culture; it is not a possibility in premodern cultures. Lawrence (1989) has properly observed that there are no premodern fundamentalists. Although it emerged first in America in its Protestant form, it emerged and can emerge in other cultures, relative to their rates of modernization. Fundamentalism can be as global as modernity is. As Gritsch (1982) has noted, the emergence of fundamentalism is a worldly phenomenon. It thus is decidedly not simply a Protestant movement, but, in Lawrence's (1989) terms, is "cross-creedal and multicultural" (p. 3).

Stereotype 6: "Fundamentalists Are Authoritarian and/or Dogmatic."

In the Introduction, we have briefly noted that efforts to identify a distinctive personality type associated with fundamentalism have often been proclaimed, but cannot stand up to close scrutiny. Over 30 years have passed since Stark (1971) noted that social scientists have a tendency to accept as true those assumptions that are congruent with their prejudices: "The widespread belief that there is a strong relationship between religious orthodoxy and authoritarianism appears to be a prominent instance of this tendency to transform suspicions and speculations into certainties" (p. 172). Given that most measures of fundamentalism are belief-oriented, "orthodoxy" is often a synonym for "fundamentalism" in empirical studies (Altemeyer, 1988; Gorsuch & Aleshire, 1974; Gregory, 1957), and thus Stark's (1971) criticism applies doubly. Neither orthodoxy nor fundamentalism is inherently authoritarian in the sense that psychologists suggest.[12] We have noted in the Introduction that the shift to right-wing authoritarianism (RWA) in the work of Altemeyer removed the psychodynamic assumptions of classical authoritarian personality research and focused instead upon socialization as a determinant of RWA. Altemeyer (1988) attempted to bypass the charge of political bias in classic authoritarian personality research "by *defining* his scale as a measure of *right-wing* authoritarianism" (Kressel, 1996, p. 225; emphases in original). Kressel goes on to say that Altemeyer "clearly prefers not only low-RWAs, but more generally, liberals, both politically and conservative" (p. 225). Ironically, the earliest authoritarian personality research was conducted in Germany by a Nazi scientist, E. R. Jaensch. He identified two character types as early as 1938. His focus upon character rather than personality emphasizes the continual value connotations that have plagued this research. However, unlike Altemeyer, Jaensch found the fatal flaw not in those types predisposed to accept Fascism who exhibited unwavering convictions with absolute certainty, but rather in those types who were less certain, easily swayed, and more open to experience and prone to accept democracy (see Brown, 1965, pp. 477–479; Kressel, 1996, p. 216). Scientists may have their preferences, but to claim that fundamentalists are necessarily conservative or "right-wing" is empirically unwarranted (Wuthnow, 1973). As conceived by Altemeyer, RWA and fundamentalism are not two independent phenomena but one construct, so that correlations (typically .70 to .80) between measures of RWA and fundamentalism are essentially reliability indices of two measures of the same construct (see Spilka et al., 2003, pp. 467–479).

However, efforts to find distinctive personality precursors of political or religious ideology have not succeeded. As much as some researchers might like to obtain such findings, neither the perpetrators of mass hatred (Kressel, 1996, pp. 211–246) nor people who carry out genocide (Waller, 2002, pp. 5–87) yield distinctive personality correlates, pathological or otherwise.

A "fundamentalist authoritarian personality," whether classic or RWA, is unsupported by the evidence despite these two distinctive research traditions. Perhaps the final blow to the claim of a distinctive authoritarian personality came from Browder's (1996) study. Using actual personnel files of 526 men who joined the German SS security service in the period 1932–1934, and examining sociocultural factors supposedly predictive of an authoritarian personality, Browder found that SS volunteers were *less* likely to have the precursors of an authoritarian personality than the general population. Browder's data are especially valuable, as they included virtually all SS officers and 62% of the total SS membership by 1934—all volunteers. When suspicions and speculations are turned into certainties, we have stereotyping, not knowledge. Social scientists are no exceptions to this rule.

Ironically, we view Rokeach's effort to develop a content-free measure of dogmatism—one that would permit the identification of an authoritarianism of the "left" as well as of the "right"—as a step in the right direction. A partial precursor of our intratextual model was suggested by Rokeach (1960) in his focus upon the process rather than the content of belief, and by Kirkpatrick et al. (1991) with a focus upon "centralized" beliefs as a less pejorative term than "dogmatic" within

Rokeach's theory. However, the inclusion of belief content items in Rokeach's Dogmatism Scale makes his measure inappropriate to separate the process of belief from the content of belief (i.e., orthodoxy). Here is one of those rare instances in the psychology of religion where a new scale is needed (see Hill & Hood, 1999). Nevertheless, even with inclusion of belief content items (indicative of orthodoxy), the relationship between dogmatism and fundamentalism is at best "weak" (Paloutzian, 1996, p. 243). We suggest that with the exclusion of belief content items, it is nonexistent.

It has been over five decades since Adorno (1951) offered the seductive metaphor of the "bicycle personality." However quaint the image of a person who bows from above but kicks from below, the simple fact is that an unbiased review of the empirical literature does not support this metaphor as a valid generalization about fundamentalists (Bruce, 2000; Kirkpatrick et al., 1991; Stark, 1971). Some fundamentalists do "kick back," but this results more often from proper frustration about modern and postmodern treatments of their beliefs, and less often from pathological tendencies presumed to be associated with adherence to such beliefs.

Our model notes that any submission to an authoritative text is not a general personality trait, even less one linked to a general trait of authoritarian aggression. The relationship must be placed within a specific cultural and historical context to be properly empirically explored. As one example, the submission of serpent handlers to their text has led them on more than one occasion to persist in handling even in the face of legal opposition (Hood & Kimbrough, 1995).

Stereotype 7: "Fundamentalism Requires a Special Explanation."

If fundamentalists are opposed by those committed to modernity, it is not necessary to assume that they are in some sense deficient in their own opposition to modernity. If Gilkey (1969, p. 39) has correctly identified the characteristics of modernity (or a "secular spirit") to include a commitment to contingency, relativity, temporality, and autonomy, then he reminds us of what fundamentalists oppose. Even the more conservative historians of fundamentalism properly understand this "secular spirit." This spirit is what their sacred text denies; thus one must either adjust one's reading of the text in light of this secular spirit, or use the text to oppose the secular spirit itself. It is only this opposition that identifies the fundamentalists within any faith tradition.

Furthermore, to describe this opposition is to offer an adequate explanation of fundamentalism. We need not assume that additional explanations are needed. This is because fundamentalist historians have *correctly identified* the tenets valued by a more liberal faith tradition; these include adjusting beliefs to new scientific advances, maintaining an open-minded tolerance for any sincere devotion to truth, holding a skeptical stance toward any claim of possessing absolute truth, and emphasizing experience over doctrine (Dollar, 1973, pp. 12–13). Fundamentalists' rejection of such values simply identifies conflicting paradigms that allow tensions to exist between what are otherwise incommensurable systems.[13] Part of our task is to understand fundamentalists' opposition to what appear to many others as obvious beliefs that positively characterize modernity and determine appropriate responses to reality (Berman, 1982).

If we are to understand fundamentalists and their opposition to modernity, it may be useful to note once more modernists' intense opposition to postmodern perspectives. While we need not delve into the nuances of postmodern thought, we can note that the refusal to accept grand metanarratives or any foundational claims to truth seems as disturbing to modernists as modernity seems to fundamentalists! How modernists feel about the idea that the achievements of the Enlightenment could be challenged by postmodern thought should suggest to them how fundamentalists feel about what they perceive as an attack upon their world.[14] In this sense, perhaps all of us can share in Schneidau's (1976) warning: "We might do well to ask if the bulk of modern [and postmodern] discourse which assumes its own enlightenment has not compounded hubris with complacency" (p. 106).

All these concerns behoove us to be empathic enough with fundamentalists to understand not only their fears and opposition to much of what others cherish, but perhaps also to allow the possibility that their refusal to grant legitimacy to either modernist or postmodernist thought is well founded in a structure in which belief is not only possible, but also liberating. As Ammerman (1987) concluded, "As long as there are people who find the world to be chaotic, there will be some who refuse to grant it legitimacy" (p. 212). Fundamentalists are such people, and their refusal is textually based and hence has a rationality that psychologists can describe. The model we have proposed is thus descriptive and not explanatory, insofar as an adequate description is itself at least the beginning of an adequate explanation.

If what we are claiming rings harshly upon the ear, it is partly because fundamentalists are often studied, but seldom study others or are allowed to have their own voice. In response to their own rhetorical question—"Why not have fundamentalists write chapters?"—the directors of the Fundamentalism Project replied, "There is no prescription against such an endeavor, but the scholars commended to us, people with coordinating skills and willingness to see each fundamentalism in the context of others, were not such fundamentalists" (Marty & Appleby, 1991, p. x). The dominant assumption that appears to guide most scholars who study fundamentalism has been well summarized by Bruce (2000):

> The temptation then is to take our analysis—the world as seen by the sort of people who study fundamentalists—as correct and suppose the fundamentalist vision so mistaken as to require an explanation quite different from the ones we would apply to ourselves. (p. 115)

However, if we apply the same criteria to fundamentalists that we would apply to ourselves, we will find that the view of fundamentalists as deficient—whether in terms of intellect, insight, or psychological health—is unwarranted. The assumption that fundamentalism needs an explanation other than one we would apply to our own beliefs is not only pejorative, but pernicious in its distortion of a proper understanding. It may be that, as Bruce (2000) suggests, "We do not need an explanation of fundamentalism as such" (p. 118). The proper question to ask is not whether fundamentalists think as we do, but whether their reasoning fits within the structure and process of their own assumptions (Bruce, 2000, pp. 115–116). This does not mean that we must accept fundamentalist beliefs as our own. It simply means that we must respect fundamentalist beliefs as logical and rational options within the total spectrum of religious alternatives—as logical and rational as extremely liberal religious beliefs are. Part of this requires an understanding of the structure and process of fundamentalist thought that not only rationalizes its way of life, but also makes fundamentalist beliefs believable.[15]

Globally, fundamentalism often stands in opposition to secular nationalist policies. As Lawrence (1989) observes, "Among the custodians of institutional religion, only fundamentalists have intuited the high stakes in this protracted struggle" (p. 84). The fundamentalist rejection of modern and postmodern worldviews is intratextually based and cannot be dismissed as either naïve or extreme (Boone, 1989, p. 44). The task of understanding fundamentalists is a challenge, especially for those whose own views are so opposed to those of various fundamentalisms. If Kressel (1996) has made the case for refusing to pathologize those who participated in the Holocaust, and Waller (2002) has made the same case for those more recently involved in the global rise of terrorism and mass hatred, then we would do well to heed the warning of Strozier (1994): "The challenge of talking with fundamentalists is to locate the appropriate meanings of whatever divisions exist, without ever describing their lives as pathological" (p. 45). To those distant from the faith, the assumptions long held—that education, faith development, psychological maturity, or social advancement would allow the obituary of fundamentalism to be written—is no longer tenable (Warner, 1979). It has been almost a quarter of a century since Marsden (1983) suggested that both "theory and wish converged" on the part of scholars to suggest that fundamentalism would "wither in the bright sun of modern culture" (p. 150). However, the scholars were proven wrong. If anything, the light of modern cultures has revealed fundamentalisms in places where many would least expect them. It is true that fundamentalists remain a minority in every tradition (Marty & Appleby, 1992, p. 5)—indeed, so much so that some self-identified fundamentalist scholars have argued that fundamentalism is dead within religious bodies and will never rise again (Dollar, 1973, p. 86). However, we contend that Dollar's obituary for fundamentalism is premature. Part of the confusion is that fundamentalists are often more silent than many suspect, and that this powerful "latent fundamentalism" can rise to the surface when inherent foundational beliefs are threatened (Gasper, 1963, p. 2). Foundational beliefs are those that are normative for life (Hood, 1995). They not only indicate what is the case, but also what ought to be done—what is "right." In this sense, fundamentalist beliefs are normative for particular forms of life.

Fundamentalists defend their forms of life as much as they defend their beliefs. For some, the defense is an attack on the larger host culture; for others, it is more individualistic, in that it seeks to separate or isolate true believers from the host culture. Nielsen (1993, pp. 12–13) has referred to these as the "two thrusts" of fundamentalism. However, for now it is sufficient to note that both "thrusts" of fundamentalism are based on a defense of a sacred text that has an identifiable structure. The structure emerges to offset the threats that modern and postmodern forms of interpretation and expression pose. Ultimately, the movement away from fundamentalism demands either a pure humanism (Gasper, 1963) or a pure naturalism (Loetscher, 1954). To strip religious fundamentalism of its supernaturalism (to put it in Protestant terms) is to lose not simply the battle but the Book, and not simply the religious structure but the Scripture (Dollar, 1973, p. 86). The antithesis of fundamentalism is a radical secularity, insofar as it admits no alternative to naturalistic explanations—not only for physical reality, but also for psychology, culture, and history (Henry, 1979, p. 135). In this sense, Loetscher (1954) is correct when he observed that "Fundamentalism emerges to oppose not simply liberalism, but the naturalism seen lurking behind it" (p. 91).

QUASI-FUNDAMENTALISM: NONRELIGIOUS EXAMPLES

There are parallels to fundamentalism that, while not strictly religious, are nevertheless worth acknowledging. The parallels include what Greil (1993) has called "quasi-religions"—groups such as Alcoholics Anonymous, Synanon, and Scientology. These groups claim not to be religions in a more formal sense, but they seem to have many of the structures of religious organizations and function in many of the same ways as churches, synagogues, and mosques, on what Greil (1994) calls the "boundaries of the sacred." We might identify as "quasi-fundamentalists" those with beliefs in a variety of contexts that appeal to more literal interpretations of authoritative texts, even when such texts endorse naturalism.

Wulff (1997, p. 635), in summarizing the current status of views in the psychology of religion, uses a fourfold classification based upon the inclusion or exclusion of the transcendent and upon literal versus symbolic means of interpretation. He rightly places fundamentalism in the quadrant that includes the transcendent (God, for Protestant fundamentalists) and acknowledges literal interpretation—not simply in terms of a text, but in the sense of literal affirmation of the reality the text affirms. He relies heavily upon James Barr (1977), who has rightly noted that Protestant fundamentalists reject any assertion that Biblical stories are myths whose meaning is symbolic.

Wulff's (1997) typology places what we refer to as "quasi-fundamentalism" in another quadrant. This one contains social-scientific theories that are themselves committed to a literalism but reject any claims to transcendence (God). Wulff includes sociobiology and classical behaviorism in this quadrant. If religious fundamentalism is characterized by "literal affirmation," then what we call "quasi-fundamentalism" Wulff identifies by the phrase "literal disaffirmation" (p. 635). The comparisons are useful, because both forms of literalism demand that the reality expressed in their texts, whether revealed or authoritatively written by theoretically oriented scientists, are the objective bases by which reality is ultimately understood. Literal disaffirmation denies the God that literal affirmation affirms, but within a methodological mirror that defines their common literalism. Johnson (1996) similarly notes how objective claims to literal truths mirror each other in the act of mutual refutation. As he says, "In the end the 'myth of Christian origins' turns out to have, in many respects, at least the same measure of historical plausibility as the theories that have been generated to replace it" (pp. 103–104).

Even more telling is perhaps the closest textual parallel in the Western world to religious fundamentalism. The U.S. Constitution has been compared to the Bible, especially by those students of the Constitution who can be identified as "strict constructionists" (Crapanzano, 2000). The comparison is not in terms of a sacred text, but rather in terms of the proper role of individuals charged with interpreting the text. Strict constructionists are quasi-fundamentalists, in that they believe the Constitution is to be interpreted in terms of original intent. That is, judges are restricted to explicating the reasonably plain intent of the framers. Of course, what makes strict constructionists is again, to use Wulff's (1997) terms above, their "literal affirmation" of the meaning of the text. Unlike a sacred text, the Constitution can be changed. Indeed, it has been, but the principle of literal affirmation applies to the changes as well. Justice Hugo Black (1969) specifically linked his view of the U.S. Constitution to issues of religious faith. In his book *A Constitutional Faith*, he referred to the Constitution as his "legal bible" and stated, "I cherish every word of it, from first to last, and I personally deplore even the slightest deviation from its least important commands" (Black, 1969, p. 66). Crapanzano (2000) has explicitly compared the literalism of religious fundamentalists with that of strict-constructionist constitutional lawyers, and finds little to support the possibility of interpretation in terms of original intent. He finds the religious fundamentalism of the pulpit and the quasi-religious fundamentalism of the bench equally untenable. He quotes one of the most conservative members of the current U.S. Supreme Court, Antonin Scalia, whose strict-constructionist orientation is easily identified with the way in which religious fundamentalists approach their text: "A text should be construed strictly, and it should not be construed leniently; it should be construed reasonably, to contain all that it fairly means" (Scalia, quoted in Crapanzano, 2000, p. 255). Crapanzano goes on to explore the difficulty in identifying a reasonably clear meaning for any text. This is to be expected, given that Crapanzano's approach is thoroughly intertextual. Compare this perspective to that of a conservative constitutional lawyer whose nomination to the Supreme Court was rejected: Robert Bork. Referring to a more intratextual approach, he states,

> Attempts to frame theories that remove from democratic control areas of life our nation's Founders intended to place there can achieve power only if abstractions are regarded as legitimately able to displace the Constitution's text and structure and the history that gives our legal right, rootedness, and meaning. (Bork, 1990, p. 353)

To refer back to Wulff's (1997) four-quadrant model of views of religion, literalism is offset by symbolic views that can either include or exclude the transcendent. Although we do not wish to confront these options here, it is sufficient to note that many schools of psychology demand an other-than-literal interpretation of transcendence in an act of restorative interpretation, if the reality of transcendence is acknowledged, or of reductive interpretation, if the reality of transcendence is denied (Wulff, 1997, p. 635). These symbolic rather than literal models are inherently intertextual, as they impose upon a text knowledge derived from other texts claimed to be inherently superior and hence genuinely "explanatory." This is another version of the fundamentalist–modernist controversy whose history we have discussed in Chapter 3.

Sorenson (2004) has noted that certain schools of psychoanalysis function as quasi-fundamentalist groups. He cites Hamilton's (1996) interview of prominent psychoanalysts in North America and Europe. Hamilton noted that Kleinians and self psychologists, while holding radically different views on substantive issues, tended to associate with their own group and to quote only from the literature of their group. Sorenson speculates that these groups behave in fundamentalist ways, out of a sense that their knowledge is partial and provisional. Thus some schools of psychoanalysis are quasi-fundamentalist. Sorenson speculates that these schools function, as do all fundamentalisms, to defensively create a system of meaning: "In the face of uncertainty, one recourse is toward certitude, to know beyond doubt, to be part of a group that knows, for which outsiders are in error and need not be read except as illustrations of false steps" (2004, p. 9). We are less sure than Sorenson of the motivations for being fundamentalist, and suggest that the certitude of fundamentalism is less fixed than suggested. What fundamentalists are most sure of is where to *search for significance*, and that is in their sacred text.

Sorenson (2004, pp. 1–11) utilized multidimensional scaling to assess the citation of over 900 authors in the three major journals devoted to three distinct schools of psychoanalysis over a 10-year period (1991–2000). Following Hamilton's work, he compared the author citations in journals of what, in terms of our model, are two largely intratextual schools (Kohutians, or self psychologists, and Kleinians) and one intertextual school (relational psychoanalysis). As predicted, Kohutians tended to cite a limited circle of self psychologists, primarily Kohut and Stolorow. Kleinians cited Klein and other Kleinians, such as Bion. The more "open" relational psychoanalysts cited a wider range of theorists, including ones who were or are not relational psychoanalysts. The conceptual maps of the quasi-fundamentalist schools (Kleinians and self psychologists) each conformed more closely to an intratextual model, and Sorenson claims that this perhaps contributed to the sociological cohesiveness of these schools as revealed by Hamilton in her interviews.

Relational psychoanalysis is intertextual, consistent with the intent of this school. Its adherents cite a wider range of theorists. However, despite identifying himself as a relational psychoanalyst, Sorenson acknowledges that intratextual schools of the quasi-fundamentalist analytical schools (as we have argued for intratextual religious fundamentalisms) "are dynamic, vibrant traditions that continue to grow and change in ways that those outside the tradition are prone to underestimate" (Sorenson, 2004, p. 10). Sorenson's own text is a marvelous example of intratextuality, as he writes as a "clinical psychoanalyst to clinical psychoanalysts" (2004, p. 1).

Sorenson's methodology can be applied directly to religious fundamentalists. One could use their literature or even sermons to see the extent to which they cite specific scriptural as opposed to nonscriptural sources. In this sense, it is meaningful to talk about the "degree of fundamentalism" of any religious group, to the extent to which it exclusively cites its own sacred text.

As we have seen, both fundamentalist Islam and Christianity note that for parts of their sacred texts, meanings are clear and straightforward. The meanings are intratextually sufficient and understandable to each believer. In other instances, interpretations are more problematic—but not so much so that reasonable agreement cannot be achieved. As Veling (1996) notes, communities of faith struggle to implement and live their understandings. To accuse fundamentalists of anti-intellectualism has its legitimacy, but not to the extent that other sources or texts cannot be consulted. However, they must be compatible with the sacred text as the ultimate arbitrator of meaning. We can do no better than to quote a saint of a church not usually identified with fundamentalism, St. Thomas Aquinas, on this matter:

> Holy teaching can borrow from the other sciences, not from any need to beg from them, but for the greater clarification of the things it conveys. For it takes its principles directly from God through revelation, not from other sciences. On that account it does not rely on them as though they were in control, for their role is subsidiary and ancillary; so an architect makes use of tradesmen as a statesman employs soldiers. That it turns to them so is not from any lack or insufficiency within itself, but because our understanding is wanting, which is the more readily guided into the world above reason, set forth in holy teaching, through the world of natural reason from which the other sciences take their course. (Aquinas, 1964, 1.1a, 1.5)

FUNDAMENTALISM AND DEATH

Finally, it is imperative to note that fundamentalism is a form of religious life judged by the text it affirms, not necessarily by more "worldly" criteria. Ultimately, in every fundamentalism is the sense of transcendence—not simply as a relationship to something larger than the self, but as some form of eternal life (Hood & Morris, 1983). Hence, in a curious turn of logic, fundamentalists are the ultimate empiricists. Their focus is upon some form of eternal life that transcends secular scientific views of personal death. The fact that the evidence for disembodied minds is meager is not the same as the claim that bodily resurrection is possible. Recent fundamentalist defenses in opposition to the conclusion of the Jesus Seminar (in which intertextually based scholars sought once again for what can be authoritatively known about the historical Jesus; Miller, 1999) affirm an intratextual interpretation of the Bible in a fashion reminiscent of *The Fundamentals*—the essays that gave Protestant fundamentalism its name (see Johnson, 1996). Intertextual analyses deny the bodily resurrection of Jesus as much as they affirm the reality of a purely secular death for us all. In Becker's (1973) sense, secular scientists recognize Christian fundamentalism as a form of "the denial of death." We need not explore the obvious—that fundamentalists' sacred texts plainly affirm the opposite—but can pause to note that even sophisticated secular philosophical defenses of an immaterial self are available (Foster, 1991). The fact that some form of eternal life is promised in fundamentalist readings of both the Bible and the Quran raise an interesting issue for those committed to some version of a falsificationist perspective on scientific claims. As Blose (1981) has noted, survival of bodily death is a hypothesis that is ultimately empirically testable, and as all fundamentalists are likely to note, testing it is an experiment we all must undergo. However, the irony is, as Blose correctly notes, that the test is asymmetrical— "allowing its truth, should it be true, but not its falsity, should it be false, to be learnt" (Blose, 1981, p. 59). This is yet another way of saying that for fundamentalists, the stakes are high and the intratextual criteria demanding. Yet the tenets of their faith can be learned, known, and accepted.

Fundamentalism constitutes not only a form of life but also a promise of another life, which informs all that fundamentalists do. This may explain the empirical link between fundamentalism and optimism in both Protestantism and Islam (Sethi & Seligman, 1993). If the empirical evidence for transcending death is asymmetrical, the evidence for the belief in some form of eternal life is not based upon an intratextual perspective. If fundamentalists are accused of not avoiding the Scylla of literalism (which we have shown to be a false accusation), they have surely avoided the Charybdis of the extreme postmodern claim, in which a text convinces one that words have no meaning. Although much remains to be done to provide a psychological understanding of fundamentalism, the beginning must be intratextually based, so that fundamentalists can recognize themselves to be fairly described—even by those outsiders purporting to offer an intertextual explanation of their thought and form of life that is somehow more adequate than the one fundamentalists provide for themselves.

Epilogue

The terrible danger for our time consists in the fact that
ours is a cut-flower civilization. Beautiful as cut flowers
may be, and much as we may use our ingenuity to keep
them looking fresh for a while, they will eventually die
because they are severed from their sustaining roots.
—TRUEBLOOD (1944, pp. 59–60)

Our intratextual model is intended to illuminate the rich tapes-
try that is fundamentalism in its various forms in the contemporary
world. Despite the stereotypes they have often adopted (and even perpe-
trated), social scientists have contributed to a greater appreciation of
some empirical aspects of this form of religious expression. For instance,
regression analyses show separate effects for measures of fundamentalism (as a belief process) versus measures of orthodoxy (as belief content). However, the effects of fundamentalism are usually negative. Fundamentalists are found to be more prejudiced than the orthodox, for
example (Kirkpatrick, 1993). However, these are typical studies done
with a selection of undergraduate psychology students, and with measures of both fundamentalism and right-wing authoritarianism that are
ideologically biased (Watson et al., 2003).

George Gallup, Jr., has painted a different picture of fundamentalists. Gallup and Jones (1992) set out to find Americans for whom "God
is a vibrant reality" (p. 11). The Gallup organization worked closely
with religious leaders and social scientists to develop a measure of what
Pope John Paul II has referred to as "hidden saints." The Gallup organization used appropriate sampling techniques and identified a minority of
Americans who either agreed or strongly agreed with all 12 items on the
survey. Included were items such as "I believe in the full authority of the
Bible," and "I try hard to put my religious beliefs into practice in all my
relations with all people regardless of their backgrounds. (People an-

swered on a 6-point scale from "strongly agree" to "strongly disagree"; a "don't know" option was also included.) According to these criteria, 13% of the sample were identified as "saints." This extrapolates to 24 million Americans, out of a total population of 182 million at the time of the survey (Gallup & Jones, 1992, p. 15). The facts that these American Christian "saints" exhibit compassion and forgiveness, and that they find joy and meaning in their lives, are not as important in the present context as the fact that they find this meaning through an intratextual understanding of the Bible. As one saint said after he had bought a Bible and began to read, "Page after page unfolded God's truth" (Gallup & Jones, 1992, 49).

We mention this survey only to note what for many social scientists is counterintuitive. The survey's data paint a radically different picture of fundamentalists from those derived from measurement studies employing undergraduate psychology students. Gallup's data indicate that a saint is more likely to be female than male, and to be nonwhite than white. The saint is probably over 50, with less than a high school education. She lives in the South. As Gallup and Jones (1992) note, "A poor, black, Southern woman is more likely to be a saint among us than an American not sharing these characteristics" (p. 98). Compared to the average American, the saints are happier, less prejudiced, more honest, and more altruistic—and although they personally follow a strict moral code, they are also more forgiving. If we take only the most extreme scorers on the 12 survey items (those who answered "strongly agree" to all items), what holds for the saints holds even more strongly for these "super saints" (Gallup & Jones, 1992, p. 41).

Although we do not uncritically endorse these survey data, they do add another dimension that needs to be considered by researchers whose work suggests the opposite. Fundamentalism has been effectively stereotyped by the predominant use of ideologically biased measurements and correlational methodologies in the empirical literature (Watson et al., 2003). The use of historical and hermeneutical approaches, in addition to traditional empirical methods, is essential. In a major project now underway, Heinz and his colleagues are using intensive interview methods to compare those who "deconvert" from fundamentalist religions with those who stay within the same fundamentalist religions, in both Germany and America (Strieb & Keller, in press). Preliminary findings suggest that for persons with various faith development styles, maintaining a fundamentalist faith can provide security and meaning in what is for many a very troublesome world. For some, fundamentalist faith becomes problematic, but even those who leave fundamentalist communities leave a life that many others still perceive as meaningful (Taslimi, Hood, & Watson, 1991).

Some readers may criticize us for defending fundamentalism, including the extreme forms of it that are more difficult to justify. Our purpose in this book has not been to defend fundamentalism as much as it has been to critique the efforts of some scholars outside fundamentalism who are quick to assume that nothing good can come of it. We recognize that fundamentalism, like any worldview or schema, varies by degree and contains both healthy and unhealthy elements. However, given that religion itself can serve as a psychological framework for understanding life and personal experience, what we have proposed in this book is a unique model that attempts to offer insight into the meaning of the fundamentalist worldview. If the readers (like ourselves) are not fundamentalists, then we will have achieved at least one aim of this text if in fact they can begin to understand fundamentalism of any type from within the parameters of the tradition's own sacred text—in a single word, *intratextually*.

Notes

CHAPTER ONE

1. Biblical passages throughout this book are taken from what many fundamentalists believe to be the only acceptable version of the Bible, the King James Version.
2. Complex issues arise with the fact of a sacred text that exists in various translated forms, as the Bible does. Issues of whether translations of "original manuscripts" are inerrant become matters of concern. However, it is sufficient that fundamentalism assumes that the existing texts are at least adequate for understanding authorial intent, even if not inerrant, as are the original versions. See Machen (1923) and Packer (1958) for two "insiders' views" and Boone (1989) for a general scholarly discussion.
3. To cite only trivial examples is unfortunate, yet nevertheless instructive. Think of how a Jungian might use the same example, employing the concept of "synchronicity," and how differently that case might be received by secular society.
4. There is a large literature on fundamentalism that uses the concept of "boundary maintenance," both conceptually and empirically, to identify beliefs that fundamentalists see as essential to protect because of intratextual considerations (Hood & Morris, 1985; Hood, Morris, & Watson, 1986; Lechner, 1989).

CHAPTER TWO

1. Protestant fundamentalists are not worried about gender-exclusive language in reference to God. The fact that the Bible uses masculine nouns (e.g., "God the Father") or pronouns to speak of God is evidence enough that it is inappropriate to refer to God as anything but masculine. To remain consistent with a primary premise of this book—namely, that we should attempt to understand fundamentalism through the interpretive lenses of fundamentalists themselves—we will, when gender-based language is used, employ only the masculine gender for God. We will do the same for Allah in the Islamic context.

CHAPTER THREE

1. This chapter is a brief distillation of more thorough historical and sociological accounts of fundamentalism, including especially that of Marsden (1980), but also those

of Ammerman (1987, 1991), Armstrong (2000), Carpenter (1997), Finke and Stark (1992), Hunter (1983, 1987), Marsden (1991), Marty (1969), Marty and Appleby (1991), and Sandeen (1970). It is not intended to add anything new to these accounts. The interested reader should consult these works for more detailed descriptions.

2. The major exception is Dollar (1973). Dollar is a self-proclaimed fundamentalist, and his work was published by the press of a university widely regarded as a fundamentalist institution. For this reason, we believe that his work should be closely consulted. Other self-identified fundamentalists include Beale (1986) and Sidwell (1998). We three authors of this volume have all had associations with fundamentalists (one was raised in a fundamentalist church), but none of us would now identify ourselves as fundamentalists.

3. The slogan "in the world but not of the world" is a favorite saying for many fundamentalists. It signifies that though they are obligated to be God's representatives here on earth, they are also to remain ideologically and behaviorally separate from a world tainted by sin. Specifically how fundamentalists handle this paradoxical tension differs from group to group.

4. This discussion of the constituent elements of modernity and modernism should not be confused with philosophical modernism, which is discussed later. As we shall see, fundamentalists, ironically, are philosophical modernists and react to a postmodern perspective.

5. This does not mean that fundamentalists represent the U.S. populace as a whole. The communities with a higher density of fundamentalist churches are likely to be lower on major socioeconomic indices. Such churches may flourish in this socioeconomic milieu.

6. This listing and our subsequent discussion of late-19th-century factors are selective and far from exhaustive. In this brief summary, it is also necessary to separate these factors from the many fascinating personalities involved, only a few of whom are identified in this chapter. For a more complete discussion of both the factors (including some not discussed here) and the role of specific leaders, see Marsden (1980).

7. We spend what may seem to be a disproportionate amount of time in such a brief review on such an esoteric subject for two reasons. First, we intend to show the extent and degree of commitment to the evangelical fervor for a high view of scripture. Second, we hope to show how sophisticated fundamentalist thinking had become in reacting to modernism.

8. Though the United States was established as a secular republic, with the separation of church and state formalized in the First Amendment to the U.S. Constitution, religion played a curiously paradoxical role both in the republic's creation and in its first century. Armstrong (2000) points out that on the one hand, the colonists were fighting for freedom of religion; on the other hand, during the days of the revolution, religion frequently became a rallying point. America, it was said, would be the land where God would establish his glorious kingdom. The tolerant philosophy of the Enlightenment (along with a good bit of pragmatism) guided the Founding Fathers, and God was relegated to a perfunctory role at best in most state constitutions; yet during the early decades of the new republic, churches with a message that countered the Age of Reason were growing rapidly. American independence, in the minds of many, was quickly sacralized as God's achievement and anointed blessing.

9. The importance of the number seven is based on numerous scriptures, primarily the book of Revelation and the prophetic books of the Old Testament. An example is the prophecy of the "seventy weeks" in Daniel 9:20–27 whereby Daniel's 70 weeks (times 7) are prophetic of 490 years—483 years from the rebuilding of Jerusalem to the time

of Christ, and a 7-year tribulation period that has yet to occur (see Marsden, 1980, for a fuller description).

10. Riesebrodt (1990/1993) and Marsden (1980) maintain—correctly, in our opinion—that the millenarian movement itself was not the major distinctive feature of 1920s fundamentalism. Though many fundamentalists were premillenialists and dispensationalism was a dominant feature of premillenialism, the fundamentalist movement of this period was much broader. In contrast, Sandeen (1970) has described dispensationalism as perhaps the primary organizational principle of fundamentalism. The difference in these perspectives probably reflects how narrowly American Protestant fundamentalism has been defined. Relative to Sandeen's, Marsden's broader conceptualization is more likely to include Biblical literalism as a primary defining characteristic (see also Marsden, 1990). Some scholars (e.g., Brereton, 1990; Dayton, 1993), however, maintain that Marsden incorrectly places historic Presbyterianism at the nexus of fundamentalism, thereby excluding Pentecostals and other Holiness groups from the fundamentalist camp. Their view is that Marsden's caricature of fundamentalism as rationalist, doctrinal, antimodern, and conservative is denominationally narrow. Dayton (1993), in particular, argues that Protestant fundamentalism is better characterized as experiential, anticreedal, doctrinally innovative with a pragmatic focus, populist, and sectarian. This debate is complex and far beyond our interests here. As we shall see, the model offered in this book will apply to both conceptions of Protestant fundamentalism.

11. The desire to quiet theological controversy is well illustrated by the life of D. L. Moody from Chicago, the premier American evangelist of his era, who developed friendships with people of several conservative theological persuasions and sought to quiet theological controversy in the interest of an unencumbered support of evangelism. He said, "I hope the motto of ministers of this country will be, 'quit your fighting and go to work and preach the simple gospel' " (Marsden, 1980, p. 33). In addition, Moody's preaching was more sentimental than most Protestant preaching in the 19th century had been. These factors allowed for a greater doctrinal latitudinarianism and, coupled with the spirit of cooperation inherited from the 19th century, made late-19th-century America ripe for the influence of liberalism.

12. Machen left Princeton under extreme pressure in 1929 and founded Westminster Theological Seminary. He eventually lost his ministerial credentials with the Presbyterian Church, and then in 1936 he started a new denomination, the Orthodox Presbyterian Church, less than a year before his unexpected death.

CHAPTER FOUR

1. We include "of Prophecy" in parentheses in the chapter title, because the present-day Church of God and Church of God of Prophecy were the same institution from its emergence in the last decades of the 19th century until 1923, when the fledgling denomination divided (largely over leadership issues, as described in later text and Note 2). Thus what is discussed in this chapter for one group also applies to the other until the 1923 disruption. After the split, however, our primary emphasis is on the Prophecy denomination, which continued under the leadership of A. J. Tomlinson—a critical figure who significantly influenced the early development and fundamentalism of both groups. For the most part, we shall continue to refer in this chapter to the Prophecy denomination as the Church of God (COG), because this was the name its members used to refer to themselves in church literature for most of the 20th century. Only

when a distinction between the two present-day groups is needed for some reason will we refer to "the present-day COG and COG(OP)." One of us (Williamson) was a product and also a clergy member of the Prophecy group, but he has not participated in the denomination for nearly 10 years.

2. Tomlinson enthusiastically endorsed the Constitution in the 1921 General Assembly (*Minutes*, 1921, p. 65), but categorically condemned its adoption as "a grave mistake" in his annual address at the 1922 Assembly (*Minutes*, 1922, p. 27). It is most probable that in the year following its adoption, limits placed on his office by the Constitution became apparent in ways he had not anticipated. Consequently, he dedicated an entire section of his 1922 annual address to the Constitution, in which he warned of its dangers as a creedal document:

> In reflecting back over the past three or four years I can now see how we have been slowly drifting toward making the Assembly a legislative body rather than merely a judicial body as has hitherto been claimed. We have claimed that the Bible contained all the laws we need and in the Assembly we have endeavored to search them out and apply them and make such explanations necessary to make them plain. This has been the chief principle and aim from the beginning. We have held pretty close to this principle all the way along and perhaps the drift toward making it legislative in practice is very slight, but it is enough to make me feel like calling a halt and give the matter sufficient consideration that we will not go that way any further. We must stick to our Bible and not weave other things in that would be the least bit displeasing to God. . . . I consider that we made a grave mistake one year ago when we adopted what we called our Constitution. . . . There is only one thing to do, and I may lose my position for saying it, and that is to abrogate the whole thing and make a record to that effect and as far as possible even erase it from our memory, and once more raise the Book high up in the air and declare, THIS IS OUR ONLY RULE OF FAITH AND PRACTICE. (*Minutes*, 1922, pp. 26, 27; emphasis in original)

The Assembly did not repeal the Constitution at that time; instead, it passed a committee resolution written by Tomlinson's opponents to strengthen it (*Minutes*, 1922, pp. 48–50, 51). Later the same day, Tomlinson submitted his resignation as General Overseer, which, of course, was refused by the unwitting delegates (p. 52). It is of interest to note that the present-day COG (the larger faction after the 1923 disruption) repealed the Constitution in 1926, 3 years after Tomlinson's impeachment and removal from office (Conn, 1996).

3. The initial name of the COG's original paper was *The Evening Light and Church of God Evangel* (the title was soon shortened to *The Church of God Evangel*), which had a reported readership of over 16,000 in 1920 (*Minutes*, 1920, p. 39). However, a new church paper, *The White Wing Messenger*, replaced it after the 1923 disruption. Tomlinson was editor of both publications except for a period between 1922 and 1923.

4. In later years, the procedure for addressing important issues changed more to one in which Assembly committees made specific recommendations that required motions, discussions, and delegate unanimity (*Minutes*, 1928, pp. 49–52). Concerning the jewelry question (and answer) of 1913, it surfaced mysteriously without further Assembly consideration in the listing of official church teachings in the back of the minutes two Assemblies later (*General Assembly Minutes 1906–1914*, 1992, p. 337). It is most likely that Tomlinson was responsible for its inclusion.

5. It should be noted that the larger faction that emerged from the 1923 disruption never embraced this interpretation of the 1903 event. In fact, until recently the present-day COG viewed Tomlinson with relative contempt, and even minimized his important contribution to the original COG through 1923. This stance was no doubt attributable to the fierce rivalry between the two groups that arose after the disruption. In

comparing recent reconstructions of the 1903 event, readers should consult Conn (1955, 1977, 1996), Davidson (1973), Stone (1977), and Williamson (2001).

6. When Tomlinson credited the Pentecostal doctrine of glossolalia to Seymour, of Azusa Street revival fame (see later text), he evidently did not know of Charles Fox Parham's role in establishing the doctrine (at least not at the time he wrote this passage).

7. *This Present Darkness* (1986), a very successful Christian novel by Frank Peretti, offers a detailed look into the spiritual warfare of this constructed fundamentalist worldview.

8. A comment on the scope of this chapter seems necessary. Our analysis has been based on the COG as led by A. J. Tomlinson, largely within, but not limited to, his lifetime. The leadership of M. A. Tomlinson, the son who succeeded him in 1943, was very similar to that of his father, except that he was more sectarian in the face of modernism, which became more of a church issue during the 1970s (Williamson, 2001). Despite increasing unrest among a younger generation, he attempted to maintain all aspects of church teachings and advices that represented the legacy of his father. By 1990, Billy D. Murray, the next General Overseer, was somewhat more willing to revisit church doctrine—at least in regard to what might be considered peripheral beliefs (e.g., the teaching against jewelry and the more restrictive membership advices). Most interesting, however, is the current push by third- and fourth-generation COG(OP) members toward reinterpreting what it means to be the "Church of God of the Bible" (*Minutes*, 2000, pp. 27–29). Their pursuit of higher education has given them constant exposure to competing views of the world, and the result may be either some degree of compromise in meaning or a reinforcement of the traditionally guarded truth. The contemporary COG still strongly advocates the authority of the Bible, holiness as a lifestyle, and Spirit baptism with speaking in tongues. However, it seems at present that modernism (and its religious child, ecumenicalism) is forcing another "taking up of the sacred text" in coming to terms with the COG's role in being the Bible church. Recent years have seen an increasing polarization among members over this issue, the full consequences of which remain to be seen. Whether the denomination eventually succeeds in achieving an intratextual reinterpretation of this truth may have major consequences in restructuring some of its worldview—and whether its worldview is restructured may also have major consequences for those among them who still claim this traditional COG truth as their own.

CHAPTER FIVE

1. It should be noted that Hensley was dismissed from the clergy of the COG as early as 1922 for family problems (Burton, 1993). By that time, U.S. membership within the COG was nearing 23,000, and serpent handling had reached its peak in popularity and was beginning to wane (Williamson & Hood, 2004). After a few years of backsliding, Hensley himself returned to serpent handling as an independent evangelist and sometimes as a pastor, and remained as such until his death in 1955 (Burton, 1993; Williamson, 2000).

2. We know of at least four congregations (one in Ohio, one in Michigan, and two in Indiana) that exist today for this reason (Williamson, 2002). We have also been informed that a serpent-handling congregation worships in Los Angeles, although we have been unable to substantiate that claim. It may well exist, since most such congregations shun publicity and outside inquiries for the sake of preserving the sacredness

of their worship and escaping the undue media criticism so often directed at these groups.

3. According to Hood and Kimbrough (1995), the most reliable records of fatalities due to serpent bite among believers approximate 80. More research is needed to document this important phenomenon accurately.

4. These interviews were videotaped and placed in the Hood–Williamson Research Archives on the Serpent Handlers of Southern Appalachia, Lupton Library, University of Tennessee at Chattanooga.

5. Based on concern for ensuring the protection and anonymity of our 16 participants, we have assigned each one a numerical code for distinction/identification in the text. Participant 1 is identified as P1, Participant 2 as P2, Participant 3 as P3, and so on.

6. Several participants in this study referred to the fact that Mark 16 does not say that believers will not experience serpent bites. The phrase "it shall not hurt them" refers only to the drinking of deadly substances.

CHAPTER SIX

1. Our purpose here is not to compete with the fine work of scholars (particularly Hostetler, 1993; Kraybill, 1989, 1998, 2001; and Nolt, 1992) who are far closer to the Amish than ourselves. Their books are substantially more thorough than our discussion in this chapter, and we rely heavily upon their insightful analyses. We encourage interested readers to consult their works. Our purpose is simply to apply the intratextual model to Amish life.

2. It should be noted that (as with other fundamentalist groups) most books written about the Amish are not written by the Amish themselves, though many of the authors are often intimately acquainted with the Amish (often through membership in a Mennonite community). This is not to say that the Amish themselves write and publish materials. There are numerous Amish publications, but they are generally intended to be written for each other on a practical level for helpful advice on everyday living. For the Amish, there is little reason to write a book for outsiders about the Amish community; indeed, such a book might damage community life by creating controversy. Furthermore, such a book might necessitate evaluations of the Amish that do not reflect a proper spirit of humility. Hence, it is not surprising that few if any books about the Amish have been written by the Amish themselves (though several books have been written by people who have left the Amish community).

3. We are indebted to the works of Hostetler (1993) and Nolt (1992) for this historical review.

4. Hostetler (1993) estimates that the largest Amish settlement in the United States during the colonial period (located in Berks County, Pennsylvania, northwest of Philadelphia) consisted of 150 to 200 members. By 1800, the Amish population in the entire United States was less than 1,000 (Nolt, 1992). By 1992, it was estimated that the number of Old Order Amish (those who have remained closest to their historic identity) alone numbered close to 145,000, despite the fact that the Amish have lost many members to other groups.

5. Hostetler (1993, pp. 290–299) provides a description of 13 divisions within a single community in Mifflin County, Pennsylvania. A stratified religious system, ranging from "low" (Old Order) to "high" (more conventionally Protestant) church orientations, exists to maintain community boundaries. With the exception of two of the divisions, there is no attempt to proselytize or recruit members from the other groups.

The threat of *Meidung*, or social avoidance, maintains each division's endogenous character. Individuals are permitted to move from one division to another, and those who might make such moves usually do so gradually and in the direction of moving from a "lower" to a "higher" group. It is less common for a person to move in the "lower" church direction or to make abrupt changes. Movement out of the lowest two Old Order groups is least common. Though other communities will have their own distinctive features, Hostetler uses Mifflin County as a fair representation of how community boundaries are established and maintained.

6. The humor of this motto, found posted in an Amish repair shop and quoted by Hostetler (1993, p. 302), is characteristically Amish. It may bring a quiet chuckle or a smile, but is not likely to evoke great displays of levity. Even humor frequently contains a subtle message of proper behavior. This does not mean that the Amish are necessarily solemn people; they often can have a rollicking good time. But the ever-present *Ordnung* helps define appropriate ways to express (and react to) humor and have fun.

7. The brief examples and discussion here are drawn largely from Kraybill (1998, 2001). For brief but insightful participant observer accounts of the "puzzles" and "riddles" of Amish life, these books are highly recommended.

CHAPTER SEVEN

1. There are no standard English spellings for Arabic terms. For instance, Koran, Qu'ran, Quran, and others are all common spellings for the name of Islam's sacred text. We have chosen simply to be consistent in the use of the English spellings we have chosen for Quran, Muhammad, and other important terms. Modifications within quotes have been made when necessary to keep this consistency. References are not modified.

2. Islam properly refers to Khomeini as "Imam," a term that all Muslims accept. Although both Sunni and Shia Muslims accept an Imam as an honored religious and prayer leader, only Shia Muslims believe an Imam to be additionally a "Caliph" (political successor to the Prophet Muhammad and an intermediary between God and humans). In the West, Khomeini is commonly known by the title "Ayatollah," referring simply to the highest religious leader in Iran (see Pipes, 1990, pp. 15, 255).

3. In a curious twist of interpretation, some have accused Rushdie of having a psychotic break weakly disguised in his own novel (see Pidcock, 1992, p. 23). We make no claims as to hidden motives. The clash between intertextual and intratextual models is sufficient to account for the tension without recourse to a psychology of hidden motives. In this sense, our model is sufficiently descriptive to be itself explanatory if one simply assumes each participant to be faithfully working with one of these perspectives.

4. Rushdie was born in India.

5. The history of concern among Protestant fundamentalists in the West, and those sympathetic to them, with blasphemy is illustrated by reactions to such works as Martin Scorsese's film *The Last Temptation of Christ,* based upon the Kazantzakis (1960) novel by that name, and the Monty Python film *The Life of Brian.* However, many Western nations have no laws against blasphemy and certainly provide at least the print media with almost unlimited freedom to criticize religion, although some Western nations (e.g., the United Kingdom) have blasphemy laws that protect only the Christian religion (see Nash, 1999). Many Muslim countries do have laws against

blasphemy, but of course they cannot be enforced in other countries without such laws (see Levy, 1993). In the United States, blasphemy is protected, whereas issues of censorship have been and continue to be applied to pornography (see Heins, 1998).

6. Since we do not challenge the "real" motivations of any participants in this debate, numerous claims about Rushdie's "conversion to Islam," his renunciation of that conversion, and his various claims to be or not to be a Muslim are of little concern. Details of Rushdie's early hiding and statements are readily available (see Pipes, 1990; Weatherby, 1990). Again, the clash between intertextual and intratextual models is sufficient if one simply assumes that each participant operates within one of these perspectives.

7. The irony here is that we ourselves must use a translation (*The Holy Qur-ān*, 1410 A.H./1989). This itself violates our principle on intratextuality, as we present the model to an audience that (like ourselves) is unlikely to be fluent in the Arabic of the Quran.

8. Rushdie, well versed in Islamic history and theology, undoubtedly knew of the offense of blasphemy. In *SV* he has the slave Bilal outside the temple of Lat answering in response to his master's demand that he enumerate the gods: " 'One,' he answered in that huge musical voice. Blasphemy, punishable by death" (Rushdie, 1989, p. 102).

9. Many Muslim groups around the world distributed excerpts from *SV*.

CHAPTER EIGHT

1. Claims of a fundamentalist "mindset" from which fundamentalists must "recover" are common (Yao, 1985). The linkage to "cult" literature is evident in Cohen's (1988) claim to have identified the basic principles of "the Evangelical mind control system" (pp. 169–405). For a critical discussion of "cults" and "mind control," see Spilka, Hood, Hunsberger, and Gorsuch (2003, pp. 394–411).

2. A comparison, for instance, can be made with Troeltsch's church–sect mysticism. Like fundamentalism as a type, Troeltsch's typology of religious organizations is both a logical possibility latent within Christianity and a particular historically contingent expression of Christianity's development (Hood, 1985, 2003).

3. While Harris (1994) makes this telling point, he does so by denying that fundamentalism is an appropriate concept for the Jewish tradition. We argue that fundamentalism does apply to the Jewish tradition. Others who identify fundamentalism within Judaism include Lawrence (1989) and Gasper (1963).

4. It is ironic that Sampson (2000) observes a dialogic aspect within rabbinic Judaism, in contrast to a monologic one in Christian individualism. Christian individualism is, as our model reveals, inherently dialogic in its fundamentalist form.

5. Sandeen (1970, p. 125) notes that Princeton theology of the early 20th century taught this as a matter of course. A major theological defense of inerrancy is found in Payne (1979).

6. Compare discussions in Barnhart (1986), Boone (1989), Dollar (1973), Frei (1974), Gilkey (1969), Hirsch (1967), Hunter (1987), Machen (1923), Packer (1958), and Schaeffer (1975).

7. As discussed in Chapter 3, *The Fundamentals* opposed primarily the new "higher criticism" from German scholars, but this was simply the opening defensive move in an ongoing debate.

8. Scholars who propose literalism, in the narrow sense, as being among the defining cri-

teria of fundamentalism are Ammerman (1987), Carpenter (1980), Marsden (1980), and Sandeen (1970).

9. Among scholars who would distinguish fundamentalism from evangelicalism are Ammerman (1987) and Marty and Appleby (1991). Among those who tend to link fundamentalism and evangelicalism are Carpenter (1980) and Hunter (1983). Self-identified fundamentalist scholars who applaud militancy (but not violence) as a defining criterion of fundamentalism are Dollar (1973), Falwell, with Dobson and Hindson (1981), and Sidwell (1998). General scholarly discussions of how to distinguish fundamentalists from evangelicals (mostly in the context of American Protestantism) include those of Ethridge and Feagin (1979), Hunter (1982, 1983), Kepel (1991/1994), Lechner (1985), Marsden (1971, 1990), Pinnock (1990), Sandeen (1970), Warner (1979), and Wilcox (1986).

10. Among scholars who argue for the antimodernist nature of fundamentalism are Ammerman (1987), Cox (1984), Lawrence (1989), and Lechner (1985). The antimodernist aspect of fundamentalism also informs the entire Fundamentalism Project. The consensus is that fundamentalists are modern but neither accept nor applaud modernity.

11. Kirkpatrick, Hood, and Hartz (1991) have made this basic argument with respect to the application of Rokeach's dogmatism theory to fundamentalism. Saucier (2000) has also argued that social attitudes may be identified that are relatively independent of personality. This suggests the need for a model that places heavy emphasis on the process of belief, especially when it interacts with specific belief contents in a unique manner. Our model reflects that fundamentalism is unique in just this way.

12. The erroneous claims that fundamentalists are necessarily authoritarian personalities are the scholarly equivalents to more popular claims of a "mindset" from which fundamentalists must "recover" (Yao, 1985). See Note 1 above.

13. In this sense, fundamentalism has much in common with the paradigm clashes that may characterize at least some aspects of the history of science and competition among scientific theories (Kuhn, 1970, 1974).

14. The literature on postmodernism and the social sciences is particularly instructive. See Gergen (1994), Kvale (1992), Rosenau (1992), and Smith (1994).

15. To prejudge the appropriateness of fundamentalists' beliefs and lifestyles does not permit a valid, "thick" description either of their beliefs or their lifestyles. Fundamentalist scholars have long argued this case (e.g., Dollar, 1973; Falwell et al., 1981; Schneidau, 1976). This view is now being supported by some social scientists (e.g., Ammerman, 1987; Bruce, 2000; Hood, 1983).

References

Aquinas, St. T. (1964). *Summa theologica*. Cambridge, UK: Blackfriars.

Adil, H. A. (2002). *Muhammad: The messenger of Islam*. Washington, DC: Islamic Supreme Council of America.

Adorno, T. W. (1951). Freudian theory and patterns of fascist propaganda. In G. Róheim (Ed.), *Psychoanalysis and the social sciences* (Vol. 3, pp. 279–300). New York: International Universities Press.

Ahmed, A. S. (1986). Death in Islam: The Hawkes Bay case. *Royal Anthropological Institute of Great Britain and Ireland, 21*, 120–134.

Ahsan, N. M., & Kidwai, A. R. (Eds.). (1993). *Sacrilege versus civility: Muslim perspectives on The Satanic Verses affair* (rev. and enlarged ed.). Markfield, UK: Islamic Foundation.

Akhtur, S. (1993). Back into the fold? In N. M. Ahsan & A. R. Kidwai (Eds.), *Sacrilege versus civility: Muslim perspectives on The Satanic Verses affair* (rev. and enlarged ed., pp. 309–317). Markfield, UK: Islamic Foundation.

Altemeyer, B. (1988). *Enemies of freedom: Understanding right-wing authoritarianism*. San Francisco: Jossey-Bass.

Ammerman, N. T. (1982). Operationalizing evangelicalism: An amendment. *Sociological Analysis, 43*, 170–172.

Ammerman, N. T. (1987). *Bible believers: Fundamentalists in the modern world*. New Brunswick, NJ: Rutgers University Press.

Ammerman, N. T. (1991). North American Protestant fundamentalism. In M. E. Marty & R. S. Appleby (Eds.), *Fundamentalisms observed* (pp. 1–65). Chicago: University of Chicago Press.

Antonovsky, A. (1987). *Unraveling the mystery of health: How people measure stress and stay well*. San Francisco: Jossey-Bass.

Appignanesi, L., & Maitland, S. (Eds.). (1989). *The Rushdie file*. London: Fourth Estate.

Armstrong, K. (2000). *The battle for God*. New York: Knopf.

Ashraf, S. A. (1993). Nihilistic, negative, Satanic. In N. M. Ahsan & A. R. Kidwai (Eds.), *Sacrilege versus civility: Muslim perspectives on The Satanic Verses affair* (rev. and enlarged ed., pp. 313–316). Markfield, UK: Islamic Foundation.

Assembly minutes. (1991). Cleveland, TN: White Wing.

Assembly minutes. (1992). Cleveland, TN: White Wing.

Baider, L., & Sarell, M. (1983). Perceptions and causal attributions of Israeli women with breast cancer concerning their illness: The effects of ethnicity and religiosity. *Psychology and Psychosomatics, 39,* 136–143.

Barnhart, J. E. (1986). *The Southern Baptist holy war.* Austin: *Texas Monthly* Press.

Barr, J. (1977). *Fundamentalism.* Philadelphia: Westminster Press.

Barr, J. (1983). *Holy scripture: Canon, authority, criticism.* Philadelphia: Westminster Press.

Barzun, J. (2000). *From dawn to decadence: 500 years of Western cultural life, 1500 to present.* New York: HarperCollins.

Baumeister, R. F. (1991). *Meanings of life.* New York: Guilford Press.

Beale, D. O. (1986). *In pursuit of purity: American fundamentalism since 1850.* Greenville, SC: Unusual.

Bebbington, D. (1994). Evangelism in its settings: The British and American movements since 1940. In M. A. Noll, D. W. Bebbington, & G. A. Rawlyk (Eds.), *Evangelism: Comparative studies of popular Protestantism in North America, the British Isles, and beyond 1700–1990* (pp. 365–388). New York: Oxford University Press.

Becker, E. (1973). *The denial of death.* New York: Free Press.

Belzen, J. A. (Ed.). (2000). *Aspects in contexts: Studies in the history of the psychology of religion.* Amsterdam/Atlanta: Rodopi.

Belzen, J. A. (Ed.). (2001). *Psychohistory in psychology of religion: Interdisciplinary studies.* Amsterdam/Atlanta: Rodopi.

Belzen, J., & Hood, R. W., Jr. (in press). Methodological issues in the psychology of religion. *Journal of Psychology.*

Berman, M. (1982). *All that is solid melts into air: The experience of modernity.* New York: Simon & Schuster.

Best, J. (2001). *Damned lies and statistics: Untangling numbers for the media, politicians, and the activists.* Berkeley: University of California Press.

Black, H. L. (1969). *A constitutional faith.* New York: Knopf.

Blose, B. L. (1981). Materialism and disembodied minds. *Philosophy and Phenomenological Research, 42,* 59–74.

Bob Jones wants to shed the fundamentalist label. (2002, March 16). *The Hutchinson News* [Greenville, SC], p. B4.

Book of minutes. (1922). Cleveland, TN: Church of God.

Boone, K. C. (1989). *The Bible tells them so: The discourse of Protestant fundamentalism.* Albany: State University of New York Press.

Bork, R. (1990). *The tempting of America.* New York: Free Press.

Bowker, J. (1973). *The sense of God: Sociological, anthropological and psychological approaches to the sense of God.* Oxford: Clarendon Press.

Bowlby, J. (1969). *Attachment and loss: Vol. 1. Attachment.* New York: Basic Books.

Brasher, B. E. (Ed.). (2001). *Encyclopedia of fundamentalism.* New York: Routledge.

Brennan, T. (1989). *Salman Rushdie and the Third World: Myths of nation.* New York: Macmillan.

Brereton, V. L. (1987). The Bible schools and evangelical higher education, 1880–1940. In J. A. Carpenter & K. W. Shipps (Eds.), *Making higher education Christian: The history and mission of evangelical colleges in America.* Grand Rapids, MI: Eerdmans.

Brereton, V. L. (1990). *The formation of the Bible schools, 1880–1940.* Bloomington: Indiana University Press.

Brians, P. (2002a). *Notes for Salman Rushdie: The Satanic Verses.* Retrieved August 18, 2003, from *www.wsu.edu:8080/~brians/anglophone/satanicverses/copyright.html*

Brians, P. (2002b). *The unity of The Satanic Verses*. Retrieved August 18, 2003, from *www.wsu.edu/~brians/anglophone/satanic-verses/unity.html*

A brief history of the Church of God. (2003). Retrieved June 20, 2003, from *www.chofgod.org/history.cfm*

Browder, G. C. (1996). *Hitler's enforcers: The Gestapo and the SS security service in the Nazi revolution*. New York: Oxford University Press.

Brown, R. (1965). *Social psychology*. New York: Free Press.

Bruce, S. (2000). *Fundamentalism*. Cambridge, UK: Polity Press.

Bulman, R. J., & Wortman, C. B. (1977). Attributions of blame and coping in the "real world": Severe accident victims react to their lot. *Journal of Personality and Social Psychology, 35*, 351–363.

Burton, T. (1993). *Serpent handling believers*. Knoxville: University of Tennessee Press.

Carpenter, J. A. (1980). Fundamentalist institutions and the rise of evangelical Protestantism, 1929–1942. *Church History, 49*, 62–75.

Carpenter, J. A. (1997). *Revive us again: The reawakening of American fundamentalism*. New York: Oxford University Press.

Carver, C. S., & Scheier, M. F. (1985). *Attention and self-regulation: A control-theory approach to human behavior*. New York: Springer-Verlag.

Chesterton, C. H. (1995). *Orthodoxy*. San Francisco: Ignatius Press. (Original work published 1908)

Choueiri, Y. F. (1990). *Islamic fundamentalism*. Boston: Twayne.

Christie, R. C., & Jahoda, M. (Eds.). (1954). *Studies in the scope and method of the authoritarian personality*. New York: Free Press.

Church of God Evangel. (1923). *14*(1), 1.

Church of God of Prophecy. (2002). *Our history*. Cleveland, TN: Pathway Press.

The Church of God is: Foundational. (2003). Retrieved June 20, 2003, from *www.chofgod.org/the_church_of_god_is.cfm*

Clark, W. H. (1958). *The psychology of religion: An introduction to religious experience and behavior*. Toronto: Macmillan.

Cohen, E. J. (1988). *The mind of the Bible-believer* (rev. ed). Buffalo, NY: Prometheus Books.

Collins, J. B. (1947). *Tennessee snake handlers*. Chattanooga, TN: *Chattanooga News–Free Press*.

Collins, R. (1986). *Methodology of the social sciences*. Cambridge, UK: Cambridge University Press.

Conn, C. W. (1955). *Like a mighty army*. Cleveland, TN: Pathway Press.

Conn, C. W. (1977). *Like a mighty army* (rev. ed.). Cleveland, TN: Pathway Press.

Conn, C. W. (1996). *Like a mighty army: A history of the Church of God* (definitive ed.). Cleveland, TN: Pathway Press.

Coreno, T. (2002). Fundamentalism as class culture. *Sociology of Religion, 63*, 335–360.

Cox, H. (1984). *Religion and the secular city*. New York: Simon & Schuster.

Crapanzano, C. R. (2000). *Serving the word: Literalism in America from the pulpit to the bench*. New York: New Press.

Curtis, E. M. (2000). *Transformed thinking: Loving God with all your mind*. Franklin, TN: JKO.

Davidson, C. T. (1973). *Upon this rock*. Cleveland, TN: White Wing.

Dayton, D. W. (1993). The search for the historic evangelicalism: George Marsden's history of Fuller Seminary as a case study. *Christian Scholar's Review, 23*, 12–33.

Deiros, P. A. (1991). Protestant fundamentalism in Latin America. In M. E. Marty &

F. S. Appleby (Eds.), *The Fundamentalism Project: Vol. 1. Fundamentalisms observed* (pp. 142–196). Chicago: University of Chicago Press.

Dekmejian, R. H. (1985). *Islam in revolution: Fundamentalism in the Arab world.* Syracuse, NY: Syracuse University Press.

Denny, F. M. (1994). *An introduction to Islam* (2nd ed.). New York: Macmillan.

Dostoevsky, F. M. (1956). Notes from underground. In W. Kaufmann (Ed.), *Existentialism from Dostoevsky to Sartre* (pp. 52–82). New York: Meridian. (Original work published 1864)

Dollar, G. W. (1973). *A history of fundamentalism in America.* Greenville, SC: Bob Jones University Press.

Duggar, L. (1964). *A. J. Tomlinson.* Cleveland, TN: White Wing.

Echoes from the eighth General Assembly. (1913). Cleveland, TN: Church of God.

Emmons, R. A. (1999). *The psychology of ultimate concerns: Motivation and spirituality in personality.* New York: Guilford Press.

Emmons, R. A. (in press). Striving for the sacred: Personal goals, life meaning and religion. *Journal of Social Issues.*

Emmons, R. A., & Paloutzian, R. F. (2003). The psychology of religion. *Annual Review of Psychology, 54,* 377–402.

Epstein, S. (1973). The self-concept revisited, or a theory of a theory. *American Psychologist, 54,* 377–402.

Epstein, S. (1994). Integration of the cognitive and psychodynamic unconscious. *American Psychologist, 28,* 404–416.

Ethridge, F. M., & Feagin, J. R. (1979). Varieties of "fundamentalism": A conceptual and empirical analysis of two Protestant denominations. *Sociological Quarterly, 20,* 37–48.

Evans, A. D. (Ed.). (1943). *A. J. Tomlinson, God's anointed prophet of wisdom: Choice writings of A. J. Tomlinson in times of his greatest anointings.* Cleveland, TN: White Wing.

The Evening Light and Church of God Evangel. (1910). *1*(1), 1.

Falwell, J., with Dobson, E., & Hindson, E. (Eds.). (1981). *The fundamentalist phenomenon: The resurgence of conservative Christianity.* Garden City, NY: Doubleday.

Feiler, B. (2002). *Abraham: A journey to the heart of three faiths.* New York: Morrow.

Finke, R., & Stark, R. (1992). *The churching of America 1776–1990: Winners and losers in our religious economy.* New Brunswick, NJ: Rutgers University Press.

Foster, J. (1991). *The immaterial self.* New York: Routledge.

Frei, H. W. (1974). *The eclipse of Biblical narrative.* New Haven, CT: Yale University Press.

Gadamer, H.-G. (1982). *Truth and method.* New York: Crossroad. (Original work published 1975)

Gallup, G. H., Jr., & Jones, T. (1992). *The saints among us.* Harrisburg, PA: Morehouse.

Gasper, L. (1963). *The fundamentalist movement, 1930–1956.* Grand Rapids, MI: Baker Book House.

Geertz, C. (1968). *Islam observed.* Chicago: University of Chicago Press.

Geertz, C. (1973). *The interpretation of cultures.* New York: Basic Books.

General Assembly minutes 1906–1914: Photographic reproductions of the first ten General Assembly minutes. (1992). Cleveland, TN: White Wing.

George, L. K., Ellison, C. G., & Larson, D. B. (2002). Exploring the relationship between religious involvement and health. *Psychological Inquiry, 13,* 190–200.

Gergen, K. (1994). Exploring the postmodern: Perils or potential? *American Psychologist, 49,* 412–416.

Gibb, H. (1963). *Arabic literature: An introduction* (2nd ed.). Oxford: University Press.

Gilkey, L. (1969). *Naming the whirlwind: The renewal of God-language.* Indianapolis, IN: Bobbs-Merrill.

Gorsuch, R. L. (2002). *Integrating psychology and spirituality?* Westport, CT: Praeger.

Gorsuch, R. L., & Aleshire, D. (1974). Christian faith and ethnic prejudice: A review and interpretation of research. *Journal for the Scientific Study of Religion, 13,* 281–307.

Gould, S. J. (1999). *Rocks of ages: Science and religion in the fullness of life.* New York: Ballantine Books.

Gregory, W. (1957). The orthodoxy of the authoritarian personality. *Journal of Social Psychology, 45,* 217–232.

Greil, A. L. (1993). Explorations along the sacred frontier: Notes on para-religious, quasi-religious, and other boundary phenomena. In D. G. Bromley & J. K. Hadden (Eds.), *Handbook of cults and sects in America: Assessing two decades of research and theory development* (pp. 153–172). Greenwich, CT: JAI Press.

Greil, A. L. (1994). Introduction: Exploring the boundaries of the sacred. In A. L. Greil & T. Robbins (Eds.), *Between sacred and secular: Research and theory on quasi-religion* (pp. 1–23). Greenwich, CT: JAI Press.

Gritsch, E. W. (1982). *Born againism: Perspectives on a movement.* Philadelphia: Fortress Press.

Guillane, A. (1987). *The life of Muhammed: A translation of Ishaq's Sirat Rasui Allah.* Oxford: Oxford University Press.

Harding, S. F. (2000). *The book of Jerry Falwell.* Princeton, NJ: Princeton University Press.

Harris, J. M. (1994). "Fundamentalism": Objections from a modern Jewish historian. In J. S. Strawley (Ed.), *Fundamentalism and gender* (pp. 137–173). New York: Oxford University Press.

Hart, M. H. (1987). *The 100: A ranking of the most influential persons in history.* Secaucus, NJ: Citadel Press.

Hassan, R. (1990). The burgeoning of Islamic fundamentalism: Toward an understanding of the phenomenon. In N. J. Cohen (Ed.), *The fundamentalist phenomenon: A view from within; a response from without* (pp. 151–171). Grand Rapids, MI: Eerdmans.

Hawley, J. S., & Proudfoot, W. (1994). Introduction. In J. S. Strawley (Ed.), *Fundamentalism and gender* (pp. 3–44). New York: Oxford University Press.

Heins, M. (1998). *Sex, sin, and blasphemy: A guide to America's censorship wars.* New York: New Press.

Henry, C. F. H. (1947). *The uneasy conscience of modern fundamentalism.* Grand Rapids, MI: Eerdmans.

Henry, C. F. H. (1979). *God, revelation and authority: God who speaks and shows* (Vol. 1). Waco, TX: Word Books.

Higgins, E. T. (1987). Self-discrepancy: A theory relating self and affect. *Psychological Review, 94,* 319–340.

Hill, P. C. (2002). Spiritual transformation: Forming the habitual center of personal energy. *Research in the Social Scientific Study of Religion, 13,* 87–108.

Hill, P. C., & Hood, R. W., Jr. (1999). *Measures of religiosity.* Birmingham, AL: Religious Education Press.

Hill, P. C., Pargament, K. I., Hood, R. W., Jr., McCullough, M. E., Swyers, J. P., Larson,

D. B., et al. (2000). Conceptualizing religion and spirituality: Points of commonality, points of departure. *Journal for the Theory of Social Behaviour, 30*, 51–77.

Hirsch, E. D., Jr. (1967). *Validity in interpretation.* New Haven, CT: Yale University Press.

Hirschman, A. O. (1991). *The rhetoric of reaction.* Cambridge, MA: Belknap Press.

Hofstadter, R. (1962). *Anti-intellectualism in American life.* New York: Knopf.

Holm, N. G. (1991). Pentecostalism: Conversion and charismata. *International Journal for the Psychology of Religion, 1*, 135–151.

Holm, N. G. (1995). Religious symbols and role taking. In N. G. Holm & J. A. Belzen (Eds.), *Sundén's role theory: An impetus to contemporary psychology of religion* (pp. 129–151). Åbo, Finland: Åbo Akademi.

The Holy Qur-ān. (1410 A.H. [After the Hegira]/1989). Al-Madinah Al-Munawarah, Saudi Arabia: King Fahd Holy Qur-ān Printing Complex.

Hood, R. W., Jr. (1983). Social psychology and religious fundamentalism. In A. W. Childs & G. B. Melton (Eds.), *Rural psychology* (pp. 169–198). New York: Plenum Press.

Hood, R. W., Jr. (1985). Mysticism. In P. Hammond (Ed.), *The sacred in a post-traditional society* (pp. 285–287). Berkeley: University of California Press.

Hood, R. W., Jr. (1995). The facilitation of religious experience. In R. W. Hood (Ed.), *Handbook of religious experience* (pp. 535–597). Birmingham, AL: Religious Education Press.

Hood, R. W., Jr. (1998). When the spirit maims and kills: Social psychological considerations of the history of serpent handling and the narrative of handlers. *International Journal for the Psychology of Religion, 87*, 71–96.

Hood, R. W., Jr. (2003). The relationship between religion and spirituality. In A. L. Greil & D. Bromley (Eds.), *Religion and the social order: Vol. 10. Defining religion: Investigating the boundaries between the sacred and secular* (pp. 241–264). Amsterdam: Elsevier.

Hood, R. W., Jr., & Kimbrough, D. L. (1995). Serpent handling Holiness sects: Theoretical considerations. *Journal for the Scientific Study of Religion, 34*(3), 311–322.

Hood, R. W., Jr., & Morris, R. J. (1983). Toward a theory of death transcendence. *Journal for the Scientific Study of Religion, 22*, 353–365.

Hood, R. W., Jr., & Morris, R. J. (1985). Boundary maintenance, social political views, and presidential preferences among high and low fundamentalists. *Review of Religious Research, 27*, 134–145.

Hood, R. W., Jr., Morris, R. J., & Watson, P. J. (1986). Maintenance of religious fundamentalism. *Psychological Reports, 59*, 547–559.

Hood, R. W., Jr., Williamson, W. P., & Morris, R. J. (2000). Changing views of serpent handling: A quasi-experimental study. *Journal for the Scientific Study of Religion, 39*(3), 287–296.

Hostetler, J. A. (1993). *Amish society* (4th ed.). Baltimore: John Hopkins University Press.

Huff, D. (1982). *How to lie with statistics.* New York: Norton.

Hunter, J. D. (1982). Operationalizing evangelicalism: A review and critique proposal. *Sociological Analysis, 42*, 363–372.

Hunter, J. D. (1983). *American evangelicalism: Conservative religion and the quandary of modernity.* New Brunswick, NJ: Rutgers University Press.

Hunter, J. D. (1987). *Evangelicalism: The coming generation.* Chicago: University of Chicago Press.

Iannaccone, L. (1994). Why strict churches are strong. *American Journal of Sociology, 99*, 1180–1211.

Igou, B. (Ed.). (1999). *The Amish in their own words: Amish writings from 25 years of Family Life magazine.* Scottdale, PA: Herald Press.

Jacobsen, D. (1987). The rise of evangelical hermeneutical pluralism. *Christian Scholar's Review, 16,* 325–335.

James, W. (1902). *The varieties of religious experience.* New York: Longmans, Green.

Johnson, L. T. (1996). *The real Jesus: The misguided quest for the historical Jesus and the truth of the traditional gospels.* San Francisco: Harper.

Jolo homecoming video. (1998, September 4). Chattanooga: Hood–Williamson Research Archives on the Serpent Handlers of Southern Appalachia, Lupton Library, University of Tennessee at Chattanooga.

Juergensmeyer, M. (2003). *Terror in the mind of God: The global rise of religious violence* (3rd ed.). Berkeley: University of California Press.

Kane, S. M. (1979). *Snake handlers of southern Appalachia.* Unpublished doctoral dissertation, Princeton University.

Kazantzakis, N. (1960). *The last temptation of Christ.* New York: Simon & Schuster.

Kelley, D. M. (1972). *Why conservative churches are growing.* New York: Harper.

Kellstedt, L., & Smidt, C. (1991). Measuring fundamentalism: An analysis of different operational strategies. *Journal for the Scientific Study of Religion, 30,* 259–278.

Kepel, G. (1994). *The revenge of God: The resurgence of Islam, Christianity and Judaism in the modern world* (A. Braley, Trans.). University Park: Pennsylvania State University Press. (Original work published 1991)

Kimbrough, D. L. (1995). *Taking up serpents.* Chapel Hill: University of North Carolina Press.

Kimbrough, D. L., & Hood, R. W., Jr. (1995). Carson Springs and the persistence of serpent handling despite the law. *Journal of Appalachian Studies, 1,* 45–65.

Kingston service video. (1995, December 2). Chattanooga: Hood–Williamson Research Archives on the Serpent Handlers of Southern Appalachia, Lupton Library, University of Tennessee at Chattanooga.

Kirkpatrick, L. A. (1993). Fundamentalism, Christian orthodoxy, and intrinsic religious orientation as predictors of discriminatory attitudes. *Journal for the Scientific Study of Religion, 36,* 207–217.

Kirkpatrick, L. A., Hood, R. W., Jr., & Hartz, G. (1991). Fundamentalist religion conceptualized in terms of Rokeach's theory of the open and closed mind: New perspectives on some old ideas. *Research in the Social Scientific Study of Religion, 3,* 157–170.

Koenig, H. G., McCullough, M. E., & Larson, D. B. (2001). *Handbook of religion and health.* New York: Oxford University Press.

Kotarba, J. A. (1983). Perceptions of death, belief systems and the process of coping with chronic pain. *Social Science and Medicine, 17,* 681–689.

Kraybill, D. B. (1989). *The riddle of Amish culture.* Baltimore: John Hopkins University Press.

Kraybill, D. B. (1998). *The puzzles of Amish life.* Intercourse, PA: Good Books.

Kraybill, D. B. (2001). *The riddle of Amish culture* (rev. ed.). Baltimore: John Hopkins University Press.

Kressel, N. J. (1996). *Mass hate: The global rise of genocide and terror.* New York: Plenum Press.

Kuhn, T. S. (1970). *The structure of scientific revolutions* (2nd ed.). Chicago: University of Chicago Press.

Kuhn, T. S. (1974). Second thoughts on paradigms. In F. Suppe (Ed.), *The structure of scientific theories* (pp. 293–319). Urbana: University of Illinois Press.

Kuortti, J. (1997). *Place of the sacred: The rhetoric of The Satanic Verses affair*. Frankfurt am Main, Germany: Lang.

Kvale, S. (1992). Postmodern psychology: A contradiction in terms? In S. Kvale (Ed.), *Psychology and postmodernism* (pp. 31–57). London: Sage.

LaPorte, V. (1999). *An attempt to understand the Muslim reaction to The Satanic Verses*. Lewiston, NY: Edwin Mellen Press.

Latour, B. (1993). *We have never been modern*. Cambridge, MA: Harvard University Press.

Lawrence, B. B. (1989). *Defenders of God: The fundamentalist revolt against the modern age*. San Francisco: Harper & Row.

Lechner, F. (1985). Fundamentalism and sociocultural revitalization in America. *Sociological Analysis, 46,* 243–260.

Lechner, F. (1989). Fundamentalism revisited. *Society, 26,* 51–59.

Lechner, F. J. (1998). Fundamentalism. In W. H. Swatos, Jr. (Ed.), *Encyclopedia of religion and society* (pp. 197–200). Walnut Creek, CA: Alta Mira Press.

Levy, L. W. (1993). *Blasphemy: Verbal offense against the sacred from Moses to Salman Rushdie*. New York: Knopf.

Ling, M. (1983). *Life of Muhammad based on early sources*. London: Allen & Unwin.

Loetscher, L. A. (1954). *The broadening church: A study of theological issues in the Presbyterian Church since 1869*. Philadelphia: University of Pennsylvania Press.

Machen, J. G. (1923). *Christianity and liberalism*. Grand Rapids, MI: Eerdmans.

Machen, J. G. (1925). *What is faith?* New York: Macmillan.

Marsden, G. M. (1971). Defining fundamentalism. *Christian Scholar's Review, 1,* 141–151.

Marsden, G. M. (1980). *Fundamentalism and American culture: The shaping of twentieth century evangelicalism 1870–1925*. New York: Oxford University Press.

Marsden, G. M. (1987). *Reforming fundamentalism: Fuller Seminary and the new evangelicalism*. Grand Rapids, MI: Eerdmans.

Marsden, G. M. (1990). Defining American fundamentalism. In N. J. Cohen (Ed.), *The fundamentalist phenomenon: A view from within; a response from without* (pp. 22–37). Grand Rapids, MI: Eerdmans.

Marsden, G. M. (1991). *Understanding fundamentalism and evangelicalism*. Grand Rapids, MI: Eerdmans.

Marty, M. E. (1969). *The modern schism*. New York: Harper & Row.

Marty, M. E. (1982). America's iconic book. In G. M. Tucker & D. M. Knight (Eds.), *Humanizing America's iconic book* (pp. 1–23). Chico, CA: Scholar's Press.

Marty, M. E., & Appleby, R. S. (Eds.). (1991). *The Fundamentalism Project: Vol. 1. Fundamentalisms observed*. Chicago: University of Chicago Press.

Marty, M. E., & Appleby, R. S. (1992). *The glory and the power*. Boston: Beacon Press.

Mazrui, A. (1993). Novelist's freedom vs. worshipper's dignity. In N. M. Ahsan & A. R. Kidwai (Eds.), *Sacrilege versus civility: Muslim perspectives on The Satanic Verses affair* (rev. and enlarged ed., pp. 210–228). Markfield, UK: Islamic Foundation.

McCauley, D. V. (1995). *Appalachian Mountain religion*. Chicago: University of Illinois Press.

McIntosh, D. N. (1995). Religion as schema, with implications for the relation between religion and coping. *International Journal of the Psychology of Religion, 5,* 1–16.

Miller, R. J. (1999). *The Jesus Seminar and its critics*. Santa Rosa, CA: Polebridge Press.

Minutes of the fifteenth annual Assembly. (1920). Cleveland, TN: Church of God.

Minutes of the fifty-third annual General Assembly. (1958). Cleveland, TN: White Wing.

Minutes of the forty-fifth annual Assembly. (1950). Cleveland, TN: White Wing.

Minutes of the ninetieth General Assembly. (1998). Cleveland, TN: White Wing.

Minutes of the ninety-first General Assembly. (2000). Cleveland, TN: White Wing.

Minutes of the seventeenth annual Assembly. (1922). Cleveland, TN: Church of God.

Minutes of the sixteenth annual Assembly. (1921). Cleveland, TN: Church of God.

Minutes of the thirteenth annual Assembly. (1917). Cleveland, TN: Church of God.

Minutes of the thirty-eighth annual Assembly. (1943). Cleveland, TN: White Wing.

Minutes of the thirty-sixth annual Assembly. (1941). Cleveland, TN: White Wing.

Minutes of the twelfth annual Assembly. (1916). Cleveland, TN: Church of God.

Minutes of the twenty-third annual Assembly. (1928). Cleveland, TN: White Wing.

Nash, D. (1999). *Blasphemy in modern Britain: 1789 to the present.* Aldershot, UK: Ashgate.

Nasr, S. H. (1987). *Traditional Islam in the modern world.* London: KPI/Methuen.

Nelson, K. (1985). *The art of reciting the Quar'an.* Austin: University of Texas Press.

Nielsen, N. C., Jr. (1993). *Fundamentalism, mythos, and world religions.* Albany: State University of New York Press.

Noll, M. A. (1996). The evangelical mind. In G. Rosell (Ed.), *The evangelical landscape: Essays on the American evangelical tradition* (pp. 13–40). Grand Rapids, MI: Baker Books.

Nolt, S. M. (1992). *A history of the Amish.* Intercourse, PA: Good Books.

Packer, J. I. (1958). *Fundamentalism and the word of God: Some evangelical principles.* Grand Rapids, MI: Eerdmans.

Paden, W. E. (1992). *Interpreting the sacred: Ways of viewing religion.* Boston: Beacon Press.

Paloutzian, R. F. (1996). *The psychology of religion* (2nd ed.). Needham Heights, MA: Allyn & Bacon.

Paloutzian, R. F., Richardson, J. T., & Rambo, L. R. (1999). Religious conversion and personality change. *Journal of Personality, 67,* 1047–1079.

Pargament, K. I. (1997). *The psychology of religion and coping: Theory, research, practice.* New York: Guilford Press.

Pargament, K. I., & Park, C. L. (1995). Merely a defense?: The variety of religious means and ends. *Journal of Social Issues, 51,* 13–32.

Park, C. L., & Cohen, L. H. (1993). Religious and nonreligious coping with the death of a friend. *Cognitive Therapy and Research, 17,* 561–577.

Parker, S. E. (1996). *Led by the Spirit: Toward a practical theology of Pentecostal discernment and decision making.* Ithaca, NY: Cornell University Press.

Payne, J. B. (1979). Higher criticism and Biblical inerrancy. In E. L. Geiser (Ed.), *Inerrancy* (pp. 84–113). Grand Rapids, MI: Zondervan.

Pelikan, J. (1990). Fundamentalism and/or orthodoxy?: Toward an understanding of the fundamentalist phenomenon. In N. J. Cohen (Ed.), *The fundamentalist phenomenon: A view from within; a response from without* (pp. 3–21). Grand Rapids, MI: Eerdmans.

Peretti, F. (1986). *This present darkness.* Westchester, IL: Crossway Books.

Pidcock, D. M. (1992). *Satanic voices ancient and modern: A surfeit of blasphemy including the Rushdie report.* Milton Keynes, UK: Mustaqim.

Pinnock, C. H. (1990). Defining American fundamentalism: A response. In N. J. Cohen (Ed.), *The fundamentalist phenomenon: A view from within; a response from without* (pp. 38–55). Grand Rapids, MI: Eerdmans.

Pipes, D. (1990). *The Rushdie affair: The novel, Ayatollah, and the West.* New York: Carol.

Powell, L. H., Shahabi, L., & Thoresen, C. E. (2003). Religion and spirituality: Linkages to physical health. *American Psychologist, 58,* 36–52.

Preus, J. S. (1987). *Explaining religion.* New Haven, CT: Yale University Press.

Pruitt, R. M. (1981). *Fundamentals of the faith.* Cleveland, TN: White Wing.

Rahman, F. (1980). *Major themes of the Qur'an.* Minneapolis, MN: Bibliotheca Islamica.

Reker, G. T., & Wong, P. T. P. (1988). Aging as an individual process. Towards a theory of relationships between religious involvement and health. In J. E. Birren & V. L. Bengston (Eds.), *Emergent theories of aging* (pp. 220–226). New York: Springer.

Riesebrodt, M. (1993). *Pious passion: The emergence of modern fundamentalism in the United States and Iran* (D. Reneau, Trans.). Berkeley: University of California Press. (Original work published 1990)

Roccas, S. (in press). Religion and value systems. *Journal of Social Issues.*

Rokeach, M. (1960). *The open and closed mind.* New York: Basic Books.

Rokeach, M. (1969). Value systems and religion. *Review of Religious Research, 11,* 2–23.

Rokeach, M. (1973). *The nature of human values.* New York: Free Press.

Rosenau, P. M. (1992). *Post-modernism and the social sciences.* Princeton, NJ: Princeton University Press.

Roth, P. A. (1987). *Meaning and method in the social sciences: The case for methodological pluralism.* Ithaca, NY: Cornell University Press.

Rushdie, S. (1989). *The Satanic verses.* New York: Viking.

Ruthven, M. (1991). *A Satanic affair: Salman Rushdie and the wrath of Islam.* London: Hogarth Press.

Sacranie, A. (1993). Q & A The Muslim case: The fuss about a fatwa evades the real issue—sacrilege. In N. M. Ahsan & A. R. Kidwai (Eds.), *Sacrilege versus civility: Muslim perspectives on The Satanic Verses affair* (rev. and enlarged ed., pp. 327–333). Markfield, UK: Islamic Foundation.

Said, E. (1979). *Orientalism.* New York: Random House.

Sampson, E. E. (2000). Reinterpreting individualism and collectivism: Their religious roots and monologic versus dialogic person–other relationships. *American Psychologist, 55,* 1425–1436.

Sand Mountain homecoming video. (1998, June 21). Chattanooga: Hood–Williamson Research Archives on the Serpent Handlers of Southern Appalachia, Lupton Library, University of Tennessee at Chattanooga.

Sandage, S. J., & Hill, P. C. (2001). The virtues of positive psychology: The rapprochement and challenges of an affirmative postmodern perspective. *Journal for the Theory of Social Behaviour, 31,* 241–260.

Sandeen, E. R. (1970). *The roots of fundamentalism: British and American millenarianism, 1800–1930.* Chicago: University of Chicago Press.

Sardar, Z. (1993). The Rushdie malaise: A critique of some writings on the Rushdie affair. In N. M. Ahsan & A. R. Kidwai (Eds.), *Sacrilege versus civility: Muslim perspectives on The Satanic Verses affair* (rev. and enlarged ed., pp. 277–308). Markfield, UK: Islamic Foundation.

Sardar, Z., & Davies, M. (1990). *Distorted imagination: Lessons from the Rushdie affair.* London: Grey Seal Books.

Saucier, G. (2000). Isms and the structure of social attitudes. *Journal of Personality and Social Psychology, 78,* 366–385.

Schaeffer, F. A. (1975). *No final conflict: The Bible without error in all that it affirms.* Downers Grove, IL: Inter-Varsity.

Scheier, M. F., & Carver, C. (1985). Optimism, coping, and health: Assessment and implication of generalized outcome expectancies. *Health Psychology, 4,* 219–247.

Schneidau, H. N. (1976). *Sacred discontent: The Bible and Western tradition.* Baton Rouge: Louisiana State University Press.

Schwartz, S. H. (1992). Universals in the content and structure of values: Theoretical advances and empirical tests in 20 countries. In M. P. Zanna (Ed.), *Advances in experimental social psychology* (Vol. 15, pp. 1–65). San Diego, CA: Academic Press.

Seguy, J. (1973). Religion and agricultural success: The vocational life of the French Anabaptists from the seventeenth to nineteenth centuries. *Mennonite Quarterly Review, 47,* 179–224.

Seeman, T. E., Dubin, L. F., & Seeman, M. (2003). Religiosity/spirituality and health: A critical review for the evidence of biological pathways. *American Psychologist, 58,* 53–63.

Sethi, S., & Seligman, M. E. P. (1993). Optimism and fundamentalism. *Psychological Science, 4,* 256–259.

Seybold, K. S., & Hill, P. C. (2001). The role of religion and spirituality in mental and physical health. *Current Directions in Psychological Science, 10,* 21–14.

Sidwell, M. (1998). *The dividing line: Understanding and applying Biblical separation.* Greenville, SC: Bob Jones University Press.

Silberman, I. (in press). Religion as a meaning-system: Implications for a new millennium. *Journal of Social Issues.*

Smith, M. B. (1994). Selfhood at risk: Postmodern perils and the peril of the postmodern. *American Psychologist, 49,* 405–411.

Smith, T. L. (1962). *Called unto holiness: The story of the Nazarenes. Vol. 1. The formative years.* Kansas City, MO: Nazarene Publishing House.

Smith, T. L. (1986). The Evangelical kaleidoscope and the call to Christian unity. *Christian Scholar's Review, 15,* 125–140.

Sorenson, R. L. (2004). *Minding spirituality.* Hillsdale, NJ: Analytic Press.

Spilka, B., Hood, R. W., Jr., Hunsberger, B., & Gorsuch, R. (2003). *The psychology of religion: An empirical approach* (3rd ed.). New York: Guilford Press.

Spurling, R. G. (1921). *The lost link.* Cleveland, TN: White Wing. (Original work not dated)

Starbuck, E. D. (1911). *The psychology of religion.* New York: Scribner's.

Stark, R. (1971). Psychopathology and religious commitment. *Review of Religious Research, 12,* 165–176.

Stark, R. (1999). A theory of revelations. *Journal for the Scientific Study of Religion, 38,* 287–308.

Stern, J. P. (1989, February 21). "By any other name." *The Guardian,* p. 21.

Stone, J. (1977). *The Church of God of Prophecy history and polity.* Cleveland, TN: White Wing.

Stott, J. R. W. (1956). *Fundamentalism and evangelism.* London: Evangelical Alliance.

Strieb, H., & Keller, B. (in press). The variety of deconversion experiences: Contours of a concept and emerging research results. *Archiv für Religionpsychologie.*

Strozier, C. B. (1994). *Apocalypse: On the psychology of fundamentalism in America.* Boston: Beacon Press.

Synan, V. (1997). *The Holiness–Pentecostal tradition: Charismatic movements in the 20th century.* Grand Rapids, MI: Eerdmans.

Tarnas, R. (1991). *The passion of the Western mind.* New York: Harmony Books.

Taslimi, C. R., Hood, R. W., Jr., & Watson, P. J. (1991). Assessment of former members of Shilo: The Adjective Check List 17 years later. *Journal for the Scientific Study of Religion, 30,* 306–311.

Tehranian, M. (1993a). Fundamentalist impact on education and the media: An overview. In M. E. Marty & R. S. Appleby (Eds.), *The Fundamentalism Project: Vol. 2.*

Fundamentalisms and society (pp. 313–340). Chicago: University of Chicago Press.

Tehranian, M. (1993b). Islamic fundamentalism in Iran and the discourse of development. In M. E. Marty & R. S. Appleby (Eds.), *The Fundamentalism Project: Vol. 2. Fundamentalisms and society* (pp. 341–373). Chicago: University of Chicago Press.

Tillich, P. (1957). *Dynamics of faith*. New York: Harper & Row.

Tomlinson, A. J. (1901–1923). *Journal of happenings*. Personal diary archived at Dixon Pentecostal Research Center, Cleveland, TN.

Tomlinson, A. J. (1914). Confusion of the scriptures: Due to natural and mental disarrangement, sanctification is the target and the battle is on (Part 2). *Church of God Evangel, 5*(24), 1–3.

Tomlinson, A. J. (1915). Receive the Holy Ghost: A glorious promise and a divine command. *Church of God Evangel, 6*(9), 1.

Tomlinson, A. J. (1931a, January 3). Editorial. *The White Wing Messenger, 8*, p. 1.

Tomlinson, A. J. (1931b, October 24). Editorial. *The White Wing Messenger, 9*, p. 1.

Tomlinson, A. J. (n.d./1984). *The last great conflict*. Cleveland, TN: White Wing.

Tracey, D. (1978). *Blessed rage for order: The new pluralism in theology*. Chicago: University of Chicago Press.

Trueblood, E. (1944). *The predicament of modern man*. New York: Harper & Row.

Van den Veer, P. (1989, Fall). Satanic or angelic?: The politics of literary liberation. *Public Culture*, pp. 100–104.

Van Doren, C. (1991). *A history of knowledge*. New York: Ballantine Books.

Veling, T. A. (1996). *Living in the margins: Intentional communities and the art of interpretation*. New York: Crossroad.

Voll, J. (1989, May 22). For scholars of Islam, interpretation need not be advocacy. *Chronicle of Higher Education*.

Waller, J. (2002). *Becoming evil: How ordinary people commit genocide and mass killing*. New York: Oxford University Press.

Warner, R. S. (1979). Theoretical barriers to the theoretical understanding of evangelical Christianity. *Sociological Analysis, 40*, 1–9.

Watson, P. J., Sawyers, P., Morris, R. J., Carpenter, M. L., Jimenez, R. S., Jonas, K. A., et al. (2003). Reanalysis within a Christian ideological surround: Relationship of intrinsic religious orientation with fundamentalism and right-wing authoritarianism. *Journal of Psychology and Theology, 31*, 315–328.

Watt, W. M. (1953). *Muhammad at Mecca*. Oxford: Clarendon Press.

Watt, W. M. (1956). *Muhammad at Medina*. Oxford: Clarendon Press.

Weatherby, W. J. (1990). *Salman Rushdie: Sentenced to death*. New York: Carroll & Graf.

Welford, A. T. (1971). *Christianity: A psychologist's interpretation*. London: Hodder & Stoughton.

Weller, J. E. (1965). *Yesterday's people: Life in contemporary Appalachia*. Lexington: University of Kentucky Press.

Wieseltier, L. (1990). The Jewish face of fundamentalism. In N. J. Cohen (Ed.), *The fundamentalist phenomenon: A view from within; a response from without* (pp. 192–196). Grand Rapids, MI: Eerdmans.

Wilcox, C. (1986). Evangelicals and fundamentalists in the new Christian right: Religious differences in the Ohio Moral Majority. *Journal for the Scientific Study of Religion, 25*, 355–363.

Williamson, W. P. (2000). The experience of religious serpent handling: A phenomen-ological study. *Dissertation Abstracts International, 62,* 1136B.

Williamson, W. P. (2001). *Fitly joined together: A concise history and polity of the Church of God of Prophecy.* Cleveland, TN: White Wing.

Williamson, W. P. (2002, July 28). [Field notes: Interview with Ron Hensley, Isom, KY]. Unpublished raw data.

Williamson, W. P., & Hood, R. W., Jr. (2004). Differential maintenance and growth of religious organizations based upon high-cost behaviors: Serpent-handling within the Church of God. *Review of Religious Research, 46,* 150–168.

Williamson, W. P., & Pollio, H. R. (1999). The phenomenology of religious serpent han-dling. *Journal for the Scientific Study of Religion, 38,* 203–218.

Wilson, B. (1970). *Religious sects.* New York: McGraw-Hill.

Wong, P. T. P. (1998). Spirituality, meaning, and successful aging. In P. T. P. Wong & P. S. Fry (Eds.), *The human quest for meaning: A handbook of psychological research and clinical applications* (pp. 359–394). Mahwah, NJ: Erlbaum.

Wulff, D. (1997). *Psychology of religion: Classic and contemporary views* (2nd ed.). New York: Wiley.

Wulff, D. (2003). A field in crisis: Is it time to start over? In H. M. P. Roelofsma, J. M. T. Corveleyn, & J. W. van Saane (Eds.), *One hundred years of psychology of religion* (pp. 11–32). Amsterdam: VU University Press.

Wuthnow, R. (1973). Religious commitment and conservatism: In search of an elusive relationship. In C. Y. Glock & R. Stark (Eds.), *Religion in sociological perspective* (pp. 117–132). Belmont, CA: Wadsworth.

Wuthnow, R. (1998). *After heaven: Spirituality in America since the 1950's.* Berkeley: University of California Press.

Yao, R. (1985). *Fundamentalism anonymous: There is a way out.* New York: Luce.

Index

Abortion, self-worth and, 44
Absolute truth
  holiness as, 94–100
  intratextual model and, 22–26,
    23f
  Protestant fundamentalism and,
    100–106
  serpent-handling sects and, 121
  Spirit baptism as, 106–113
Acts 28, 128, 130–132. *See also*
    Bible; Serpent-handling sects
Afterlife, 39–40
"Age of grace," 58
"Age of law," 58
American Council of Churches
  Graham, Billy and, 77–78
  history of, 75–76
Amish fundamentalism
  efficacy and, 43
  history of, 137–142
  maintaining beliefs of, 143–
    146
  meaning systems and, 187–190
  overview, 6, 8, 133, 134–137,
    146–153, 153–154, 220n–
    221n
  purpose in life and, 40
  self-worth and, 45
  sense of coherence and, 37
  unifying philosophy of life and,
    35–36
  values and, 41–42
Ammann, Jakob, 139–140. *See also*
    Amish fundamentalism

Anabaptist tradition. *See also* Amish
    fundamentalism
  farming and, 149
  history of, 137–142
Anxiety, 18–19
Arabian Nights, 161–162
Authoritarianism
  intratextual model and, 25
  overview, 4
  stereotypes regarding
    fundamentalism and, 199–201

B

Baptism. *See also* Spirit baptism
  Anabaptist tradition and, 137–138
  shunning and, 147
  unifying philosophy of life and, 35
Behavioral regulation
  Ordnung and, 135–137, 144
  sacred texts as the sole source of
    meaning and, 31–32
Belief system
  intratextual model and, 25
  stereotypes regarding
    fundamentalism and, 198–199
Beliefs, peripheral
  intertextual model and, 26–28, 27f
  overview, 23f, 24–26
Bible. *See also* Sacred texts
  Amish fundamentalism and, 134–
    135
  Church of God and, 86–87, 113–
    114
  common-sense realism and, 55

Bible (*continued*)
  history of fundamentalism and,
    50–51
  literal reading of, 80–82
  19th-century views of, 64–65
  Ordnung and, 135–137
  purpose in life and, 39–40
  serpent-handling sects and, 118–
    119, 119–122, 122–132
  shunning and, 146–147
  as the sole source of meaning, 31
  Tomlinson, A. J., and, 103–104
"Bible church", 100–106. *See also*
  Church of God
Biblical literalism, 80–82
Blasphemy, 171–172
Boundary maintenance, 215*n*
Bryant, W. F., 88, 101–102. *See also*
  Church of God

C

Calvinists, 50
Career achievement
  Amish fundamentalism and, 149–151
  higher purpose and, 32
  sacred texts as the sole source of
    meaning and, 30–31
Cashwell, C. B., 107. *See also*
  Church of God
Character, 143, 145–146
Child rearing
  Amish fundamentalism and, 148–
    149
  as a divinely conferred
    responsibility, 32
  overview, 30–31
Christ, second coming of. *See*
  Eschatology
Christian fundamentalism
  afterlife and, 39–40
  19th-century views, 53–60
  orality of, 24
  self-worth and, 44
Christian Union, 88. *See also* Church
  of God
Christianity
  defining fundamentalism from
    within, 49–50

history of fundamentalism and,
    50–51
  19th-century views and, 53–60
  Quran and, 178–179
Church of God. *See also* Pentecostal
  fundamentalism
  efficacy and, 43
  fundamentals of being the "Bible
    church" and, 100–106
  history of, 87–91
  holiness and, 94–100
  intratextual model and, 186
  meaning systems and, 187–190
  overview, 84–87, 93–94, 113–114,
    217*n*–219*n*
  peripheral beliefs and, 24
  purpose in life and, 40
  self-worth and, 44–45
  sense of coherence and, 37
  serpent-handling sects and, 116–
    117
  Spirit baptism and, 106–113
  Tomlinson, A. J., and, 91–93
  unifying philosophy of life and, 35
Church of God (of Prophecy), 87–91.
  See also Church of God
Cognitive–experiential self theory,
    14–15
Coherence, sense of
  overview, 17–19, 187, 188–189
  sacred texts and, 36–38
Common-sense realism, 55
Comprehensiveness of religion, 19–21
Conservatism
  intellectual, 72–74
  stereotypes regarding
    fundamentalism and, 199–201
Constitution of the United States of
  America, 205–206
Context of fundamentalism, 51–53
Controlling of behavior
  Ordnung and, 135–137, 144
  sacred texts as the sole source of
    meaning and, 31–32
Conversion, of A. J. Tomlinson, 95
Countertext of fundamentalism, 51–
    53
Creativity, 30–31
Crusades, Graham, Billy and, 76–78

D

Darwinism
  history of, 66–67
  Protestant fundamentalism and,
    60–63
  rejection of, 56
  teaching of, 63–64, 65–66
Death, 208–209
Decision-making, 25
Defining fundamentalism, 49–50
Depression, 18–19
Dispensationalism, 56–59
Divine being
  behavior regulation and, 32
  intratextual model and, 23–24
Dogmatism, 200–201, 223n
Dwelling, spirituality of, 18–19

E

Ecclesiastes 10:8, 126–130. *See also*
    Bible; Serpent-handling sects
Education
  Amish fundamentalism and, 45,
    148–149
  higher purpose and, 32
  intratextual model and, 25–26
  Protestant fundamentalism and,
    43
  teaching of evolution and, 63–64,
    65–66
Efficacy
  Amish fundamentalism and, 143
  as a need for meaning, 16, 42–44,
    189–190
Electricity use, 152–153. *See also*
    Amish fundamentalism
Empiricism, 6, 209
End times. *See* Eschatology
Eschatology
  19th-century views of, 56–59
  overview, 79
Evangelicalism
  as distinct from fundamentalism,
    70–72, 78–82
  historical development of, 70–78
Evangelism
  from 1950s on, 70–78, 71f
  age of revivals and, 69

Graham, Billy and, 76–78
  overview, 57–58, 78–79
  separatism and, 79–80
Evolution
  history of, 66–67
  Protestant fundamentalism and,
    60–63
  rejection of, 56
  teaching of, 63–64, 65–66

F

Falwell, Jerry, 12
Farming, 149–151
Fatwa
  overview, 164–167, 175, 186
  The Satanic Verses (Rushdie) and,
    159
Fisher, Fred S., Sr., 90–91. *See also*
    Church of God
Fuller, Charles E., 73–74
Fundamentalism Project, 2–3
The Fundamentals: A Testimony to
    the Truth, 61–63

G

Gemeinde, 40
Gender-based language, 215n
Global orientation, 17
Glossolalia, 106–113. *See also* Spirit
    baptism
Goals, 17
Graham, Billy, 76–78

H

Hadith, 40–41, 170–172. *See also*
    Sacred texts
Handling of snakes. *See* Serpent-
    handling sects
Hawkes Bay incident, 157–158. *See*
    also The Satanic Verses
    (Rushdie)
Heaven, 39–40
Hell, 39–40
Hensley, George Went. *See also*
    Serpent-handling sects
  overview, 116–117, 219n
  Sundén's role theory and, 118

History of Protestant
fundamentalism. *See*
Protestant fundamentalism,
history of
Holiness, 94–100
Holiness Church at Camp Creek, 88.
See also Church of God
Holiness movement
Church of God and, 87, 106
19th-century views and, 59–60
serpent-handling sects and, 120
Holy Spirit
Church of God and, 86
19th-century views of, 59–60
Holy war
Quran and, 179
Shariah and, 172
Home schooling
Amish fundamentalism and, 148–
149
Protestant fundamentalism and, 43
Humanism, 204
Humility, 145–146

I

Identity, 4–5
Ideology, fundamentalism as, 198–
199
"In the world but not of the world"
Amish fundamentalism and, 153–
154
overview, 51, 216*n*
Protestant fundamentalism and,
184
Induction, scientific, 55–56
Inerrancy of scripture. *See also*
Scripture
Church of God and, 85
overview, 78
stereotypes regarding
fundamentalism and, 192–194
Intellectual conservatism, 72–74
Intertextual model
compared to the intratextual
model, 26–28, 27*f*
Islam fundamentalism and, 173–
179
Tomlinson, A. J., and, 97

Intratextual model. *See also*
Intratextuality
Amish fundamentalism and, 136–
137
intertextual alternative to, 26–28,
27*f*
Islam fundamentalism and, 179–181
overview, 2–3, 9, 12, 22–26, 23*f*,
28–29, 211–213
serpent-handling sects and, 132
Sundén's role theory and, 93
Intratextuality. *See also* Intratextual
model
assumptions of, 184–187
meaning systems and, 187–190
overview, 28–29
serpent-handling sects and, 118–
119, 119–122, 122–132
Tomlinson, A. J., and, 97
Islam fundamentalism
behavior regulation and, 33
efficacy and, 43–44
hadith and, 170–172
history of, 49
intertextuality and, 173–179
intratextual model and, 179–181,
184, 186
overview, 2, 6, 155–157, 181–182,
221*n*-222*n*
philosophy of life and, 188
purpose in life and, 40–41
Quran and, 167–170
sacred texts as the sole source of
meaning and, 31
The Satanic Verses (Rushdie) and,
157–167
sense of coherence and, 37–38
Shariah and, 172–173
values and, 42
worldview of, 38
Isolation, 48

J

Jihad
Quran and, 179
Shariah and, 172
Jones, Bob, III, 12
Jones, Bob, Sr., 77–78

K

Keswick movement, 59

L

The Last Great Conflict (Tomlinson), 104–105. *See also* Church of God; Tomlinson, A. J.
League of Nations, 63
Liberalism
  intellectual conservatism and, 72–74
  stereotypes regarding fundamentalism and, 199–201
Loneliness, 18–19
Luke 10:19, 125–126. *See also* Bible

M

Machen, J. Gresham
  intellectual conservatism and, 72–73
  overview, 217*n*
Magical realism, 157–159
Mark 16. *See also* Bible; Serpent-handling sects
  Acts 28 and, 130–132
  Ecclesiastes 10:8 and, 127–129
  overview, 123–125, 220*n*
Matthew 18, 147. *See also* Bible
McIntire, Carl, 77–78
Meaning. *See also* Meaning system
  Amish fundamentalism and, 143, 145–146
  how fundamentalism provides, 33–45
  needs for, 16, 38–45, 45–46
  overview, 4–5
  religion's ability to provide, 20–21
  of a sacred text, 193–194
  sacred texts as the sole source of, 30–33
  Tomlinson, A. J. and, 96
Meaning system. *See also* Meaning
  Amish fundamentalism and, 134–135
  fundamentalism as, 187–190
  overview, 14–15
  religion as, 12–21

Mennonites, 138–139, 142
Methodist label, 12–13
Militant aspect of fundamentalism, 194–196
Millenarianism, 56–57, 79, 217*n*
Modernism
  Amish fundamentalism and, 151–153
  fundamentalism as a response to, 48
  "in the world but not of the world" and, 51–52
  overview, 216*n*
  social scientific literature and, 185–186
  stereotypes regarding fundamentalism and, 196–198, 201–204
  Tomlinson, A. J., and, 99
"Monkey Trial", 65–66, 66–67. *See also* Scopes, John
Morality
  sense of coherence and, 17–18
  unifying philosophy of life and, 34–36
Murray, Billy D., 90–91. *See also* Church of God
Muslims. *See also* Islam fundamentalism
  absolute truth and, 24
  sacred texts and, 3

N

National Association of Evangelicals, 76
Naturalism, 204
Needs for meaning, 16, 38–45, 45–46, 189–190. *See also* Meaning system
Neo-orthodoxy
  overview, 74–75
  separatism and, 79–80
New Testament church. *See* Church of God
19th-century views
  Amish fundamentalism and, 140–142
  Church of God and, 87–88

19th-century views (*continued*)
   cultural understandings of truth
      during, 64
   overview, 53–60
Nonreligious fundamentalism, 205–
   208
Normative behavior, 3

O

Occupation
   Amish fundamentalism and, 149–
      151
   higher purpose and, 32
   sacred texts as the sole source of
      meaning and, 30–31
Ordnung. See also Amish
      fundamentalism
   child rearing and education and,
      148–149
   efficacy and, 43
   humor and, 221*n*
   overview, 135–137
   philosophy of life and, 188
   purpose and, 40, 143–144
   self-worth and, 45
   separatism and, 144
   shunning and, 146–148
   unifying philosophy of life and,
      35–36
   values and, 42
Organizational developments, 75–76
Orientalism, 174–175
Orthodoxy, 192, 199–200

P

Parenting
   Amish fundamentalism and, 148–
      149
   as a divinely conferred
      responsibility, 32
   overview, 30–31
Pentecostal fundamentalism. *See also*
      Church of God
   fundamentals of being the "Bible
      church" and, 100–106
   history of, 87–91
   holiness and, 94–100
   overview, 84–87, 93–94, 113–114

peripheral beliefs and, 24
   Spirit baptism and, 106–113
   Tomlinson, A. J., and, 91–93
Peripheral beliefs
   intertextual model and, 26–28, 27*f*
   overview, 23*f*, 24–26
Personality traits, 25
Philosophical orientation, 19–20
Philosophy of life, 188
Pluralism
   overview, 81
   stereotypes regarding
      fundamentalism and, 194–
      196, 197–198
Possessions, 150
Postmillennialism, 56–57, 79
Premillennialism, 56–57, 79
Protestant fundamentalism. *See also*
      Church of God; Serpent-
      handling sects
   distinguishing from others, 1–2
   efficacy and, 42–43
   gender-exclusive language and, 215*n*
   intratextual model and, 184
   overview, 78–82, 205
   sacred texts as the sole source of
      meaning and, 31
   stereotypes regarding
      fundamentalism and, 198–199
Protestant fundamentalism, history of
   during the 1930s and 1940s, 67–70
   current state of, 78–82
   early 20th century, 60–67
   19th-century views, 53–60
   overview, 47–51
   rise of evangelicalism and, 70–78,
      71*f*
Psychoanalysis theories, 207–208
Puritans
   history of fundamentalism and,
      50–51
   overview, 12–13
Purpose in life
   Amish fundamentalism and, 143,
      145–146
   as a need for meaning, 16, 39–41,
      189–190
   overview, 4–5
   religion's claim to have, 20–21

Q

Quasi-fundamentalism, 205–208
Quran. *See also* Sacred texts
  efficacy and, 43–44
  hadith and, 170–172
  intertextuality and, 173–179
  intratextual model and, 179–181
  Islam fundamentalism and, 167–170
  orality of, 24
  overview, 3, 190, 221*n*-222*n*
  philosophy of life and, 188
  purpose in life and, 40
  The Satanic Verses (Rushdie) and, 158–159, 160–161
  self-worth and, 45
  Shariah and, 172–173
  as the sole source of meaning, 31

R

Rapture, 58
Realism, common-sense, 55
Redemption, 40
Regulation of behavior
  Ordnung and, 135–137, 144
  sacred texts as the sole source of meaning and, 31–32
Reist, Hans, 139–140. *See also* Amish fundamentalism
Relational psychoanalysis, 207–208
Relationships
  Amish fundamentalism and, 37
  sacred texts as the sole source of meaning and, 30–31
  shunning and, 146–148
Religion
  distinctions among, 13
  fundamentalism as, 191–192
  as a meaning system, 12–21
  sense of coherence and, 17
Resources
  intratextual model and, 186
  sense of coherence and, 17
Revivals
  overview, 69
  Tomlinson, A. J., and, 110

Right-wing authoritarianism
  overview, 4–5
  stereotypes regarding fundamentalism and, 199–201
Rituals, 143–144
Roles, Sundén's theory regarding. *See* Sundén's role theory
Rushdie, Salman, 157–159, 221*n*-222*n*. *See also* *The Satanic Verses* (Rushdie)

S

Sacred texts. *See also* Bible; Quran; Scripture
  Church of God and, 86–87, 113–114
  coherence of, 188–189
  intertextual model and, 26–28, 27*f*
  intratextuality and, 2–3
  meaning systems and, 187–190
  overview, 183–184, 184–185
  quasi-fundamentalism and, 206–208
  sense of coherence and, 36–38
  as the sole source of meaning, 30–33, 38–39
  stereotypes regarding fundamentalism and, 190–204
  Tomlinson, A. J., and, 91
  translation of, 215*n*
  in understanding fundamentalism, 21–28, 23*f*, 27*f*
  unifying philosophy of life and, 35
  values and, 41–42
Sanctification, Tomlinson, A. J., and, 94–99
Satan, Church of God and, 86, 112
The Satanic Verses (Rushdie)
  intertextuality and, 173–179
  Islam fundamentalism and, 156
  offense of, 159–164
  overview, 157–159, 181–182
Schema, 19–20
Schools. *See also* Education
  Amish fundamentalism and, 148–149
  Protestant fundamentalism and, 43
  teaching of evolution and, 63–64, 65–66

Science, 19th-century views of, 54–
    56
Scientific induction, 55–56
Scopes, John, 65–66, 66–67
Scripture. *See also* Sacred texts
    Biblical literalism and, 80–82
    dispensationalism and, 58–59
    inerrancy of, 78, 85, 192–194
    19th-century views of, 53–54
    Tomlinson, A. J., and, 103–104
Second coming of Christ. *See*
        Eschatology
Seeking, spirituality of, 18–19
Self-worth
    Amish fundamentalism and, 143
    as a need for meaning, 16, 44–45,
        189–190
Separatism
    Amish fundamentalism and, 144
    Protestant fundamentalism and,
        79–80
Serpent-handling sects. *See also*
        Protestant fundamentalism
    fundamentals of, 122–132
    history of, 116–122
    intratextual model and, 186
    meaning systems and, 187–190
    overview, 115–116, 132, 219*n*–
        220*n*
    purpose in life and, 40
    self-worth and, 44–45
    sense of coherence and, 37
    unifying philosophy of life and,
        35
Shariah, 172–173. *See also* Islam
        fundamentalism; Quran
Shia Islam. *See* Islam fundamentalism
Shunning, 146–148
Significance
    of a sacred text, 193–194
    search for, 15–19, 207
Sin
    Biblical literalism and, 81–82
    Church of God and, 86
    19th-century views of, 59–60
    Tomlinson, A. J., and, 97
Smith, Wilbur M., 73–74
Snake handling. *See* Serpent-handling
        sects

Social scientific theory
    intratextual model and, 185–186,
        211–213
    overview, 183–184
    as quasi-fundamentalism, 205
Social support
    intratextual model and, 186
    shunning and, 146–148
    spirituality orientations and, 18–19
Socioeconomic status
    overview, 216*n*
    Pentecostal fundamentalism and,
        111
    serpent-handling sects and, 119
Speaking in tongues, 106–113. *See
        also* Spirit baptism
Spirit baptism. *See also* Baptism
    Church of God and, 86, 106–113
    speaking in tongues and, 106–
        113
    unifying philosophy of life and, 35
Spirituality, 18–19
Spurling, Richard, 88, 101. *See also*
        Church of God
Statistics, 185–186
Stereotypes regarding
        fundamentalists, 13, 190–204
Sundén's role theory
    overview, 92–93
    serpent-handling sects and, 118
    Spirit baptism and, 108
    Tomlinson, A. J., and, 96–97, 102–
        103
Sunni Islam. *See* Islam
        fundamentalism

T

Telephone use, Amish
        fundamentalism and, 152
Terminology
    history of, 61, 66
    overview, 2–3
Terrorism
    Islam fundamentalism and, 156
    stereotypes regarding
        fundamentalism and, 194–
        196, 203–204
Theological liberalism, 65

Tomlinson, A. J. *See also* Church of God
  Church of God and, 88–90
  fundamentals of being the "Bible church" and, 100–106
  holiness and, 94–100
  influence of on Church of God, 91–93
  overview, 93–94, 113–114, 218*n*, 219*n*
  Spirit baptism and, 106–113
Tomlinson, M. A., 90. *See also* Church of God
Transcendence
  issues of, 20
  overview, 208–209
  unifying philosophy of life and, 35
Tribulation, 58
True-Hearted People, 139. *See also* Amish fundamentalism
Truth, absolute
  fundamentals of being the "Bible church" as, 100–106
  holiness as, 94–100
  intratextual model and, 22–26, 23*f*
  serpent-handling sects and, 121
  Spirit baptism as, 106–113
Truth, cultural understandings of, 64
20th century
  evangelism during, 70–78, 71*f*
  Protestant fundamentalism during, 60–67
  resurrection of fundamentalism during, 67–70

U

U.S. Constitution, 205–206
Unifying philosophy of life, 34–36

V

Value
  Amish fundamentalism and, 143
  Islam fundamentalism and, 156
  as a need for meaning, 16, 41–42, 189–190
  spirituality orientations and, 18–19
Violence
  Islam fundamentalism and, 156
  stereotypes regarding fundamentalism and, 194–196, 203–204
Vocation
  Amish fundamentalism and, 149–151
  higher purpose and, 32
  sacred texts as the sole source of meaning and, 30–31

W

Wealth, Amish fundamentalism and, 150
Wesleyan Holiness tradition
  Church of God and, 87, 106
  serpent-handling sects and, 120
Wesley's Methodist perfectionism model, 60
"In the world but not of the world"
  Amish fundamentalism and, 153–154
  overview, 51, 216*n*
  Protestant fundamentalism and, 184
World War I
  neo-orthodoxy and, 75
  Protestant fundamentalism and, 63
Worldview
  of Islam fundamentalism, 38
  overview, 185
Wrongness, sense of, 96